BIBLE LIFE SERIES

BOOK ONE

BRINGING THE EXODUS TO LIFE

PHILIP COTTRAUX

Published by Innovo Publishing, LLC
www.innovopublishing.com
1-888-546-2111

Providing Full-Service Publishing Services for Christian Authors, Artists & Ministries:
Books, eBooks, Audiobooks, Music, Film & Courses

BRINGING THE EXODUS TO LIFE
Book 1 in the Bible Life Series

Copyright © 2019 by Philip Cottraux
All rights reserved.

No part of this publication may be reproduced, stored in a retrieval system, or transmitted in any form or by any means electronic, mechanical, photocopying, recording, or otherwise, without the prior written permission of the author.

Unless otherwise noted, all scripture is taken from the King James Version (KJV) of the Bible.

Library of Congress Control Number: 2018963388
ISBN: 978-1-61314-453-4

Cover Design & Interior Layout: Innovo Publishing, LLC

Printed in the United States of America
U.S. Printing History
First Edition: 2019

For God, family, and church, in that order.

CONTENTS

Introduction 7

    1: THE MIGRATION 27

    2: THE BIRTH OF MOSES 35

    3: MOSES IN THE WILDERNESS 43

    4: THE BURNING BUSH 49

    5: THE TEN PLAGUES 73

    6: THE RED SEA 109

    7: NOW WHAT? 127

    8: MOUNT SINAI 143

    9: LEAVING SINAI 201

    10: CONCLUSION 219

Author's Afterword 223
Index 227
Endnotes 237

INTRODUCTION

The title may throw people off. To say that I intend to "bring the Exodus to life" may sound presumptuous. Worse still, it may sound heretical, indicating the story is somehow dead and in need of resurrecting. It is not. Like every tale in the Bible, it is very much alive. The characters and events may be long gone, but their legacy itself is a living, breathing part of the Word of God. It transcends time and will live forever.

But that doesn't mean everything in the Word is alive *to people*. And I don't just mean unbelievers. The Word is life for Christians, but not if we don't apply it to our lives. Manna was supposed to be heaven's miraculous food, but Moses warned the Israelites it would go bad if they didn't eat it. How could something created in heaven decay? What good is bread if it isn't eaten? What good is the Word if we don't read it? A perfect gift from God is dead if it sits on your shelf, gathering dust.

The skeptic needs to see evidence that the story is true. But the lukewarm Christian needs to be reminded that the same God who smote Egypt with ten plagues and parted the Red Sea is here to do the same for them.

I couldn't begin to describe the influence of the book of Exodus. The epic tale of Moses leading the children of Israel out of Egypt is more than just an ancient legend, representing the dichotomies of human nature. It is more than just a classic myth in the same vein as Homer's *Iliad* or the works of Shakespeare. It transcends all of those in precisely how it has shaped civilization along the way. Even if the story itself didn't happen (and I will, of course, argue that it did), it still changed the course of human history forever, serving as the foundation of the world's three major monotheistic religions: Judaism, Christianity, and Islam.

And still today, it has a legacy that endures beyond the writings of the Greeks or Romans. Its lessons of faith, leadership, and courage still resonate with people. We still can relate to Moses' self-doubt before the burning bush. We can see Pharaoh's hard-heartedness in our enemies. I see no reason why the story still won't be relevant in another four thousand years.

The Founding Fathers looked to Exodus and saw the same drama playing out with the British. George Washington likely saw himself in Moses and King George III in Pharaoh. I can easily picture him in the darkest days at Valley Forge, wondering if the cause of freedom was hopeless, drawing inspiration as he poured over his Bible by candlelight in his tent.

And no doubt, a few years later, African American slaves saw themselves as the children of Israel in bondage, demanding freedom. Look at any great leader who stood up and led his people to a new life—from

Harriet Tubman to Gandhi to Martin Luther King, Jr.—and you will see a familiar play acted out on different stages.

When I chose the Exodus as the subject for my first book (in what I aspire to be a series), I had little idea what I was getting into. *There's plenty of material in the book itself,* I mused. *This will be a cinch to write!* I quickly learned that this was like choosing Mount Everest for my first climb.

I do this to myself all the time, as anyone who knows me can vouch for. I kept telling myself that I had enough, yet kept finding so much irresistible information. I scoured thrift stores for any book I could find on archaeology or Bible history. I spent hours on the internet, poring over pictures of ancient scrolls and broken pottery, intently looking for *anything else* that might contribute to this project.

It was exhausting and demoralizing. There was plenty of self-doubt along the way. And I wouldn't have traded the experience for the world.

Now, I could have just made this book a Bible commentary. But plenty of those already exist (and I consulted many of them). I could have written a pure history book, stacks of which now occupy my living room. But neither of those seemed like enough. This is why this book turned out the way it did. Instead of just lessons from Exodus for our daily lives, or a historical examination of whether it happened, or a study of the influence it has had on civilization, my intent eventually came to make it about *all* of those things. Quite simply, I wanted it to be the best book on the subject I could write. The title says it all.

Frankly it was discouraging to look at Bible commentaries that produced marvelous practical applications but copped out on historical evidence. In fact, many great scholars today take that same approach: often when a rabbi or pastor is asked whether or not the stories are factual, a common response is, "I don't know, and I don't care." The point they make is that whether or not the stories are true is beside the point; it's the spiritual lesson we gain from them—the *meta-truth,* if you will. Yes?

No. Buddhists may be able to accept that premise, but historicity has always been a crucial foundation of Christianity. I can't compromise that. Call me an extremist, but my feelings are that you either believe in *all* the Bible or *none* of it. Jesus Himself said, "He that is not with me is against me" (Matthew 12:30).

Of course, I fully admit that being raised in a Christian home, I'm biased. But I genuinely did not set out to prove the Exodus; the initial purpose of this book was to craft a spiritual commentary with my unique approach. But I'm also a history buff, and that lure of historical research kept pulling me in. I snuck a little bit of it in the book . . . then more. Before long, those aspects ended up taking up a large portion of the book. Seeing how ancient history synchronizes with the stories of the Bible proved to be too good to pass up.

INTRODUCTION

And there you have the reasoning behind this book, *Bringing the Exodus to Life*. It was never intended to be a definitive reference book or a doctrinal change that denominations across the world must adapt to. I don't want to see Sunday school literature change to accommodate the theories of Philip Cottraux. This book is, quite simply, my take on Exodus. I'll try to make persuasive arguments and present facts to back up my claims, but I don't demand that anyone believe it. This is what years of researching the subject has led to. I hope you get just as much out of reading this book as I did writing it.

Of course, by writing this book as an amalgamation, I ran the risk of it turning out unfocused and discombobulated. It needed structure and logic. So I planned it all out: First of all, each chapter will focus on the major events in Exodus—the checkpoints, if you will. Some of it will look at other areas of scripture. It starts with the migration of Jacob's family to Egypt and ends with Exodus 40. Later events, such as the brass pole or conquest of Canaan, might be briefly touched on but won't be the main focus. Second, each chapter will break down, scripture by scripture, its topic. The scriptures are set apart in blocked text and are followed by one or a combination of four categories:

1. *The Practical Application:* The most important question Christians can ask while reading the Bible is, *How does this apply to me?* In these sections, we'll look at the lessons we can learn from Exodus and apply to our own lives and relationships with God. Moses' walk with the Lord isn't wholly different from what we will experience walking with Him too.

2. *The Ties that Bind:* The Word of God is a living organism; and seeing how, like fibrous tissue, it is webbed to itself from beginning to end and everything in-between is enormously fascinating. You can find connections to Exodus and the ministry of Jesus, the Acts of the Apostles, and even Revelation.

3. *Middle Kingdom Dynamics:* A better phrase for this might have been, "Did it really happen?" This is history brought to life. Although many scholars today would argue that it doesn't matter whether or not the story is true, as long as we learn from its universal truths, I respond that I don't want to put my faith in a lie. If there is genuine archaeological evidence to support a historical exodus, it needs to be shown to the world. The phrase *Middle Kingdom Dynamics* refers to the most compelling argument that I have found, that the evidence for a historical exodus can be found in the Middle Kingdom era of Egypt's history. I'll explain later.

4. *The Naturalist Theories:* This may be the most controversial section. Some historians attribute miraculous events in the Bible to natural phenomena. The ten plagues are a perfect example, as

we'll learn later. Some claim that natural explanations debunk the supernatural altogether, but they build my faith in God even more. Sometimes science can explain the *how*, but it can never explain the *why*. Even if a natural explanation can affirm the story, that doesn't mean God wasn't behind the scenes, orchestrating the events. As Christians, we need to understand the difference between *miracles* (God violates the laws of nature to make His will happen) and divine *providence* (God uses the laws of nature to make His will happen). A natural blowing wind could have driven back the water enough for the Israelites to pass through. But its occurring just as they were about to be destroyed by Pharaoh is an extraordinary coincidence. When you add coincidental event after event, the divine hand guiding the elements along the way becomes more and more apparent.

Ultimately, whether or not you're a Christian, I hope this book changes the way you look at the book of Exodus. My goal as a teacher and blogger has always been to get people excited about the Bible again—because we find the heart of God in the secrets of its pages. If Christians want better direction in their lives, they need to start by looking at the foundation of their faith. It's there, whispering to us through the ancient tales of Abraham, Jacob, Joseph, and Moses. And it will not just be for our edification but for the better of the body of Christ as a whole.

Let's begin!

A HISTORY OF EXODUS

Ancient Mesopotamia—the land between the two rivers. Its deserts form an alien world; yet for many who travel there, they feel a kinship with the land, almost as if they have arrived at a home they never knew existed. Something is truly mystical about its brutal, wind-driven heat and cold, starry nights. The faint voices of ancient peoples can still be heard, echoing through its mountains, caves, and canyons. It is not just a place but a journey—a spiritual destination where a man gets in touch with his origins. One thing both archaeologists and people of faith agree on is that this is where the dawn of man took place. Evolutionists call it the cradle of civilization. Creationists call it Eden.

Stories began to emerge from this ancient land. They were timeless tales of heroic figures whose journeys speak to basic truths in all people. They may have lived in a foreign land, speaking a distant language, but we can still project ourselves onto them. They thought like we think and speak like we still speak and live lives that we still live. And perhaps that is why the tales of the patriarchs have such a lasting legacy. You will take something new out of them each time you read them.

INTRODUCTION

One tale in particular has endured the test of time. We call it the Torah. Something is remarkable about it. While hardly anyone remembers the other primitive legends of early man, the Torah has a lasting power so great that the majority of people in the world still swear by it as absolutely inspired by the Almighty. Christians, Jews, and Muslims all describe it as the first five books of the Old Testament.

Exodus, of course, is the second book of this five-volume series. In understanding it, we have to start by examining the history of the Torah itself. In their structure, these five books are inseparable. The name *Exodus* is Greek, meaning simply "the exit" or "departure." However its original Hebrew title is *Shemoth*, which is derivative of the first six words: "And these are the names of,"[1] indicating Genesis and Exodus were never meant to be two separate works. Genesis ends with the death of Joseph while Exodus immediately picks up with the twelve tribes of Israel migrating to Egypt.

> *So Joseph died, being a hundred and ten years old: and they embalmed him, and he was put in a coffin in Egypt. (Genesis 50:26)*

> *Now, these are the names of the children of Israel, which came into Egypt; every man and his household came with Jacob. (Exodus 1:1)*

For many centuries, the events in the Bible were accepted as fact. Today, however, skepticism is at an all-time high. What happened?

Ironically the field of archaeology was invented by the Europeans with two express purposes: to find the works of Homer, and to prove the Bible.[2] However a good archaeologist acts like an unbiased scientist rather than one who uses findings to support his already-determined agenda. Sensational stories of amazing discoveries wowed the public for decades as many diggers jumped to conclusions too fast in their quests for the publicity.

The real damage started in the late 1950s when a British archaeologist named Kathleen Kenyon explored the ruins of Jericho, which, according to the Bible, was a land conquered by Joshua after God brought the walls tumbling down. Kenyon shocked the world when she announced that, according to her findings, no such event occurred in the time frame given and therefore didn't happen.[3] By the 1960s, a backlash against the Bible had started. New archaeologists began intensely criticizing it, claiming no historical evidence supports any of its stories, and the entire book must be a complete fabrication. This is now the consensus among archaeologists; like Frankenstein's monster turning on its creator, a field created to prove the Bible has now become devoted to its destruction.

But much to their dismay, Bible archaeology is seeing resurgence due to a new generation who has entered the field and is questioning their methods. Even Kenyon's conclusions, the origin of most modern Bible skepticism, have been challenged due to further explorations that found her work incomplete. This has given way to two categories on the subject: *Bible minimalists* who believe the stories to be pure fantasy, and *Bible maximalists* who believe them to have at least a grain of historical reality.

The reason this is important is that, while Jericho may have been the start of the controversy, the Exodus is really at the center of it. After years of digging through the ruins of ancient Egypt, Bible minimalists have been adamant for decades that there is no mention of Israelite slaves, Moses, or any plagues.

As this has become the proclamation of so many historians, Christians have shied away from the subject. As a Sunday school teacher, I've read through much teaching material in preparation for my classes, and little, if any, ever addresses it.

Of course, the problem at the heart of the division is common among sciences of the past. We will never know for sure who is right or wrong. Just like a dinosaur will never emerge from the past to show paleontologists whether it has scales or feathers, Abraham is never going to step out of a time machine with a business card and confirm his identity. Unlike other scientific fields where experiments can confirm or disprove hypotheses, archaeology is always going to require a certain amount of guesswork. This is why nothing ever seems settled, and no matter how much evidence is found, contradictory statements can still hold some water. History is constantly being rewritten by new discoveries.

Bible minimalists claim that the Bible does not have its origins in ancient Mesopotamia but that it was likely first penned thousands of years later during the seventy-year Babylonian exilic period (after Nebuchadnezzar's armies conquered Jerusalem and the people were banished from their homeland). The theory holds that Jewish scholars began making up legends to restore pride among the people's heritage in order to rally them behind the cause of returning to their homeland.

So let's tackle this first. How old, exactly, is the Torah?

THE HISTORY OF THE TEXT ITSELF

Our picture of life in Old Testament days is more complete than our picture of the Dark Ages. Historians have over thirty thousand ancient documents to study and piece together from Mesopotamia. There are less than 10,000 from Medieval Europe.[4] The number of historical artifacts from Egypt is even greater. This sounds incredible, but consider the dawn of man as a time when humans were frantically building great art and achieving knowledge; they would make careful records of their day and time. But thousands of years later, few Europeans were even literate, and humanity was mired in death and superstition.

We think of the scribes as Jesus' enemies, lumping them together with the Pharisees as examples of religious authority gone corrupt.

INTRODUCTION

Woe unto you, scribes and Pharisees, hypocrites! For ye are as graves which appear not, and the men that walk over them are not aware of them. (Luke 11:44)

But they played an important role in Jewish history, making copies of and interpreting the law. Scribes were extremely meticulous in preserving the ancient texts of the Old Testament in exact detail; it is said that they would even measure the distance between each letter, fearing God's wrath if one tiny word was off.[5] Without their hard work, we wouldn't have the holy scriptures.

The Old Testament is so important to the Jews that they spent many centuries writing and expanding on it, eventually forming a massive body of work completed around 500 AD called the Talmud, which exists in two forms: the Palestinian and the Babylonian.[6] The Talmud is an invaluable resource in understanding the history of Judaism.

While most ancient documents were written on papyrus, much of the Old Testament was written on durable sheepskin that had been stretched out and stitched together (called vellum) to ensure its longevity.[7] Most of it was written in ancient Hebrew (the Greek translation is called the Septuagint, which means "seventy," as it was believed to have over seventy translators[8]); this, however, leads to many problems in translating it to modern languages. Hebrew did not contain vowels. It wasn't until the AD 600s that Jewish scholars saw the need to attempt to update the scriptures into something modern readers could understand. Much disagreement was already in place over the exact wording, so a thorough amount of work and research was put into rewriting the ancient texts, determining which vowels needed to be inserted where without changing any of the original meaning.[9] The men in charge of this massive task were known as the Masoretes, a name that derives from the word for "tradition," *masorah*.[10] These manuscripts came to be known as the Masoretic Text. Every Protestant Bible takes this version as its Old Testament.

Predating the Masoretes, the oldest known writing to contain any part of Exodus (before the Dead Sea Scroll discovery) was the Nash Papyrus, discovered by Dr. Walter Nash in 1903. Dated at around 200 BC, this twenty-four-line message fragment of a papyrus leaf contains the Ten Commandments, as well as parts of Exodus and Deuteronomy, leading some to believe that it was likely a short excerpt of scriptures stored inside tefillin (small boxes Jewish rabbis carry with them that contain prayers and scriptures).[11] A few tatters of other books of the Torah exist, dating back much farther; the oldest currently known is the Ketef Hinnom, a copy of the priestly blessing from Numbers 6:24-26 that has been dated back to the 600s BC.[12] On the other hand, the oldest known *complete* Torah is a scroll from only about 1150–1200 AD.[13]

But in 1947, a Bedouin shepherd threw a rock into a cave on the northwestern shore of the Dead Sea, and instead of an echo, he heard a curious breaking sound. Upon entering the cave, he found a trove of pottery containing ancient scrolls. Originally he sold them on the streets of Qumran, but fortunately, many of them were tracked down by archaeologists before being lost forever. News of the discovery quickly spread, leading to a "gold rush" to the area, and after decades of excavations (still going on to this day), over 970 ancient texts and documents were found hidden in eleven different caves around the Dead Sea.[14]

Referring to the history of Judaism in "temple periods" points to two different eras wherein the people worshiped at Solomon's temple. The first began when the temple was completed around 1000 BC and ended with its destruction during the Babylonian invasion of Nebuchadnezzar in 586 BC. The Second Temple period started when it was rebuilt after the "Second Exodus" (covered by the books of Ezra and Nehemiah) seventy years later and resumed until the Roman emperor Titus destroyed it for good in 70 AD.[15] Today the Palestinians control the land and have erected the Dome of the Rock Mosque on the site where the magnificent Jewish temple once stood.

Since the temple was the site of the worship of God and the operations of the priesthood, it was a storehouse for the sacred texts that form the Word of God. Most of these original copies were likely lost or destroyed by the Roman army. Fortunately, for centuries a cult of radical Jews called the Essenes had been making copies of the Old Testament and storing them in the safety of the caves surrounding the Dead Sea.

Most of the Dead Sea Scrolls are from the Second Temple period, some dating back as far as almost 200 BC. It is the most comprehensive find in biblical archaeology; dozens of copies of every book in the Old Testament (except for Esther) were found and are now on display at various museums around the world. More importantly, through forensic analysis, most have now been dated, translated, and published. Not all of the finds were books of the Bible; many are historical records that give us insight into Judaic daily life.[16]

The Dead Sea Scroll discovery is perhaps one of the most important moments in the history of modern Judaism and Christianity because it largely verifies the accuracy of the Bible we read. Since the Masoretic text was translated throughout the AD 600s, critics of the Bible could easily claim that it was written too soon to accurately represent scriptures from two millennia before. A collection of stories that had been retranslated over thousands of years would never resemble their original versions, would they? Most of the Dead Sea Scrolls predate the Masoretic Text, some by as many as eight hundred years, and the evidence shows that the Masoretes got the translation exactly right.

Furthermore, the idea that the Old Testament texts were invented stories written during the period of exile runs into major problems when examining the details. First of all, let's look at God's covenant with

INTRODUCTION

Abraham. The concept of forming a covenant with one's gods wasn't unique to Semites; many ancient cultures, including the Canaanites and Hittites, did this.[17] Evangelism didn't quite exist yet; each kingdom served its own gods, and one didn't try to convert other cultures to worship theirs (conquest to prove whose gods were superior was more common), and the idea of contracts with deities over who controls which land wasn't uncommon. In this context, it doesn't seem unusual that Abraham would form such an agreement with God, and this isn't something that the scholars of the exilic period many centuries later could have dreamt up.

There's more, of course. The story of Noah is just one of many flood legends to emerge from Mesopotamia; in fact, including the Babylonian epic of Gilgamesh, over 217 from around the ancient world existed, many of them bearing great similarities to Genesis.[18] While some critics would say that this proves that Noah's Flood is a work of fiction, a product of many other spreading tales of gods destroying the earth with water but saving humanity through one man, I maintain that it seems a little too coincidental. If over two hundred legends from the ancient world emerged from the same time period, all bearing a striking resemblance, doesn't that tell us that some cataclysmic flood event *did* happen, and the story must have an element of truth behind it?

But I digress; Noah's Ark is another topic for another book. More evidence that the Bible is at the very least a product of the ancient time it claims to be lies within the Exodus story. Take the forty years of wandering through the wilderness. Many details are unique to the Sinai Peninsula; for example, both manna and getting water from rocks are actual naturally-occurring phenomena common in the region. It's hard for me to believe that such stories didn't appear in the book of Exodus from real-life events that occurred during the long journey through the wilderness towards the Promised Land.

Of course, this is the important reason behind the "Naturalist Theories" that are discussed in this book. Many miraculous events in Exodus can have a scientific explanation. But this doesn't prove that God didn't perform them; if anything, it verifies the authenticity of the Bible, that this book *was* written in the ancient deserts describing historical events of real nomadic peoples. Personally it doesn't diminish my faith but has quite the opposite effect, making the story more plausible, and therefore more *real*.

Look at it this way. With each story in the Bible, we are presented with three possibilities. One is that the story never happened and is a made-up legend. Another is that it is largely exaggerated but based on some real-life occurrence. And the third, of course, is that every word is true and happened exactly as described. The critics of the Bible usually make the first claim. In our arguments with them, they will proudly and defiantly state that there is not a shred of evidence to support such ludicrous fiction. But what if we can point to some real phenomenon or ancient artifact that, while not necessarily proving that the Bible is absolutely true, at least supports the second possibility? This may seem like a copout. But we have eliminated the first possibility and have now planted the seed of doubt in the critic's mind. And this is very important as we go through this book and add up all the archaeological evidence; the doubter simply *can't* walk away, ignoring it all.

And the question that biblical maximalists will still argue, permeating every point I just made, is, *Why?* If the exilic writers invented the stories of the Bible to rally national pride and convince the Jewish people to migrate back to their homeland and rebuild their temple, why would they portray their ancestors as slaves? Most nations would be inclined to greatly exaggerate the greatness of their origins—that they were born of gods or descendants of divinity. The Jewish history, however, shows a nation of dirty slaves who begrudgingly followed God while stubbornly rebelling against Him and repeatedly enduring His wrath along the way. Hardly typical of ancient cultures, imagining a great forging of their kingdom.

So if the exilic Jewish scribes didn't write the Torah, who did?

THE AUTHOR

Since I mentioned earlier that our oldest known copy of even a shred of the Torah dates back to the 600s BC, and I will contend later that the Exodus actually occurred sometime in the 1400s BC, we are still left with a gap of around eight hundred years between the historical event and the earliest writing that describes it. This sounds like a sizable gap, but such discrepancies aren't uncommon among ancient historical documents and the events they chronicle. However it still presents a monumental challenge for the Bible maximalist trying to make the case that the story is based on fact instead of legend.

Reading the Torah itself, we see that while Genesis paints a vivid picture of Creation, as a history book it is a hodgepodge of quickly glossed-over stories of early man. The patriarchs are iconic, but very few take up much space in the Bible itself. Noah appears in six chapters. Abraham's life covers thirteen. Jacob's goes on for eleven before Joseph steals the spotlight and occupies the remaining fourteen chapters. Then, in Exodus, Moses emerges and dominates the next four entire books. He is truly the central figure of the Torah, the protagonist around which the entire story revolves. More of the Bible is devoted to him than any other figure until Jesus, so it's not difficult to see why tradition holds that he is the author of the first five books of the Bible.

But scriptural evidence supports it as well.

INTRODUCTION

And the Lord said unto Moses, Write this for a memorial in a book, and rehearse it in the ears of Joshua: for I will utterly put out the remembrance of Amalek from under heaven. (Exodus 17:14)

Here, the Lord instructs Moses to chronicle the victory over the Amalekites, and this is the first indication of a book of records of the events of the time. This could well have been the dawn of the Bible we hold in our hands today (with the exception for Job, which predates the Torah).

These are the journeys of the children of Israel, which went forth out of the land of Egypt with their armies under the hand of Moses and Aaron. And Moses wrote their goings out according to their journeys by the commandment of the LORD: and these are their journeys according to their goings out. (Numbers 33:1-2)

While this passage doesn't mention Genesis or the early chapters of Exodus, it indicates that Moses recorded every event taking place from the exit from Egypt to the arrival at Canaan.

And Moses wrote this law, and delivered it unto the priests the sons of Levi, which bare the ark of the covenant of the Lord, and unto all the elders of Israel. (Deuteronomy 31:9)

This verse leads us to safely conclude that Moses also wrote about the giving of the law and the book of Leviticus.
But scriptures outside of the Torah also support Mosaic authorship.

Only be thou strong and very courageous, that thou mayest observe to do according to all the law, which Moses my servant commanded thee: turn not from it to the right hand or the left, that thou mayest prosper withersoever thou goest. This book of the law shall not depart out of thy mouth; but thou shalt meditate therein day and night, that thou mayest observe to do according to all that is written therein: for then thou shalt make thy way prosperous, and then thou shalt have good success. (Joshua 1:7-8)

By this point, we can see that all of Moses' writings were collected and read aloud by Joshua to the people to remind them what the law stated. In the Bible's mysterious origins, this is the first time on record of it being given to people as a guide for how they should live.

And keep the charge of the Lord thy God, to walk in his ways, to keep his statutes, and his commandments, and his judgments, and his testimonies, as it is written in the law of Moses, that thou mayest prosper in all that thou doest, and whithersoever thou turnest thyself. (1 Kings 2:3)

The description "as it is written in the law of Moses" is preceded by "statutes, commandments, judgments, and testimonies." Such broad terms wouldn't cover a small portion of the Torah. Again, this does not state that everything from Genesis to Deuteronomy was written by Moses but supports that at least the majority of the first five books were.

> *And they set the priests in their divisions, and the Levites in their courses, for the service of God, which is at Jerusalem; as it is written in the book of Moses. (Ezra 6:18)*

Ezra was written during the time of the resettling of Jerusalem after the Babylonian exile, about one thousand years after the Exodus took place.[19] It chronicles the rediscovery of Judah's spiritual heritage as they rebuilt the temple and reestablished the priesthood. *Book of Moses* in singular form could refer to Leviticus, or it could indicate that at one time, the five books of the Torah were originally one (an idea that is further supported by the fluid structure that binds them together).

> *As it is written in the law of Moses all this evil has come upon us: yet made we, not our prayer before the Lord our God, that we might turn from our iniquities, and understand thy truth. (Daniel 9:13)*

Daniel declares that judgment has fallen because God's people have forsaken His Word and worshiped idols. He points to the "law of Moses" to explain why "evil has come upon us." It would be extraordinarily difficult to pinpoint one particular instance of this covenant in the Torah, as the promise of God that He will bless the people as long as they serve Him and curse them if they turn from Him is found consistently throughout the latter four books.

Jesus Himself and even Paul weighed in on the matter in the New Testament.

> *Have ye not read in the book of Moses, how in the bush God spake unto him, saying, I am the God of Abraham, and the God of Isaac, and the God of Jacob? (Mark 12:26)*

Just like Ezra, Jesus refers to a single "book of Moses" and God's appearance in the burning bush, which would support Moses' authorship of the early chapters of Exodus.

> *For Moses describeth the righteousness which is of the law, That the man which doeth those things shall live by them. (Romans 10:5)*

There are exceptions, of course. As Moses dies in Deuteronomy 34, the completion of that book was taken over by another author, probably Joshua.

INTRODUCTION

But with all the evidence within the Bible itself, it is hard to conclude that anyone other than Moses wrote at least the majority of the Torah. Why then, the challenge to that traditional view?

An increasingly common theory is that the Torah doesn't have a single "author" in the sense of the word but was composed over a span of time by several different men (called the "compositional view").[20] Sections might have been written by Moses, but others were compiled by his followers or written down while he dictated what to say.

With concrete evidence of the scripture's origins in short supply, let's take a hard look at the compositional view. Our oldest shreds date back some twenty-six hundred years, but even those were later copies. Who knows how old the very first written texts were? Unless we can find original copies of the Torah consisting of Moses' authenticated handwriting (allegedly, Josephus was in possession of these once, though that can hardly be verified), the Bible is considered to be a product of legends first amalgamated many centuries later.

The first problem with that is that it assumes that the Israelites were illiterate. The absence of ancient scrolls doesn't mean such scrolls didn't exist; to the contrary, by the midsecond century BC (the same period in which the Exodus likely took place), proto-Sinaitic had developed into one of the most sophisticated alphabets of the ancient world.[21] While the Egyptians had hieroglyphics, a discombobulated means of writing, to say the least, the Hebrew language was the first to match individual letters to represent each syllable. With this revolutionary form of communication in its earliest days, why wouldn't they be frantically writing down every major event that occurred? It would make perfect sense for Moses to keep a careful record of the critical points of God forging His nation on the earth.

Genesis, of course, is a possible exception. Moses was not present during Creation or the times of any of the patriarchs, so this book could well be a product of passed-down stories of how the world began. At the very least I would contend that he was still the author of the first book, due to the connection between the end of Genesis and the beginning of Exodus. So while I accept that he authored most of the last four books of the Torah, the next question we're left with is, How and why did he write Genesis?

It's entirely possible that while Moses was recording the events of the Exodus and the law, he decided now would be a good time to record the Creation and Semitic history. Is oral history reliable? Maybe. After starting this book, I was firmly against the idea. But during my research, I came across a startling fact that softened my stance. In German history is a series of legends called the *Niebelungs*, dating back at least as far as 800 AD. The story has survived, passed down from generation to generation, for over twelve hundred years, rarely written down and almost unchanged. Many people (including Hitler) have tried to add their spins, yet it remains largely unscathed from its original form.[22]

Even still, it seems more credible to me, as a Christian, that the Holy Spirit moved on Moses and told him what to write, even telling him the stories of Creation, the fall of man, and the Flood (though the prevalence of so many flood legends from the ancient world indicates that the great deluge was a well-known event in Mesopotamian culture). This would eliminate the possibility of the Word of God being tainted by man's imagination over the years. In 2 Timothy 3:16-17, Paul wrote,

> *All scripture is given by inspiration of God and is profitable for doctrine, for reproof, for correction, for instruction in righteousness: That the man of God may be perfect, thoroughly furnished unto all good works.*

It would certainly give their journey through the wilderness a greater sense of purpose, of God's greater plan being revealed through their endurance as a nation.

If we've established Moses as the author of the Torah, though, we've provided Bible minimalists with their next line of ammunition. A common claim against the Torah is that it is written in varied and different styles, sometimes even within chapters, as if written by several different people. So let's address that criticism next.

As I said earlier, not all of the Torah could have been written by Moses, as some of it takes place after his death. But what about the rest of it? It's not hard to believe that Moses could have had different scribes to whom he dictated what to write—like secretaries. This wouldn't be unique to the Torah, as Paul was known to do the same. If several different writers were following Moses, diligently recording the events, each one might have brought a slightly different wording to their respective passages.

Attempts have been made to decipher the alleged "different styles" of the Torah as well, but all of them have proven fruitless. One effort even divided the entire book into four different colors, with each color representing a unique style, to try to break down who wrote which parts.[23] The results, however, are incomprehensible. One can't read just the red, blue, or yellow texts and understand what is being said.

Even still, this point is made moot by the fact that one author can often write in different styles at different times. Sometimes the Torah is a history book, at times it is poetic, and at times it is a book of laws. It is what it needs to be, whenever it needs to be.

Which brings us to the ultimate conclusion of the authorship of the Torah: while Moses may have been the one to write it down, like the rest of the Bible, the entire book came straight from the mind of God.

DID THE EXODUS HAPPEN?

And finally, we get to my favorite part! While I loved studying the practical applications of Exodus for our daily lives, this particular topic was the biggest adventure. Each time I opened my reference books was like forging down a new path, with exciting discoveries at every turn. Earlier I mentioned the Middle Kingdom theory and stated that it would play a major role throughout the book. Now let me explain.

Since Kenyon's pronouncement that the Jericho story is a myth, archaeology has never been the same. The majority of professors excavating ancient sites defiantly claim that they have found no evidence to support any of the Bible's stories—no mention of the Israelite slaves, Moses, or any of the ten plagues. And this has led to several generations plagued with growing skepticism in the Word of God, while Christians and Jews alike slink away from the subject, murmuring that either archaeologists are devil-possessed or that it doesn't matter. Meanwhile, atheists around the world have seized this, triumphantly proclaiming to the world that the Bible is a lie.

But what if I told you that all of their claims may be based on a misreading of the scriptures?

The first question that will help us is this: who was the Pharaoh of the Exodus? Since the Bible frustratingly never names him, we're left to figure it out for ourselves. This, of course, is so important because it's our starting point.

Most people never make it past the first clue in Exodus 1:11:

> *Therefore they did set over them taskmasters to afflict them with their burdens. And they built for Pharaoh treasure cities, Pithom and Raamses.*

Ramses II, also known as Ramses the Great, was the most powerful Pharaoh in Egyptian history and built the magnificent city that bore his name. Therefore tradition has held for years that he must be the one that refused to let the Hebrews go. After all, he was played by Yule Brenner in a great performance in Cecil B. Demille's *The Ten Commandments*.

This is very easy to accept because the word *Pharaoh* is immediately synonymous with "Ramses." It makes for great drama; one of the world's greatest leaders versus one of the key figures in the Bible. It's why some biblical archaeologists like Kenneth Kitchen are drawn to naming Ramses in our quest to find the unnamed Egyptian ruler. It's a perfectly human reaction to imagine Moses confronting one of the most famous kings in history.

But this is where the problem comes in. Under the assumption that Ramses is the Exodus Pharaoh, based on one scripture and a considerable amount of influence from TV and movies, archaeologists have diligently searched for clues amongst Ramses-era ruins. And their searches have turned up nothing. Not a reference. Not a statue. No mention of it in any ancient records. No Jewish slaves, no Moses, no plagues, and no army drowning in the Red Sea. Therefore the story must be a myth. And most abandon the search from there.

However it's possible that we've been reading Exodus 1:11 wrong. Let's explore the possibility that the verse is an *anachronism*, which Webster's dictionary defines as "something (such as a word, an object, or an event) that is mistakenly placed in a time where it does not belong in a story, movie, etc."[24] In this case, the cities mentioned, Pithom and Ramses, may be names inappropriately given to older cities from a different time period.

Anachronisms are more common in ancient texts than people realize, which can make deciphering the Bible's timelines very confusing. It's entirely possible that somewhere along the way, a scribe inserted the name of a contemporary city in place of a city that didn't exist anymore to make the geography of the story make sense. If, in the eighth century BC, your priest read, "Our ancestors built the city of Avaris," you would respond, "What? Where's that?" because Avaris hadn't existed in ages. But if he read, "Our ancestors built the city of Ramses," which is a similar city *near* where Avaris once stood, you would know to where he was referring.

There's evidence within the Bible itself to support this. In 2 Kings 22, King Josiah starts to renovate the temple, and the priests discover ancient scrolls of the Torah. Shaphan the scribe reads Josiah the Word of God, moving the king deeply as he realizes how far the people have strayed.

> *And Shaphan the scribe shewed the king, saying, Hilkiah the priest hath delivered me a book. And Shaphan read it before the king. And it came to pass when the king had heard the words of the book of the law, that he rent his clothes. (2 Kings 22:10-11)*

The law is read aloud, moving the people to great spiritual reformation. They burn idols and destroy temples to Baal. Worship of the one true God is restored. The scribes began feverishly making updated copies of the Torah, and this is a clue to when the anachronisms would be inserted.

So if Exodus 1:11 is an anachronism, we have been looking for years in the wrong place for the Exodus.

On a timeline, we can divide the history of ancient Egypt into three eras: the Old Kingdom, the Middle Kingdom, and the New Kingdom. Traditional dating has placed the Old from 2700–2200 BC, the Middle at 2050–1800 BC, and the New Kingdom at 1550–1100 BC.[25] Notice, however, that there is a gap of several hundred years between each. These are referred to as the *intermediate periods*, when Egypt collapsed, plunging into poverty and sometimes even being conquered by outside kingdoms.

We have great historical records during the days that Egypt flourished but very little covering the periods of darkness, indicating that maybe, just maybe, our classical chronology of Egypt is off. This was first brought forward by Edwin Thiele in his 1943 book, *The Mysterious Numbers of the Hebrew Kings*. In 1996 Egyptologist David Rohl took this further with a controversial book, *A Test of Time*, wherein he proposed a radically changed Egyptian timeline (henceforth known as the "New Chronology"). You'll notice that several of Rohl's books appear in the sources sections this one:

of all the historians I read, he made the most compelling case for the new date of the Exodus.

One of the reasons Ramses is named the Exodus Pharaoh is that on top of being the most infamous Pharaoh, he was also the last great one. He is the symbol of the New Kingdom when Egypt reached the height of its power. After his death, it slowly declined and eventually collapsed altogether. It's thrilling to think that the ten plagues and Ramses drowning in the Red Sea might have been what caused Egypt's downfall. But it's also very improbable.

The new timeline hasn't gained widespread acceptance yet within the archaeological community; although most archaeologists are sympathetic to Rohl's premise, they aren't willing to take it quite as far as he does. It places the reign of Ramses about three hundred years in the future, from 943–877 BC.[26] Since we don't know how long the periods of darkness between each era lasted, and our traditional timetable has been essentially guesswork, this isn't as far-fetched as it sounds.

But even more outrageous is that the Middle Kingdom theory gives the Exodus a new date at five hundred years before Ramses (about 1447 BC). If this is true, it explains why archaeologists aren't finding any mention of the Exodus in the Ramses-era ruins. However searches among Middle Kingdom ruins have told a completely different story. This was the critical flaw of Kathleen Kenyon's excavation of Jericho. She decreed that a cataclysmic event followed by an invasion and burning of the city *did* happen; but under the assumption that Ramses was the Exodus Pharaoh, her dating didn't match that timeline.[27] But the newly proposed Middle Kingdom timeline perfectly synchronizes Bible chronology and archaeological history!

Of course, I can understand why so many Bible commentaries would want to shy away from such a controversial topic. For my book, the opportunity to bring Middle Kingdom dynamics into the fold was too good to pass up, especially as I saw more hard evidence to support the story. So while it may seem like I'm taking sides, my real goal truly is just for people to believe in the Bible again; it is truly the best hope for humanity.

And I fully admit that some of the entries in the Middle Kingdom sections will be not as much hard fact as speculation. The circumstantial evidence is quite overwhelming, but I won't pretend that it's something it isn't. For an example that I'll give more detail on later, we'll never know for sure if the mysterious Egyptian vizier given unprecedented power during the reign of Amenhemhat III was Joseph, but the parallels between the two are uncanny, and doesn't that at least deserve a second look?

So before actually getting into the book itself, let me begin with two specific things to help us date the Exodus in our new timeline. These are very helpful in matching up Egyptology with Jewish history and serve as our starting points in examining the evidence for the Middle Kingdom theory. And both of them start after the Exodus, as we work our way backward.

Setting aside Exodus 1:11, another scripture puts the Exodus at a completely different date (that for some reason archaeologists largely ignore).

> *And it came to pass in the four hundred and eightieth year after the children of Israel were come out of the land of Egypt, in the fourth year of Solomon's reign over Israel, in the month Zif, which is the second month, that he began to build the house of the* LORD. *(1 Kings 6:1)*

If the Exodus took place 480 years before Solomon began building the temple of God (according to Thiele, about 967 BC), we're winding the clock back to somewhere in the mid-1400s BC, exactly when the Middle Kingdom theory suggests.

The other is a more tantalizing possibility. It starts with a story described in both 1 Kings 14 and 2 Chronicles 12. After the death of King Solomon (931 BC), the nation of Israel is divided into two kingdoms; the ten tribes of the North stay Israel, but the kingdom in the South, which includes both largest and smallest tribes (Judah and Benjamin), becomes Judah. Jerusalem remains the capital and is the location of Solomon's temple, but during the division, the city is attacked and plundered by a mysterious Egyptian king.

> *So Shishak king of Egypt came up against Jerusalem, and took away the treasures of the house of the* LORD, *and the treasures of the king's house; he took all: he carried away also the shields of gold which Solomon had made. (2 Chronicles 12:9)*

Bible critics will point out that no Pharaoh named Shishak ever ruled Egypt, leading to a great deal of speculation by Christians and Jews to find out who exactly the Bible is describing here. A popular theory is that this might have been Shoshenk I, mainly due to the similarity in name, but the evidence for this is flimsy at best. Shoshenk was the founder of the twenty-second dynasty, reigning from 822–802 BC (new chronology), ruling over Egypt in the twilight of its waning years.[28] He did engage in military campaigns, but Ramses the Great he was not. The biggest case of mistaken identity here is that Shoshenk did invade the Northern Kingdom of Israel during his lifetime, but a common misconception is that this was a full-fledged invasion (it was more of a touring campaign and show-of-force for his allies). But the main reason that he could not be Shishak becomes clear when examining a map of his conquests; he never set foot in the kingdom of Judah nor came anywhere near Jerusalem or Solomon's temple.[29]

However let's examine the name a little closer. Believe it or not, *hypocoristics* (the shortening of one's name) existed in the ancient world, just like today. Even for world leaders. We called Princess Diana, "Lady Di." We call the most powerful Pharaoh in Egyptian history, "Ramses," but this is the Greek translation of an ancient name in a dead language. As close as we can determine, the exact pronunciation of Ramses' name was "Riamashisha."[30] See where I'm going with this?

In Egyptian, the hypocoristic of his name would have ended in *aw*, "Sysw." The Hebrew version of this is "Shysha." The *k*, then, was probably added during the retranslations under King Josiah (interestingly enough, the Semitic word *shakak* means "to plunder").[31]

If you believe in the traditional chronology, then Ramses the Great ruled in the 1200s BC, but under the new chronology, he is placed three hundred years later in the 900s BC. This would place his reign right at the time when King Solomon died and makes him a perfect candidate for Shishak.

As it stands, there is hard evidence that Ramses is the Egyptian king that plundered Solomon's temple. A large Egyptian tablet, called the Merneptah Stela, currently located at the Cairo Museum, is a campaign relief depicting the military victories of the Pharaoh and his family. Merneptah was the son of Ramses, but the Western side of the wall depicts the military victories of his father. It contains epic descriptions of the enemies beaten, including this intriguing passage in hieroglyphics: *Israel is laid waste, his seed is no more.*[32]

Whether or not Ramses is the biblical Shishak, this should definitively lay to rest the Ramses Exodus chronology. How could the man have led a military victory against a nation that didn't exist yet? That was just now being released from slavery and still had forty more years of wandering before they would reach their homeland? The results of the Exodus must have been devastating for Egypt, but Egypt prospered during the reign of Ramses and continued to thrive after his immediate death. It just doesn't make sense.

Now let's get back to the original question: just who was the Pharaoh of the Exodus?

If we're going by the traditional chronology, the Pharaoh who reigned in the mid-1400s BC is also the second-most popular candidate: Thutmose III. Thutmose is often referred to as the "Napoleon of ancient Egypt," mainly because, like Ramses, he conquered many nations. Thutmose also has the distinction of having a powerful aunt named Hatshepsut, whom some attribute as the daughter of Pharaoh that raised Moses as a child in the palace.[33]

However, just like Ramses, the evidence doesn't quite back it up. This is another example of taking an infamous Pharaoh and, for the sake of drama, tagging him as the one who refused to let the slaves go. People gravitate towards a familiar figure or recognizable name in history in these situations, and Thutmose certainly left his imprint on Egyptian history. But this may be exactly where he falls short. We tend to forget that there were hundreds of Pharaohs who ruled for thousands of years of Egyptian history; what are the odds that the Exodus figure would just happen to be one of the few immediately recognizable ones? Our most logical candidate is going to be someone who took control of a powerful kingdom and, during or towards the end of his reign, saw Egypt collapsing from the devastating effects of the ten plagues and the slaves escaping to freedom.

Under the new chronology, we find a perfect candidate reigning during the proposed date for the Exodus: Dudimose II. Now I'm sure you're wondering, *Who?* Dudimose, also referred to as "Tutimaos" by the Jewish historian Josephus, is not one of the more well-known Pharaohs. He is obviously not as recognizable as Thutmose or Ramses; in fact, in all my research, I have yet to see a picture of any statues or engravings of him.

But this is encouraging: if the Exodus Pharaoh existed, he took over an Egypt with a firm grip on the world's most powerful army—but he died with an empire crumbling all around him. And with the shame of failing to prevent the Hebrew slaves from leaving, he likely would have faded into obscurity.

Now, granted, our knowledge of the late Middle Kingdom is very limited by the lack of cohesive remains. But what we do know about Dudimose is helpful. We could call his reign the climax of the Middle Kingdom era; he took control at the height of Egypt's military might. But there is evidence of a series of cataclysmic events during his reign, and shortly after his death, Egypt was invaded and conquered by a foreign army, the Hyksos.[34] Where was their mighty army? The oppressive rule of the Hyksos signaled the beginning of the next period of darkness between the Middle and New Kingdom eras. It was Ahmose II who would finally drive out the Hyksos, allowing Egypt to be reborn.[35]

So we have a new chronology, a new place in Egypt's timeline, and a perfect candidate for the Pharaoh. Now, to find archaeological evidence for the Exodus, we need to take a closer look at the Middle Kingdom and examine historical records during the reign of Dudimose II. And here is where things get interesting.

But I don't want to spoil it all here in the introduction. This will all be explored further during the Middle Kingdom Dynamics sections of the book, corresponding to each major event. After thoroughly diving into the archaeology, I was surprised at all there is and even more amazed that there remains any doubt to the truth of the story. But most archaeologists are well-entrenched in the Bible minimalist belief and have been since Kenyon's proclamation. Discovery requires an open mind, and for archaeologists—the world over—to admit to being wrong on this issue may never happen. But in the meantime, I hope I can make a convincing argument in favor of the Middle Kingdom theory for believers and nonbelievers alike—the world over!

Chapter 1

THE MIGRATION

INTRODUCTION

It had been God's plan from the beginning.

Abraham (still called Abram at the time) was promised to be the father of many nations, but times would not always be good for his children.

> *And he [God] said unto Abram, Know of a surety that thy seed shall be a stranger in a land that is not theirs, and shall serve them; and they shall afflict them four hundred years; And also that nation [Egypt], whom they shall serve, will I judge: and afterward shall they come out with great substance. (Genesis 15:13-14)*

The entire story had been written before Abraham's wife, Sarah, even gave birth to Isaac. His seed would forever inhabit the land of Canaan; but first, they would migrate to Egypt during a great famine and then endure four hundred years of slavery before God's hand brought them back.

But technically, the story begins with Joseph.

> *And God spake unto Israel in the visions of the night, and said, Jacob, Jacob. And he said, Here am I. And he said, I am God, the God of thy father: fear not to go down into Egypt; for I will there make of thee a great nation: I will go down with thee into Egypt, and I will also surely bring*

thee up again: and Joseph shall put his hand upon thine eyes. And Jacob rose up from Beersheba: and the sons of Israel carried Jacob, their father, and their little ones, and their wives, in the wagons which Pharaoh had sent to carry him. And they took their cattle, and their goods, which they had gotten in the land of Canaan, and came into Egypt, Jacob, and all his seed with him: His sons, and his sons' sons with him, his daughters, and his sons' daughters, and all his seed brought he with him into Egypt. (Genesis 46:2-7)

The scripture then goes on to label all the family of Jacob and each of his twelve sons. Altogether, a clan of about seventy migrated to Egypt. God was bringing them to this land during the time of great famine, but Egypt was only a temporary place; Canaan would always be their home.

MIDDLE KINGDOM DYNAMICS

So did Joseph exist? Was he a real historical figure or a product of Jewish myth as they invented their own history?

Let's face it; there couldn't have been an exodus without a sojourn. So I want to begin with the same method we used in dating the Exodus (mid-1400s BC), looking for evidence by deducing which Pharaoh was ruling during this time.

We find ourselves in the reign of Amenemhat III, one of the last Pharaohs of the twelfth dynasty. The traditional chronology places him from 1817–1772 BC, but the new timeline dates his reign from 1678–1631 BC.[36] The Bible tells us that Joseph was sold into Egyptian slavery by his brothers, then rose to power in the house of Potiphar, before being imprisoned due to a false accusation. Years later he was able to free himself by interpreting the Pharaoh's disturbing dream, a warning from God that seven years of plenty were coming followed by seven years of famine. Pharaoh needed to build storehouses and gather a great harvest for Egypt to survive. The king was so impressed that he freed Joseph and made him the second in command over the whole kingdom, with the specific task of storing grain in preparation. When the famine came, his older brothers came crawling to Egypt to beg for food, fulfilling Joseph's dream that one day they would bow to him. Joseph ultimately forgave them, inviting the entire family to live in Egypt.

Amenemhat is a perfect candidate for the Pharaoh of Joseph, as events during his reign eerily echo the biblical story. Even statues of him are unusual among ancient kings: his face is depicted not as that of a great conqueror or mighty warrior but as a concerned man with worried features. His scrawnier-than-usual waistline indicates a time of famine during his reign, and his enlarged ears show that he was known for being attentive to the needs of the people.[37]

THE MIGRATION

Amenemhat's reign was the longest of the twelfth dynasty, and there was, in fact, a period of great plenty that preceded a terrible famine. Further exploration of the cause can help shed light on some intriguing details that match the biblical account. Flooding from the Nile River had inundated crops and covered harvest fields with several feet of water, bringing a massive agricultural shortage.[38] Compare this to Genesis 45:6, which gives us a clue for the cause of the famine:

> *For these two years hath the famine been in the land: and yet there are five years, in the which there shall neither be earing nor harvest.*

Logically, a deluge rather than drought would be the most likely reason for the lack of plowing.

What's more is that leading up to the famine, Amenemhat's government began preparing for it, almost as if by premonition. During the great abundance, they confiscated farmlands and seized crops, constructing storehouses all across Egypt to hoard mass quantities of food.[39] A canal to divert the water away from the crops and combat the shortage was also built and is still in Egypt today. Its name? The *Bahr Yussef*, which translates to "Waterway of Joseph."[40]

But Amenemhat did not order these major projects by himself. During his reign, a mysterious vizier came to power who served as the chief orchestrator overseeing this construction. The Bible tells us that Joseph was given an Egyptian name:

> *And Pharaoh called Joseph's name Zaphnathpaaneah, and he gave him to wife Asenath, the daughter of Potipherah priest of On. And Joseph went out over all the land of Egypt. (Genesis 41:45)*

The first part of his name, *Zaphnath*, loosely translates in Egyptian to "He who is called," while *pa-Aneah* means "The one who lives."[41] The symbol of life in Egyptian hieroglyphics is known as an *ankh*.

Which brings us to our next intriguing clue. Just like "Sishack" could be a hypocoristic of "Ramses," the name of our mysterious vizier who emerged during Amenemhat's reign could well be a hypocoristic of "pa-Aneah," *Ankhu*.

Was Ankhu Joseph? The resemblance is remarkable. Not only did Ankhu suddenly emerge from obscurity to an unprecedented amount of power, but he was also the one charged with constructing the grain houses (his official title in historical records reads "Ankhu, Overseer of the Fields").[42] The Bible tells us that Joseph had two sons, Ephraim and Manasseh. Ankhu too had two sons, named in Egyptian "Resseneb" and "Iymeru."[43]

When Ankhu died, his two sons took over his position as co-viziers of Egypt and became so powerful that they overshadowed the Pharaoh himself. After Amenemhat had also died, the following line of Pharaohs had short-lived reigns, as their governments were more or less puppet regimes of the children of Ankhu.

The Bible says that after some generations,

> *Now there arose up a new king over Egypt, which knew not Joseph. And he said unto his people, Behold, the people of the children of Israel, are more and mightier than we: Come on, let us deal wisely with them; lest they multiply, and it come to pass, that, when there falleth out any war, they also join unto our enemies, and fight against us, and so get them up out of the land. (Exodus 1:8-10)*

If Ankhu was Joseph, his two sons had gained so much power over a weakened throne that there was a backlash and power struggle after their deaths. The twelfth dynasty was then brought to an end, as the throne was seized by the Luxor family, ushering in the thirteenth dynasty. Since Egypt had been shadow-ruled by a foreign family, the Luxors would have dethroned Joseph's descendants and put the Israelites into slavery, ensuring that native Egyptians would rule once again.[44]

THE CITY OF AVARIS

All of this may sound like speculation and coincidence, but now let's get to the key piece of evidence. At the centerpiece of the Middle Kingdom theory is the city of Avaris. The ruins of this ancient settlement were first discovered by Austrian archaeologist Manfred Bietak in 1966.[45] Bietak's team made several more excavations at this amazing site and made startling discoveries that I will be covering in the rest of the book in conjunction with the events of the Exodus.

The Bible calls the Israelite settlement "the land of Goshen." Avaris sprang up during the reign of Amenhemhat III, the same Pharaoh we've deduced ruled during the time of Joseph. But the words *Jew* or even *Israelite* didn't exist yet. The population of Avaris were foreigners, as the architecture of its buildings was not Egyptian. Natives called its citizens *Asiatics*, which refers to immigrants from the Levant, specifically the Syrio-Canaan region (where Jacob's family would have come from).[46] "Avaris" is a Greek translation of the original Egyptian "Haware," which loosely means "Office of the Region."[47] If this city were built for Joseph and his family, it clearly would have been an extension of the capital.

Avaris originally had a small population of about seventy to one hundred. A beautiful palace was built at the center of the town of immigrants. Throughout the city were also eleven more houses with eleven tombs, almost as if the settlement was run by twelve patriarchs, with one of them being more powerful than the others.[48] The contents of the palace are telling; within its walls was a magnificent tomb with the kind of décor only reserved for Pharaoh himself (and unprecedented for a foreign leader), including a pyramid. Over the tomb was discovered the broken remains of a large statue, with the four-thousand-year-old traces of paint still visible. Upon reconstruction, the details reveal the palace resident holding a throw stick, the symbol of Asiatics, with red hair (Egyptians were always depicted with black hair) and wearing a coat of many colors![49]

Inside the tomb, the bones of this great ruler were missing.[50] But their removal was a pious act; destructive grave robbers would have been interested in the priceless treasures buried alongside Egyptian kings, not the bones themselves.

> *And Joseph took an oath of the children of Israel, saying, God will surely visit you, and ye shall carry up my bones from hence. (Genesis 50:25)*

Moses was careful to fulfill this request when the Israelites finally won their freedom and escaped Egypt:

> *And Moses took the bones of Joseph with him: for he had straitly sworn the children of Israel, saying, God will surely visit you; and ye shall carry up my bones away hence with you. (Exodus 13:19)*

EXODUS 1:1-22

> *Now these are the names of the children of Israel, which came into Egypt; every man and his household came with Jacob. Reuben, Simeon, Levi, and Judah, Issachar, Zebulun, and Benjamin, Dan, and Naphtali, Gad, and Asher. And all the souls that came out of the loins of Jacob were seventy souls: for Joseph was in Egypt already. And Joseph died, and all his brethren, and all that generation. And the children of Israel were fruitful, and increased abundantly, and multiplied, and waxed exceeding mighty, and the land was filled with them. (Exodus 1:1-7)*

Among Jacob, his twelve sons, daughters, in-laws, and grandchildren, about seventy people moved to Egypt altogether. But as the Lord promised to do with His people, He multiplied them greatly, until they exploded into a population that overtook a sizable portion of the land.

THE PRACTICAL APPLICATION

If Egypt represents the world, the children of Israel represent us. We are not commanded to stay in our churches and just have services among ourselves but are to be sent out into the world to multiply the body of Christ.

> *And he said unto them, Go ye into all the world, and preach the gospel to every creature. (Mark 16:15)*

MIDDLE KINGDOM DYNAMICS

Since Avaris housed Joseph and his family, it represented wealth and aristocracy. Some years later, the city did indeed see a population explosion due to a combination of a mass migration of Asiatics and a dramatic increase in childbirth from its settlers. It was forced to expand, swelling fast from a small village to a sprawling metropolis that became the economic center of the Pelusiac branch of the Nile River.[51] This was an ideal place to live, but its magnificence was to be short-lived.

> *Now there arose up a new king over Egypt, which knew not Joseph. And he said unto his people, Behold, the people of the children of Israel, are more and mightier than we: Come on, let us deal wisely with them; lest they multiply, and it come to pass, that, when there falleth out any war, they also join unto our enemies and fight against us, and so get them up out of the land. Therefore they did set over them taskmasters to afflict them with their burdens. And they built for Pharaoh treasure cities, Pithom and Raamses. (Exodus 1:8-11)*

THE PRACTICAL APPLICATION

This is the same attitude the world has towards Christianity today. We don't pose a threat as long as we stay in the church and sing to ourselves. But the minute we go out on the streets and begin proclaiming the gospel to every creature, we start a movement, and they feel threatened. Why else would they fight evangelism so hard? Why else file a lawsuit every time they see a plastic manger scene? Why else try to remove the very name of God from every sect of public life, under the false guise of "separation of church and state"? The mantra of secularism is, "Keep religion in the churches," and by doing so, they try to contain us. The devil, through them, wants to keep us under control; but Exodus teaches us that this isn't anything new.

> *But the more they afflicted them, the more they multiplied and grew. And they were grieved because of the children of Israel. (Exodus 1:12)*

The more the Egyptians tried to cull the Israelite population, the more it grew. Persecution has a way of making God's people more powerful. The harder the Pharisees tried to stamp out the early church, the more were saved. The more the Romans tried to stop Christianity, feeding them to lions in front of cheering crowds, the stronger it became. Pastors tried to warn their congregations to stay away from the Pentecostal revival that broke out of Azusa Street, yet thousands flocked from all over America to see what it was all about. The Christian Church in China today is exploding more than any other in the world, not the least of which is because of the great persecution they suffer. If the American church is at a standstill, it's because we have become too comfortable and lost the fire that drives us.

> *And the Egyptians made the children of Israel serve with rigor: And they made their lives bitter with hard bondage, in morter, and in brick, and in all manner of service in the field: all their service, wherein they made them serve, was with rigour. (Exodus 1:13-14)*

But the greater the burden, the more the Israelites grew in number. Eventually Pharaoh was forced to come up with a sinister plan to stifle the population growth of his enemies.

MIDDLE KINGDOM DYNAMICS

For years, archaeologists have claimed that there is no evidence that any Jewish slaves lived in Egypt. Therefore Exodus itself must be a work of fiction. But remember, this claim is made under the assumption that Ramses was the Exodus Pharaoh and that the events would have taken place towards the end of the New Kingdom.

However an ancient Egyptian papyrus dating from the Middle Kingdom at the Brooklyn Museum tells a different story. The papyrus dates from the reign of Sobekhotep III, in the middle of the thirteenth dynasty after the Asiatic rulers would have been overthrown and enslaved by the Luxor family. The document contains a list of slave names from a wealthy Theban estate in southern Egypt (remember that the Bible says the Israelites spread throughout the land). About half of the names are Semitic, including "Shiphrah," "Asher," "Menahem," and "Issachar."[52]

Furthermore, exploring the timeline of Avaris, Bietak's team found that the population was originally large and prosperous. But after a few generations, the conditions inside tombs told a compelling story. Skeletons were suddenly malnourished, and mortality rates indicate that the citizens were dying much younger, usually a tell of poverty, starvation, and perhaps even slavery. The evidence is clear that the citizens of Avaris suddenly turned from wealthy aristocratic immigrants to starving paupers forced to work to death in miserable conditions.[53]

THE MIDWIVES

> *But the midwives feared God, and did not as the king of Egypt commanded them, but saved the men children alive. And the king of Egypt called for the midwives, and said unto them, Why have ye done this thing, and have saved the men children alive? And the midwives said unto Pharaoh, Because*

the Hebrew women are not as the Egyptian women; for they are lively, and are delivered ere the midwives come in unto them. (Exodus 1:17-19)

These Hebrew midwives refused to carry out Pharaoh's commandment, much to his ire. After all, he was considered a god to the Egyptians, and to disobey him would be heresy. But Shiprah and Puah knew they could not dishonor the one true God to please this worldly king.

Therefore God dealt well with the midwives: and the people multiplied, and waxed very mighty. And it came to pass, because the midwives feared God, that he made them houses. (Exodus 1:20-21)

THE PRACTICAL APPLICATION

Pharaoh's plan failed, his enemies grew even mightier, and God blessed the midwives. These women knew they could lose their lives by refusing to obey Pharaoh, but just like Shadrach, Meshach, and Abednego (Daniel 3), they would not bow. Would that the church had that uncompromising spirit today! If we Christians allow the world to influence us, we will end up destroying our children.

MIDDLE KINGDOM DYNAMICS

Exploring the graves of Avaris indicates that not only were its citizens suddenly oppressed with poverty but that infant mortality rates instantly skyrocketed for no apparent reason. At the climax of this period, the population of males declined to almost nothing, as if every male baby had been killed; for every three female skeletons, there are only two males.[54] Why the sudden shift in gender ratio? It seems clear that the ruler of Egypt had ordered every male child killed to curb what he saw as a growing threat, exactly as the Bible describes!

CONCLUSION

In only twenty-two verses of Exodus, we already have a profound lesson. The Lord has sent us forth into Egypt (the world) with the same message: multiply. Grow His kingdom and win the lost. The world won't care at first and may even welcome us until we start to increase in size and power truly. First they will try to destroy us, then our children; but if we trust in God and refuse to compromise, He will bless us greatly even in the midst of great persecution.

Chapter 2

THE BIRTH OF MOSES

INTRODUCTION

The Hebrew midwives refused to obey Pharaoh, but the rest of Israel was not quite so steadfast. We have no record of any of them, other than Moses' parents, resisting the commandment to throw their newborn babies into the Nile River. Living in Egypt for four hundred years had given them the mindset of pleasing Pharaoh first; the real tragedy is that their babies died as a result.

It's difficult for us to comprehend gruesomely murdering our children because a worldly leader tells us to. But so many of us today are doing just that, in a spiritual sense. If we don't raise them according to biblical standards, especially where discipline is concerned, we are tossing them out into the Nile of this world where Satan's army of crocs awaits, salivating mouths open in anticipation. How different are we from the Israelites when we send our children out to public schools to be indoctrinated that the Bible is a lie? Or to concerts where drugs and alcohol are freely passed out as harmless?

Jacob had two wives and two concubines, bearing him a combined total of twelve sons (how many daughters is never revealed), each becoming the head of the twelve tribes of Israel. He loved Rachel but had been tricked into marrying her older sister, Leah, first.

> *And he went in also unto Rachel, and he also loved Rachel more than Leah and served with him yet seven other years. And when the LORD saw*

> *that Leah was hated, he opened her womb: but Rachel was barren. (Genesis 29:30-31)*

Leah bore more children for Jacob than any other, and Levi was their third son.

> *And she conceived again, and bare a son; and said, Now this time will my husband be joined unto me because I have born him three sons: therefore was his name called Levi. (Genesis 29:34)*

What she hoped was that the third child would finally cause her husband to love her above his other wives, so she named him "Levi," which means "to adhere." Levi was the living embodiment of his mother's desire to win the heart of the father. How interesting that from this child would come the sacred priests, which were the representatives of the people before the Father. Moses, also being a Levite, would lead his people to freedom, and just like the priesthood, he would stand before God's wrath as an intercessor. We can see the type and shadow of Christ, our Royal Priest interceding on our behalf before the Father, saving us from judgment.

Before we delve into the lesson, however, I need to get an important issue out of the way. One of the de facto criticisms of the Bible is that its stories are not original. The claim is that the biblical tales are borrowed from other ancient legends. This is especially true of the Flood, as skeptics often point to numerous other flood legends that predate Genesis and contain many eerie similarities to the story of Noah, including the Babylonian Epic of Gilgamesh. The birth of Moses, however, is also one of the most cited examples.

In 2117 BC, in Mesopotamia's Early Dynastic period, a mighty Semitic conqueror named Sargon of Akkad conquered much of Southern Mesopotamia. City after city fell under his invading armies as he carved out the largest empire up to that time. This coincided with the decline and eventual fall of Old Kingdom Egypt. The Akkad dynasty (who gave us one of the most common languages of the time, Akkadian), would rule the region for the next one hundred eighty years.[55]

If Sargon's status in the Sumerian Empire was legendary, his ego was probably even more legendary. His epic tale of his own life, the infamous *Legend of Sargon of Akkad*, contains many great escapades, even a version of his birth that sounds similar to the birth of Moses:

> Sargon, the mighty king, king of Akkad, am I . . . my mother, the high priestess, conceived me. In secret, she bore me. She placed me in a basket of rushes. With bitumen, she sealed my lid. She cast me into the river which rose not over me. The river bore me up and carried me to Akki, the drawer of water. Akki, the drawer of water, lifted me out of the river as he dipped his ewer. Akki, the drawer of water, appointed me as his gardener.

> While I was a gardener, Ishtar (ancient fertility goddess) granted
> me her love, and for four and fifty years I exercised kingship.[56]

So according to Sargon, he had been born of a high priestess and placed in a basket along the river, and the current carried him to a palace gardener named Akki, who took him and raised him as his own. The rest of the story involves his meteoric rise to power.

The similarities to the birth of Moses in Exodus are too obvious to be ignored, and Bible critics are quick to jump on this as proof that Moses' legendary origins were borrowed from a much older mythological tale, therefore proving that the story didn't happen.

But not so fast. That Sargon predates Moses by many centuries is undeniable, but writing off Exodus as untrue is jumping to conclusions far too quickly. Let's consider the historical context. At this point, it had been about five hundred years since the Akkadian dynasty. Just because the mid-second century BC Israelites were slaves doesn't mean they were stupid and uneducated. Quite the contrary; while originally sojourning to Egypt as a traveling tribe, they still carried with them a rich and proud oral history. One must also take into account that as Semites (descendants of Shem), they were blood relatives of Sargon, a Sumerian. (I will argue in a later book that the similarities of the names Shem and Sume indicate the Sumerians and Semites of early Genesis were the same.) In all probability, the tribes of Israel were well-versed in tales of ancestors past, especially the *Legend of Sargon of Akkad*. Perhaps they looked to this past story as a source of inspiration for their heritage, considering the hopeless situation they now found themselves in as a people.

So when Pharaoh ordered the infanticide, it is within reason to assume that Moses' parents were inspired by the legend to save their baby by putting him in a basket and setting him afloat down the Nile. The Bible critic may say that this is only wishful thinking on the part of the Bible defender, but I have to point to the overwhelming amount of evidence support of so many other details of the Exodus at this time detailed in this book. I have no doubt that the Exodus took place and that the Bible has given us a reliable depiction of what happened. There is no real reason, then, to discount its version of Moses' birth, either, even if it does bear resemblance to another ancient Middle Eastern tale.

EXODUS 2:1-9

> *And there went a man of the house of Levi, and took to wife a daughter of Levi. And the woman conceived, and bare a son: and when she saw him that he was a goodly child, she hid him three months. (Exodus 2:1-2)*

WHO WERE MOSES' PARENTS?

We do know that Moses was from the tribe that would eventually produce the priesthood, but the identity of his parents is not initially revealed. The issue is not addressed until Exodus 6:20, when describing the generations and genealogies of the Israelites:

> *And Amram took him Jochebed his father's sister to wife, and she bares him Aaron and Moses: and the years of the life of Amram were a hundred and thirty and seven years. (Exodus 6:20)*

It would be easy to interpret this as Moses being a product of a peculiar incestuous relationship between a Levite and his aunt, but if we investigate the scriptures a little more, we find this problematic.

Kohath was the son of Levi, born before the migration to Egypt (Genesis 46:11); and in Exodus 6:18, two verses before describing Moses' birth, Amram is declared to be one of four sons of Kohath.

> *And the sons of Kohath; Amram, and Izhar, and Hebron, and Uzziel: and the years of the life of Kohath were a hundred thirty and three years. (Exodus 6:18)*

If Amram was the direct grandson of Levi, Jochebed was a daughter.

> *And the name of Amram's wife was Jochebed, the daughter of Levi, whom her mother bare to Levi in Egypt: and she bares unto Amram Aaron and Moses, and Miriam their sister. (Numbers 26:59)*

The problem is that Moses was born some three hundred fifty years after these people lived.

This leaves us with two distinct possibilities: (1) Amram and Jochebed were not direct children of Levi but were descendants of his, or (2) Moses' parents were both direct descendants of Levi but came from different ancestries of his children; the father was from the branch of Kohath and the mother from Jochebed. As the scripture is more precise, labeling these two with Levi's other children and grandchildren, the latter seems a more plausible explanation.

Since his parents are not specifically named in Exodus 2, a certain air of mystery surrounds Moses' parentage; the only thing we can conclude is that he was the middle of three children, with an older sister named Miriam and a younger brother named Aaron.

Out of all Israel, we only have a record of one who did not obey Pharaoh's order. But the child could not be hidden forever.

> *And when she could not longer hide him, she took for him an ark of bulrushes, and daubed it with slime and with a pitch, and put the child therein; and she laid it in the flags by the river's brink. (Exodus 2:3)*

Just like God had instructed Noah to build an ark to save one remnant of humanity, the Spirit moves on Moses' mother to build a small basket to save her son. Satan did his best to get rid of the man who would lead the Hebrews to freedom, but God would not allow it.

But was a basket enough to save the child? The Nile crocodile, after all, is the largest crocodilian species in the world. None of us would feel safe allowing our newborn baby to be put in a small basket to float down a river swarming with the world's biggest crocs. She surely had to have faith in God as she embarked on this, even allowing Moses' older sister, Miriam, to wade into the dangerous waters to watch where the basket ended up.

> *And his sister stood afar off, to wit what would be done to him. (Exodus 2:4)*

So many babies died needlessly, but the hand of God was over this precious one. Just like the angel of the Lord would shut the mouths of the lions when Daniel was thrown into their den someday (Daniel 6), no doubt that same angel came down and shut the mouths of the crocodiles as that baby, with his sister not far behind, floated down the river.

> *And the daughter of Pharaoh came down to wash at the river; and her maidens walked along by the river's side, and when she saw the ark among the flags, she sent her maid to fetch it. And when she had opened it, she saw the child: and, behold, the babe wept. And she had compassion on him, and said, This is one of the Hebrews' children. (Exodus 2:5-6)*

It isn't explained how Pharaoh's daughter knew that the child was Hebrew. Was it his style of clothes? His features, perhaps? Did the Spirit whisper it to her? Or did this mean something deeper? The world should immediately be able to recognize us as children of God. The people we encounter on a daily basis should know we're Christians before we say anything because of His glory shining from our faces. It used to be said on Sundays, and one could stand on a high building and look down at crowds of churchgoers leaving and differentiate the Pentecostals above all the others because of the glow they had. Do we still have that glow?

MIDDLE KINGDOM DYNAMICS

As our new timeline perfectly synchronizes the story with real-life historical events, we find more names to assign to biblical characters. The twenty-eighth ruler of the thirteenth dynasty was Palmanothes, who never had any sons to continue his reign. His only biological offspring was one daughter, Merestekhi. Therefore the next Pharaoh would be the future queen's husband, Khaneferre. Upon marrying the daughter of the king and ascending to the throne, he took the royal name Sobekhotep IV.[57] Reigning from 1530–1508 BC (New Chronology), he was one of the most powerful kings of the Middle Kingdom; his colossal statues still haunt its ruins.

Merestekhi could certainly well be the biblical "daughter of Pharaoh," and we now find an intriguing drama playing out during the Sobekhotep's that mirrors the second chapter of Exodus.

Unfortunately, the most conclusive evidence we could find to demonstrate the validity of the Bible would be an exact reference to Moses; however, that name does not appear in Egyptian records. Nevertheless, it is tempting to match him with the oldest son of Merestekhi and Sobekhotep, who grew up in the house of Pharaoh as a favorite prince of Egypt.

> *And the child grew, and she brought him unto Pharaoh's daughter, and he became her son. And she called his name Moses: and she said Because I drew him out of the water. (Exodus 2:10)*

"Moses" is not traditionally a Jewish name; the Egyptian *Munius* means "drawn from the water," which the Torah translates into Hebrew as "Moshe."[58]

Egyptian archives called the son of Merestekhi and Sobekhotep "Mio," which is very similar to "Mo," the Egyptian word for "water." Mio was the oldest of four and clearly in line to become Pharaoh. Historically, he was educated in the best schools and highly trained in the role of leadership, being taught diplomacy and military leadership. His three younger brothers were incredibly jealous; however, upon deeper inspection, we learn there is more to the story than simply sibling rivalry. Mio does not show up in any of the royal lists of bloodlines, indicating that like Moses, he was likely adopted.[59] The brothers would have seethed with resentment that a future Pharaoh would rule with blood foreign to the royal family.

Mio was also a military hero. Late in the reign of Sobekhotep, Egypt was subject to two different invasions from the South by the Kushites; as it was customary for Pharaohs and their sons to lead Egypt's armies in battle, Mio fought and won a striking victory.[60] With each battle, he returned home a triumphant hero, the people lavishly celebrating his arrival.

Another clue in identifying Mio as Moses is examining many of the strategic moves Moses would later make in leading the Israelite people through the wilderness, suggesting at least some military experience on his part.

Perhaps most telling, though, is that despite being the favored prince of Egypt, Mio never actually became Pharaoh. A short time after his victories, he vanished mysteriously from Egyptian record and is never mentioned again.[61] It's almost as though he had brought disgrace to the royal family, to be stricken from history forever. The second-oldest son, Merhotepre, would be the next Pharaoh and take the moniker of Sobekhotep V.

The only thing quite stopping us from concluding that Mio *is* Moses is the dating; the Bible tells us that Moses spent forty years in the wilderness before returning to Egypt to save his people. In our new chronology, the banishment of Moses would have taken place in about 1487 BC, but the disappearance of Mio occurs about ten to fifteen years before that. Nevertheless, in the grand scheme of thousands of years of Egyptian history, I'm open to the possibility that some dating might be slightly off, and we could adjust a few years here and there, bringing the two events closer together.

> *Then said his sister to Pharaoh's daughter, Shall I go and call to thee a nurse of the Hebrew women, that she may nurse the child for thee? And Pharaoh's daughter said to her, Go. And the maid went and called the child's mother. And Pharaoh's daughter said unto her, Take this child away, and nurse it for me, and I will give thee thy wages. And the women took the child and nursed it. (Exodus 2:7-9)*

THE PRACTICAL APPLICATION

The Lord will bless those who obey His commandments over the world's. He did this for the Hebrew midwives and then helps Moses' mother. She was living as a slave, but He saw to it that she was rewarded for not killing her child like everyone else. This lowly woman became a servant in the house of Pharaoh, only doing what was natural: nursing her baby. But she was paid wages for this, keeping her out of the poverty and suffering of the rest of the people.

CONCLUSION

God works in mysterious ways. In the midst of child slaughter, He was able to save one and raise him up to be the savior of his people. It's not by coincidence that this would repeat itself many years later: when Herod ordered the massacre of every male child in Bethlehem, Jesus was saved by fleeing to Egypt. And from great tragedy, the greatest miracle of salvation arose.

The devil hates the youth. He wants to destroy them because they represent the future; and in the future, God can raise saviors. We look at abortion, at the tens of millions of babies who have been slaughtered since *Roe v. Wade* was passed. But God very well could have raised the next savior out of that tragedy. Just like Jesus ascended out of the massacre at Bethlehem and Moses out of the Egyptian slaughter, our next great leader who will bring His people to the Promised Land could well have been born out of this cynical youthful age, rising from the ashes of an aborted generation.

But the parallels between Jesus and Moses don't end there, and the next step is very important. Jesus was saved from massacre and baptized by John at the start of His ministry. But first He had to go through a wilderness time. That period is essential for people going into God's work. He fasted forty days and was tempted by the devil before He could do great things. Moses was going to endure forty years of darkness before he could be counted worthy to set his people free.

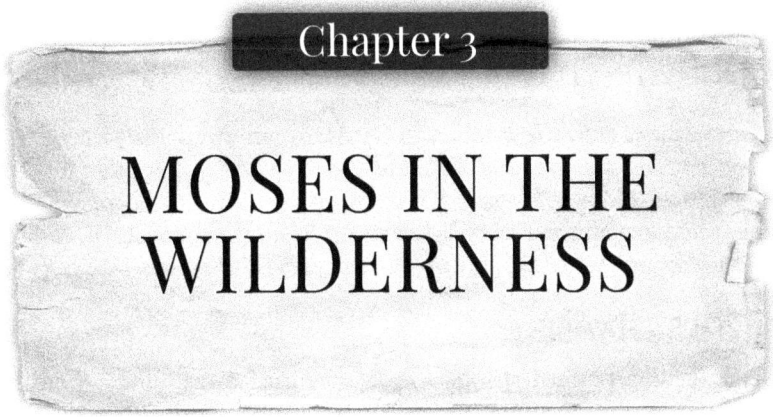

MOSES IN THE WILDERNESS

INTRODUCTION

A story as old as time itself starts here. A man is destined for greatness; but first, he spends years on a journey of self-discovery, before returning ready to accept his destiny. Moses left Egypt but returned decades later after the ultimate downfall and humiliation. I already mentioned that this character arc is repeated throughout the Bible. David was anointed king as a young man but then spent the next ten years on the run for his life, sleeping in caves and clinging to survival with a band of rogue soldiers. From the psalms he wrote during this time, we can tell he spent plenty of nights looking to the sky and crying,

> *Hear, O LORD when I cry with my voice: have mercy also upon me and answer me. (Psalm 27:7)*

And this journey still resonates into modern times. When Theodore Roosevelt's wife and mother both died, he left New York and spent years in the Midwest, living as a lowly cowboy on the plains and completely rediscovering himself. His tragedy and years of self-imposed exile molded and shaped him into the eccentric figure he was to become, and he returned to New York City with the vigor to run for mayor. It was this drive that eventually made him one of the most influential presidents in American history.

The basic plot of Exodus is one of the most archetypal stories of all time. Moses spent a third of his life as a fallen prince who became a lowly shepherd. Let's look closely at what we do know about those years to find out what shaped him, and most importantly, what we can learn from it.

EXODUS 2:11-25

> *And it came to pass in those days, when Moses was grown, that he went out unto his brethren, and looked on their burdens: and he spied an Egyptian smiting a Hebrew, one of his brethren. And he looked this way and that way, and when he saw that there was no man, he slew the Egyptian and hid him in the sand. (Exodus 2:11-12)*

THE TIES THAT BIND

We see a distinct pattern among God's greatest; almost all of them had troubled pasts. Here was the great leader of the Exodus, but he was a murderer in his former life. Abraham made a mistake with Hagar, Jacob deceived his father, Elijah hid from Jezebel, Peter denied Christ, and Paul persecuted the first Christians. But the Lord is a God of redemption.

> *And when he went out the second day, behold, two men of the Hebrews strove together: and he said to him that did the wrong, Wherefore smitest thou thy fellow? And he said, Who made thee a prince and a judge over us? Intendest thou to kill me, as thou killedst the Egyptian? And Moses feared, and said, Surely this thing is known. (Exodus 2:13-14)*

THE PRACTICAL APPLICATION

We can also see the spiritual condition of the Israelites. When he was questioned for smiting a fellow child of God, this Hebrew retorted with the classic line people use today to justify their sin: "Don't judge me!"

It's bad enough if the world lives by this mantra, twisting the words of Jesus to make themselves immune from all criticism; but when God's people do it, we have a problem. "Don't judge me!" is one of modernism's most common mottos, and it is leading millions on a path straight to hell. Sure, Moses had no right to kill someone, but did that excuse this man from striking a fellow child of God?

> *Now when Pharaoh heard this thing, he sought to slay Moses. But Moses fled from the face of Pharaoh, and dwelt in the land of Midian: and he sat down by a well. (Exodus 2:15)*

The exile begins. Many great men of God have to endure it first. Jonah fled from God and spent three days in the belly of a whale before he finally did what the Lord wanted. After David was anointed a king, he went back to tending his sheep in the fields. Elijah hid from Jezebel under the juniper tree. Even Jesus had to fast and be tempted by the devil before He could start His ministry.

When God has His hand on our lives, we're sometimes not even aware of it and will spend years in this wilderness, feeling like fugitives. We may even be there for decades, not knowing that He's patiently waiting for the right time to reveal Himself.

> *Now the priest of Midian had seven daughters: and they came and drew water, and filled the troughs to water their father's flock. And the shepherds came and drove them away: but Moses stood up and helped them, and watered their flock. And when they came to Reuel, their father, he said, How is it that ye come so soon today? And they said, An Egyptian delivered us out of the hand of the shepherds, and also drew water enough for us, and watered the flock. And he said unto his daughters, And where is he? Why is it that ye have left the man? Call him, that he may eat bread. And Moses was content to dwell with the man, and he gave Moses Zipporah his daughter. (Exodus 2:16-21)*

Who were the Midianites? In Genesis, after Abraham's wife, Sarah (mother of the promised child, Isaac), died, he remarried Keturah, who bore him six sons.

> *Then again Abraham took a wife, and her name was Keturah. And she bares him Zimran, and Jokshan, and Medan, and Midian, and Ishbak, and Shuah. (Genesis 25:1-2)*

Since the Midianites were blood relatives of the Israelites, Moses was not taking a heathen wife by marrying Zipporah.[62]

Moses' father-in-law, referred to as a "priest of Midian," is intriguing for an apparent contradiction that pertains to God's perfect number. Not only did he have seven daughters, but he is referred to by seven different names in the Old Testament.

1. This passage in Exodus refers to him as "Reuel," which means "Friend of God."
2. Exodus 3:1 calls him "Jethro," which in Hebrew means that he "Flowed with good deeds."
3. Exodus 4:18 in the King James Version lists him again as "Jethro," but the original Hebrew more accurately translated to "Jether," indicating that he was responsible for "an addition" to the Torah.
4. Exodus 6:25 refers to Aaron taking one of his daughters as a wife as well but names the Priest of Midian as "Putiel," referring to one that has renounced idolatry.

5. Numbers 10:29 calls Moses' father-in-law "Hobab," the "Beloved son of God."
6. Outside of the Torah, Judges 1:16 calls him a "Kenite," indicating he was "Zealous for God."
7. Finally, Judges 4:11 names "Heber," or "Associate of God." However this could refer not specifically to Jethro but to one of his sons. At the very least, it still indicates a family name.[63]

History also indicates that the Midianites were just as in-tune with the laws of God as the Israelites at this point. Circumcision, for example, had been a commandment of Abraham's descendants since the beginning.

This is my covenant, which ye shall keep, between you and me and thy seed after thee; Every man child among you shall be circumcised. (Genesis 17:10)

It represents cutting away the flesh, a sacrifice that identifies God's children as His own. (We Christians today do not necessarily have to be physically circumcised, but according to Romans 2:29 we must undergo a circumcision of the heart.)

Some mistakenly attribute Jethro as a descendant of Ishmael. This is due to some confusion over Genesis 37:28, which refers to the band of nomads (both Midianites and Ishmaelites) to whom Joseph's brothers sold him as a slave.

Then there passed by Midianites merchantmen, and they drew and lifted up Joseph out of the pit, and sold Joseph to the Ishmaelites for twenty pieces of silver: and they brought Joseph into Egypt. (Genesis 37:28)

This likely indicates that the band was comprised of a mixture of both tribes, not that Midianites and Ishmaelites were the same.

By all accounts in the Word, Jethro was a true man of God, with even seven different names given to him, devoted to describing his greatness as a servant of the Lord.

So from where did Moses' knowledge of God come? It certainly was not during his time as a child of Pharaoh. Was he taught the ways, history, and laws of his people by his mother during his early childhood? Possibly. But we can't help but determine that Jethro, who was a powerful servant of God, had much influence on him during his forty years in the wilderness as a shepherd. His father-in-law shaped him into becoming the true deliverer of his people, instructing him on the knowledge and nature of the God of their forefathers.

Even during our wilderness times, when we have separated ourselves far from the will of God, the Lord still has people placed in our lives who are helping us every step of the way. One can almost imagine Jethro acting on behalf of the Holy Spirit, whispering over Moses' shoulder as he worked, teaching him right from wrong.

And she bare him a son, and he called his name Gershom: for he said, I have been a stranger in a strange land. (Exodus 2:22)

The name "Gershom" literally means "a stranger there."[64] It indicates that Moses had accepted his fate, living in a strange land. It had been a lesson in humility, going from prince to shepherd, and it certainly seemed he had no chance of ever returning to the land he called home.

THE PRACTICAL APPLICATION

We try to give our children names to bear our sins. Moses gave his child a name that showed he thought his past deeds unforgivable. It was almost a curse, an expectation that his seed was doomed for all eternity. He had settled down for a life as a shepherd, expecting his children to be shepherds, and their children shepherds after that, forever. But God was undoing that curse before it even started. Moses would, in fact, be a shepherd for the rest of his life. But he would not be herding sheep.

And it came to pass in the process of time, that the king of Egypt died: and the children of Israel sighed by reason of the bondage, and they cried, and their cry came up unto God by reason of the bondage. And God heard their groaning, and God remembered his covenant with Abraham, with Isaac, and with Jacob. And God looked upon the children of Israel, and God had respect unto them. (Exodus 2:23-25)

God's plan from the beginning was coming together. He had promised in His covenant with Abraham that his descendants would be in bondage for many generations in a foreign land, but now deliverance was coming. One of the most important events in human history was about to lay the foundation of God's nation on planet Earth.

MIDDLE KINGDOM DYNAMICS

Unfortunately, films and TV series such as *The Ten Commandments* and *Prince of Egypt* have portrayed Moses and Pharaoh as two brothers growing up in the Egyptian court, only to become bitter enemies years later. It makes for great theater, and read literally, the Bible almost seems to support it. Verse 23 describes the death of the Pharaoh who raised Moses, and no other Pharaoh is mentioned between this and Moses' return. How much more dramatic is it to depict Ramses as this brother-turned-mortal-enemy? But it doesn't hold up historically.

After the death of Sobekhotep IV, his second-oldest son (not Mio) took over. Remember, however, that Moses spent forty years as a refugee from Egypt; Sobekhotep V only ruled for twenty-two years. By the time of the Exodus, several Pharaohs with very short reigns have come and gone. If Dudimose II was the king of Egypt during the Exodus, he had probably heard of Moses but never met him personally.

CONCLUSION

Throughout human history, whenever the Jews have cried out to the Lord for deliverance, He has remembered His covenant with Abraham. The enslavement wouldn't be the last time their light was almost snuffed out. The Egyptians almost accomplished it. The Assyrians and Babylonians nearly destroyed them. The Seleucid kings almost extinguished them, and the Romans thought they had broken them forever. Hitler came close to exterminating them. Today Israel's enemies all around want to wipe them off the face of the earth. But God will not allow it.

No one will ever be able to destroy the Jewish people. God keeps His Word for all eternity. If the Lord has made you a promise and you are discouraged that it has not yet come to pass, remember this: five thousand years after Abraham, the covenant is still in effect.

A new Pharaoh had taken over; but this one was even crueler than before, only increasing their workload. Discouragement grew as they cried out to the Lord. After four hundred years, surely they questioned whether anyone was hearing them. But all the while, God was molding and shaping the man he had ordained to be the deliverer.

You may have been praying for many years for the Lord's help. It could be for an unsaved loved one, a healing, or a financial miracle. Maybe your prayers have gone unanswered for so long that no one seems to be listening. But be of good courage; before you even came before Him, He already knew the need and was moving. He will answer it at the perfect time, and you can claim in faith, believing that it is already done.

> *And it shall come to pass, that before they call, I will answer; and while they are yet speaking, I will hear. (Isaiah 65:24)*

Chapter 4
THE BURNING BUSH

INTRODUCTION

Moses was only doing his job, keeping the flock, when the Lord suddenly intervened. God often sweeps us into our callings when we least expect it. Peter and Andrew were fishing when Jesus first appeared to them.

> *And Jesus, walking by the sea of Galilee, saw two brethren, Simon called Peter, and Andrew his brother, casting a net into the sea: for they were fishers. And he saith unto them, Follow me, and I will make you fishers of men. (Matthew 4:18-19)*

He didn't give them time to say goodbye to loved ones or make preparations.

> *And they straightway left their nets, and followed him. (Matthew 4:20)*

They dropped what they were doing, abandoned their very livelihood and the only thing they'd ever known, and followed Him. Something was clearly different about this Man.

In Luke 9 Jesus made this same sudden call to another man to follow Him but was met with an excuse:

> *And he said unto another, Follow me. But he said, Lord, suffer me first to go and bury my father. Jesus said unto him, Let the dead bury their dead: but go thou and preach the kingdom of God. (Luke 9:59-60)*

He wasn't even given a chance to take care of very important business first. But we can't even afford to say goodbye to family when He calls. It is just looking back, the same sin that turned Lot's wife into a pillar of salt.

> *Another also said, Lord, I will follow thee; but let me first bid them farewell, which is at home at my house. And Jesus said unto him, No man, having put his hand to the plow, and looking back, is fit for the kingdom of God. (Luke 9:61-62)*

And when that trumpet sounds,

> *In a moment, in the twinkling of an eye, at the last trump: for the trumpet shall sound, and the dead shall be raised incorruptible, and we shall be changed. (1 Corinthians 15:52)*

We won't have time to prepare when the Lord returns. We can't say one last-minute sinner's prayer and make the Rapture.

> *For yourselves know perfectly that the day of the Lord so cometh as a thief in the night. (1 Thessalonians 5:2)*

EXODUS 3:1

Mount Horeb

> *Now Moses kept the flock of Jethro his father in law, the priest of Midian: and he led the flock to the backside of the desert, and came to the mountain of God, even to Horeb. (Exodus 3:1)*

"Mount Horeb" or "the mountain of God, in Horeb" appears several times in the Old Testament. Biblical scholars disagree on its exact location, or whether it is even different from the famed Mount Sinai later in scripture. The name *Horeb* may be an ancient Sumerian word for "glowing heat," which indicates a mountain of the sun, while *Sinai* could be derived from "Sin," a lunar pagan deity. Thus "Horeb" and "Sinai" would be mountains of the sun and moon, respectively. Some have posited that the names may suggest different sides of the same mountain, with the sun rising on one slope and the moon appearing from the other.[65]

Biblical evidence seems to support this. Malachi 4:4 tells us to,

> *Remember ye the law of Moses, my servant, which I commanded unto him in Horeb for all Israel, with the statutes and judgments. (Malachi 4:4)*

"Horeb" rather than "Sinai" is mentioned as the place where God gave Moses the law, rather than appearing in the burning bush. Moses' father-in-law, Jethro, was present at Sinai in Exodus 18. First Kings 8:9 also describes God giving Moses the law at Mount Horeb:

> *There was nothing in the ark save the two tables of stone, which Moses put there at Horeb, when the* LORD *made a covenant with the children of Israel, when they came out of the land of Egypt. (1 Kings 8:9; also see 2 Chronicles 5:10)*

THE TIES THAT BIND

Horeb is where Elijah hid from Jezebel.

> *And he arose, and did eat and drink, and went in the strength of that meat forty days and forty nights unto Horeb the mount of God. (1 Kings 19:8)*

It is worth noting that where God appeared to Moses in the burning bush, and possibly later gave him the Ten Commandments, Elijah also went on a forty-day fast while hiding from the armies that sought to kill him. This mountain was a holy place in the Old Testament, where two of the greatest men of God who ever lived heard from the Lord! As two of the greatest prophets in the Bible, Moses and Elijah are intrinsically linked. They both appeared at the Mount of Transfiguration in the New Testament.

> *And it came to pass about an eight days after these sayings, he took Peter and John and James, and went up into a mountain to pray. And as he prayed, the fashion of his countenance was altered, and his raiment was white and glistering. And, behold, there talked with him two men, which were Moses and Elias: Who appeared in glory, and spake of his decease which he should accomplish at Jerusalem. (Luke 9:28-31)*

It's profound that Moses and Elijah were discussing the coming crucifixion with Jesus on top of the mountain. Mountains play an important role in the Word of God. Noah's Ark landed on one when the flood waters receded. God appeared to Moses in the burning bush and gave him the law possibly on the same mountain. Years later Elijah hid from Jezebel at the same location. Jesus revealed Himself in His glorified state to the disciples on the Mount of Transfiguration. And all of them point to the greatest mountain of all: Calvary, the holiest of all mountains, where the Lamb of God was slaughtered for the sins of humanity.

Because of this bond between them, many believe that Moses and Elijah are the two witnesses described in Revelation 11 who will prophesy against the antichrist and his followers during the Tribulation period. God does nothing by coincidence!

EXODUS 3:2-10

And the angel of the LORD *appeared unto him in a flame of fire out of the midst of a bush, and he looked, and, behold, the bush burned with fire, and the bush was not consumed. (Exodus 3:2)*

In the hot desert, seeing a bush catch fire wasn't uncommon. But this is no ordinary fire. It drew Moses to take a closer look.

"The angel of the Lord" seemed to bring some confusion as to who was in the flame. While it seemed to describe an angel, the voice coming from the bush belonged to God Himself. The word *angel* here in Hebrew more accurately translates to "the messenger,"[66] a title often assigned to Gabriel. However this isn't the only time in the Old Testament that "the angel of the Lord" is used to describe a being that may be synonymous with God. In Genesis 16 such a "messenger" was sent to deliver the news to Abraham that he and Sarah would bear a child even in their old age. Whenever "the angel of the Lord" is mentioned appearing, followed by being referred to as "the Lord," we can almost imagine Jesus Himself appearing to Old Testament figures to bring news to them from heaven.

And Moses said, I will now turn aside, and see this great sight, why the bush is not burnt. (Exodus 3:3)

One helpful key in any Bible study is to remember types and shadows, especially in the Old Testament. Wood, for example, may represent the cross; we see a picture of Jesus carrying His cross up Calvary in Isaac carrying the wood for his own sacrifice (Genesis 22). The Holy Spirit appeared in three different forms: oil, a dove, or fire; anytime these are mentioned in the Old Testament, we can safely venture that it is symbolic of the Holy Ghost.

What draws us to Calvary? Jesus told the disciples,

But if I depart, I will send him [the Holy Spirit] unto you. And when he come, he will reprove the world of sin, and of righteousness, and of judgment. (John 16:7-8)

The Holy Spirit convicts, ultimately leading each and every one of us to the cross, and that is foreshadowed in the burning bush attracting Moses to the mountain.

And when the Lord saw that he turned aside to see, God called unto him out of the midst of the bush, and said, Moses, Moses. And he said, Here am I. (Exodus 3:4)

THE TIES THAT BIND

When God calls a name twice, it is of extra significance. The Lord double-names seven different persons throughout the Bible (again, God's perfect number). The first four are in the Old Testament: Abraham (Genesis 22:11), Jacob (Genesis 46:2 and 35:9-15), Moses (Exodus 3:4), and Samuel (1 Samuel 3:10). It then occurs three times in the New Testament: Martha (Luke 10:41), Simon (Luke 22:31), and Saul (Acts 9:4).

Moses had to see and hear from the fire of God before he could answer, "Here am I." This also occurs elsewhere in scripture. When Isaiah had his vision in chapter 6, God was so huge that even the massive temple was only big enough to hold the train of His robe.

> *In the year that king Uzziah died I saw also the Lord sitting upon a throne, high and lifted up, and his train filled the temple. (Isaiah 6:1)*

So awesome was the sight of the Almighty that even the holiest prophet in Judah fell before Him, unworthy.

> *Then said I, Woe is me! For I am undone; because I am a man of unclean lips, and I dwell in the midst of a people of unclean lips: for mine eyes have seen the King, the LORD of hosts. (Isaiah 6:5)*

In this condition, the prophet was not ready to tell anyone what he'd seen. But coal from the fire of God's altar made all the difference.

> *Then flew one of the seraphims unto me, having a live coal in his hand, which he had taken with the tongs from off the altar: And he laid it upon my mouth, and said, Lo, this hath touched thy lips; and thine iniquity is taken away, and thy sin purged. (Isaiah 6:6-7)*

Once the fire of God touched his lips, Isaiah was transformed.

> *Also, I heard the voice of the Lord, saying, Whom shall I send, and who will go for us? Then said I, Here am I; send me. (Isaiah 6:8)*

He had gone from crumpled in worthlessness to boldly answering the call to go forth and deliver the Lord's message. It was the same cry of "Here am I!" that Moses made before the burning bush.

When the disciples received the Holy Ghost on the day of Pentecost, they were transformed from a band of refugees to the founders of Christianity.

> *And there appeared unto them cloven tongues like as of fire, and it sat upon each of them. And they were all filled with the Holy Ghost and began to speak with other tongues, as the Spirit gave them utterance. (Acts 2:3-4)*

Peter went from the man who denied Christ to the man who won three thousand souls to the Lord in one day and was so anointed that people were healed merely by touching his shadow. That's the difference the Holy Ghost makes. Moses' experience at the burning bush and Isaiah's vision of the coals before the altar of the Lord both foreshadow the outpouring of the Holy Spirit through speaking in tongues. One must have the Holy Ghost before going into the ministry; they cannot obey God without His fire.

And he said, Draw not nigh hither: put off thy shoes from off thy feet, for the place whereon thou standest is holy ground. (Exodus 3:5)

THE TIES THAT BIND

Adam and Eve ate the forbidden fruit in Eden:

And the eyes of them both were opened, and they knew that they were naked; and they sewed fig leaves together, and made themselves aprons. (Genesis 3:7)

Once sin entered the picture, mankind was no longer fully allowed to be in God's presence, and they had to put up fig leaves as aprons to separate themselves from Him.

The partition appears throughout the Bible. In the temple, the presence of the Lord dwelt the strongest in the Holiest of Holies, a room in the innermost part of the building. But a veil at the entrance stood between the glory of God and man, and only the priest was allowed to enter once a year on the Day of Atonement.

But into the second went the high priest alone once every year, not without blood, which he offered for himself, and for the errors of the people. (Hebrews 9:7)

When Jesus died on the cross, the veil was torn, representing the separation between God and man being brought down.

Jesus, when he had cried again with a loud voice, yielded up the ghost. And, behold, the veil of the temple was rent in twain from the top to the bottom; and the earth did quake, and the rocks rent. (Matthew 27:50-51)

Notice that it was rent from top to bottom, proving that God tore it down, not man. His presence is now fully given to man without measure.

However we continue to put up barriers between ourselves and God. Anything we do that stands between us and Him is a veil, and He cries for us to let them down.

Nevertheless when it shall turn to the Lord, the vail shall be taken away. (2 Corinthians 3:16)

This is why Moses had to take off his shoes. The presence of God emanating from the burning bush was so powerful that the ground surrounding it was holy. The soles of his shoes are small things, but the Lord wanted *nothing* between them. That's the only condition in which He's able to move in our lives.

> *Moreover he said, I am the God of thy father, the God of Abraham, the God of Isaac, and the God of Jacob. And Moses hid his face; for he was afraid to look upon God. (Exodus 3:6)*

The Lord reminded Moses who He was, mentioning His father and ancestors. Our God is the God of all of our fathers, going back to the beginning of time, and farther. He is also the God of our children, grandchildren, and their grandchildren, forever and ever.

> *I am Alpha and Omega, the beginning and the end, the first and the last. (Revelation 22:13)*

No wonder the simple and profound phrase, "I am," is one of His many titles!

THE TIES THAT BIND

To look upon Him and hear His voice is so overwhelming that Moses hid his face, just like Isaiah when he was transported to the throne. It's also why John wrote that when he first saw Jesus in His glorified state,

> *I fell at his feet as dead. And he laid his right hand upon me, saying unto me, Fear not; I am the first and the last. (Revelation 1:17)*

When we get so deep into His glory, our knees become weak, and we can fall over as one dead. Pentecostals call this experience being slain in the Spirit. If John, who knew Jesus personally, was still knocked over by seeing Him in such a powerful way, how much more of an impact will His presence have on us?

But the Lord had good news for Moses.

> *And the LORD said, I have surely seen the affliction of my people which are in Egypt, and have heard their cry by reason of their taskmasters; for I know their sorrows; And I am come down to deliver them out of the hand of the Egyptians, and to bring them up out of that land unto a good land and a large, unto a land flowing with milk and honey; unto the place of the Canaanites, and the Hittites, and the Amorites, and the Perizzites, and the Hivites, and the Jebusites. Now, therefore, behold, the cry of the children of Israel comes unto me: and I have also seen the oppression wherewith the Egyptians oppress them. Come now therefore, and I will send thee unto Pharaoh, that thou mayest bring forth my people the children of Israel out of Egypt. (Exodus 3:7-10)*

Not only did God proclaim the great things that He was about to do, but He also invited all of us with the personal call, "Come now, therefore." We should consider it a privilege to travel into the darkness to break the chains of bondage the enemy has on people.

But all too often, our response is similar to Moses'.

EXODUS 3:11-22

Moses Argues with God

> *And Moses said unto God, Who am I, that I should go unto Pharaoh, and that I should bring forth the children of Israel out of Egypt? (Exodus 3:11)*

Moses would go on to do more for the Lord's children than any other until Jesus. But right now he was a murderer, hiding from the authorities. But God often chooses the people we'd least expect. The Bible stands as a living testament to God's transformative power—how He can take the least among us and raise them up to be His most powerful warriors.

THE PRACTICAL APPLICATION

When the Lord calls us to ministry, we often don't answer with joy so much as doubt. Not so much in Him but in ourselves. Moses' question, "Who am I?" is met with one of God's greatest promises, one that shines through every scripture of both Old and New Testaments:

> *I will be with thee. (Exodus 3:12)*

This permeates the entire Bible, breaking the fourth wall into today. No matter how afraid we are to step forward, His Spirit whispers those five simple words into our ears to strengthen us.

> *I can do all things through Christ which strengtheneth me. (Philippians 4:13)*

But Moses still had questions.

> *And Moses said unto God, Behold, when I come unto the children of Israel, and shall say unto them, The God of your fathers hath sent me unto you; and they shall say to me, What is his name? What shall I say unto them? (Exodus 3:13)*

After four hundred years in slavery, their cries of salvation going unanswered, the Israelites were doubtful about who their Lord was. Unfortunately, it would take more than just miraculous deliverance to shake that doubt. Moses instinctively knew that the first question he'd be faced with on his mission was who God is in the first place.

The Tetragrammaton

> *And God said unto Moses, I AM THAT I AM: and he said, Thus shalt thou say unto the children of Israel, I AM hath sent me unto you. (Exodus 3:14)*

"I am" is the shortest possible complete sentence in the English language, yet it says so much about God. It signifies His omnipotence; He is everywhere, all the time, seeing, hearing, and knowing all. When He sends us out into the world to proclaim the Good News, they may ask the same question: *Who is He?* We even call Him the "Great I Am." It is beyond the comprehension of the human mind; He simply is.

There is some debate over God's exact wording here. The root word "to be" in Hebrew, *hyh*, is derivative of the phrase *I am*, or *'ehyeh*. We can see a clear connection with the actual name of God. The four letters that spell out YHWH is called the Tetragrammaton. The name was forbidden from being spoken aloud in ancient Judaism; just as God's presence was so powerful in the Holiest of Holies that anyone other than the priest could die from entering, the name of God was considered to have power beyond what the human body could handle.[67]

Interestingly enough, ancient writings reflect this change in the Almighty's moniker. The Hebrew God is referred to as *El* before Moses' experience at the burning bush; afterward, He is called Yahweh. Inscriptions in the Syrio-Canaan region dating before the Middle Bronze Age have been found referring to God, *El-Olam* ("God the Eternal").[68]

> *And God said moreover unto Moses, Thus shalt thou say unto the children of Israel, the LORD God of your fathers, the God of Abraham, the God of Isaac, and the God of Jacob, hath sent me unto you: this is my name forever, and this is my memorial unto all generations. (Exodus 3:15)*

Since the Lord stated, "This is my name forever," we could take that to mean He's just declared a secret, never-before-revealed title to Moses. On the other hand, He could merely have been reminding Moses that He would forever be remembered as the Lord of the patriarchs. Either way, we are left with a powerful impression of His awesome nature.

God declared this shall be a "memorial for all generations." Here we are, thirty-five hundred years later, still analyzing what the story means. Generations into eternity will know about what He did for Abraham, Isaac, and Jacob. They will still discuss the revelation to Moses on Mount Horeb. And they will sing of the story of Exodus forever.

> *Go, and gather the elders of Israel together, and say unto them, The LORD God of your fathers, the God of Abraham, of Isaac, and of Jacob, appeared unto me, saying, I have surely visited you, and seen that which is done to you in Egypt: And I have said, I will bring you up out of the affliction of Egypt*

> *unto the land of the Canaanites, and the Hittites, and the Amorites, and the Perizzites, and the Hivites, and the Jebusites, unto a land flowing with milk and honey. And they shall hearken to thy voice: and thou shalt come, thou and the elders of Israel, unto the king of Egypt, and ye shall say unto him, The* LORD *God of the Hebrews hath met with us: and now let us go, we beseech thee, three days' journey into the wilderness, that we may sacrifice to the* LORD *our God. (Exodus 3:16-18)*

Moses was to tell the children of Israel one story but then something else entirely to Pharaoh. While promising freedom, he was to ask Pharaoh permission to venture into the wilderness for three days to make sacrifices. Was this a lie? Is God deceitful? No. It was a test; He knew Pharaoh wasn't about to lose three days' worth of labor while the slaves went unguarded into the desert. But the Lord was willing to give Pharaoh one more opportunity before judging Egypt.

> *And I am sure that the king of Egypt will not let you go, no, not by a mighty hand. (Exodus 3:19)*

The plan was ordained from the beginning. God knew Pharaoh's heart. The king of Egypt had a "mighty hand," or was a strong ruler, and would not show perceived weakness by respecting the customs of slaves. After all, Pharaoh was supposedly a god. But the Lord was setting this vanity up to demonstrate just who the one true God is.

> *And I will give these people favor in the sight of the Egyptians:, and it shall come to pass, that, when ye go, ye shall not go empty. But every woman shall borrow of her neighbor, and of her that sojourneth in her house, jewels of silver, and jewels of gold, and raiment: and ye shall put them upon your sons, and upon your daughters; and ye shall spoil the Egyptians. (Exodus 3:21-22)*

The Israelites wouldn't just be freed; they would take the spoils of Egypt with them. We go through great darkness, hoping the Lord will allow us to barely survive. We limit Him with this kind of thinking. Little do we know that His nature is to bring us out with greater blessings than we had before!

THE TIES THAT BIND

In 2 Chronicles 20, the Moabites and Ammonites came together to attack the Jews.

> *It came to pass after this also, that the children of Moab, and the children of Ammon, and with them other beside the Ammonites, came against Jehoshaphat to battle. (2 Chronicles 20:1)*

THE BURNING BUSH

Outnumbered and facing destruction, King Jehoshaphat and all the people gathered together to fast and pray before God. He answered through a prophecy, as the Holy Ghost took over one in the congregation.

> *Then upon Jahaziel the son of Zechariah, the son of Benaiah, the son of Jeiel, the son of Mattaniah, a Levite of the sons of Asaph, came the Spirit of the LORD in the midst of the congregation; And he said, Hearken ye, all Judah, and ye inhabitants of Jerusalem, and thou king Jehoshaphat, Thus saith the LORD unto you, Be not afraid nor dismayed by reason of this great multitude; for the battle is not yours, but God's. (2 Chronicles 20:14-15)*

The message through Jahaziel was clear; God would win the battle for them.

> *And when he had consulted with the people, he appointed singers unto the LORD, and that should praise the beauty of holiness, as they went out before the army, and to say, Praise the LORD; for his mercy endureth forever. (2 Chronicles 20:21)*

The people had such great faith that Jehoshaphat sent the singers out before the army, praising the Lord in advance for the victory.

> *But the LORD honored that faith, killing the enemy before they even arrived at the battlefield. And when Judah came toward the watch tower in the wilderness, they looked unto the multitude, and, behold, they were dead bodies fallen to the earth, and none escaped. (2 Chronicles 20:24)*

They wouldn't even have to fight.
Verses 25-26 tell us,

> *And when Jehoshaphat and his people came to take away the spoil of them, they found among them in abundance both riches with the dead bodies, and precious jewels, which they stripped off for themselves, more than they could carry away: and they were three days in gathering of the spoil, it was so much. And on the fourth day they assembled themselves in the valley of Berachah; for there they blessed the LORD: therefore the name of the same place was called, The valley of Berachah, unto this day. (2 Chronicles 20:25-26)*

The riches and spoils of battle gathered from the slain enemy were so great that it took three days to carry it all back. The valley of Beracah had been a place designated for their destruction but became where they received their greatest blessing. That is the power of faith!

But God still wasn't done; His greatest act was using it to prove Himself to the world.

> *And the fear of God was on all the kingdoms of those countries when they had heard that the LORD fought against the enemies of Israel. (2 Chronicles 20:29)*

Our problems may look insurmountable. We may feel just like the children of Israel after four hundred years of slavery, or the kingdom of Judah surrounded and outnumbered by a hostile enemy. But the Lord won't just get us through it barely alive; He will bring us out with blessings beyond our wildest comprehension. And the world will not be able to help but see what a great God He is. Our victories will be testimonies.

EXODUS 4:1-16

The Tests

When God told Abram to leave his home, family, and everything he'd ever known for a promised land, he went without question.

> *Now the* LORD *had said unto Abram, Get thee out of thy country, and from thy kindred, and from thy father's house, unto a land that I will shew thee. . . . So Abram departed, as the* LORD *had spoken unto him; and Lot went with him: and Abram was seventy and five years old when he departed out of Haran. (Genesis 12:1, 4)*

This was Abram's first encounter with God, and he had come from a family of idol worshipers, but his faith in this Being was so great that he simply obeyed. Moses, however, was lacking.

> *And Moses answered and said, But, behold, they will not believe me, nor hearken unto my voice: for they will say, The* LORD *hath not appeared unto thee. (Exodus 4:1)*

Moses' questions earlier were at least legitimate: first, whether he was able, then whether the Israelites would recognize he was sent by God (3:11). Then his questions got bolder, asking God whether or not they would recognize the One who'd sent him (3:13). Now, despite looking straight into the fire of God, he was still uncertain.

> *And the* LORD *said unto him, What is that in thine hand? And he said, A rod. And he said Cast it on the ground. And he cast it on the ground, and it became a serpent, and Moses fled from before it. And the* LORD *said unto Moses, Put forth thine hand, and take it by the tail. And he put forth his hand and caught it, and it became a rod in his hand. That they may believe that the* LORD *God of their fathers, the God of Abraham, the God of Isaac, and the God of Jacob, hath appeared unto thee. (Exodus 4:2-5)*

This is the first of three signs that God would give to prove beyond a shadow of a doubt that He was sending Moses on this mission. Each sign foreshadowed a miraculous event that would take place later in Egypt. With one breath, the Lord could shake the earth with a massive earthquake or make fire fall from heaven or conjure up terrifying beasts. Instead, He performs a small trick that even the Pharaoh's magicians could replicate. Moses throws his staff on the ground, and it turns into a snake. Then Moses grabs its tail as it becomes a staff again. We tend to think that serpents represent Satan, but the Lord is master over every animal—the devil is not.

> *And the LORD said furthermore unto him, Put now thine hand into thy bosom. And he put his hand into his bosom: and when he took it out, behold, his hand was leprous as snow. And he said, Put thine hand into thy bosom again. And he put his hand into his bosom again; and plucked it out of his bosom, and, behold, it was turned again as his other flesh. (Exodus 4:6-7)*

Leprosy was a common term to describe many different skin diseases in Bible days.[69] It had no cure at the time, so to prevent spread of the disease, lepers were placed in colonies outside of cities where they became outcasts. This demonstrates the Lord's mastery over both sickness and health; Moses' hand is perfectly healthy when placed into his coat, made leprous upon removal, then restored to normal "again as his other flesh."

THE TIES THAT BIND

While leprosy could be punishment from God (in Numbers 12, Moses' sister was stricken for grumbling out of jealousy of his leadership), God used lepers to do great things. In 2 Kings 7, the Syrians had come to destroy Israel, and Samaria was under siege. Four lepers sat outside the city. But little did they know that God had placed them in the right place at the right time—poised to become heroes.

> *And there were four leprous men at the entering in of the gate: and they said one to another, Why sit we here until we die? If we say, We will enter into the city, then the famine is in the city, and we shall die there: and if we sit still here, we die also. Now therefore come, and let us fall unto the host of the Syrians: if they save us alive, we shall live; and if they kill us, we shall but die. (2 Kings 7:4-5)*

Deciding they had nothing to lose, they bravely ventured to the enemy camp, only to find it abandoned.

God had scared the Syrians away, and no one hiding in the besieged city even knew it.

> *For the LORD had made the host of the Syrians to hear a noise of chariots, and a noise of horses, even the noise of a great host: and they said one to another, Lo, the king of Israel hath hired against us the kings of the Hittites, and the kings of the Egyptians, to come upon us. (2 Kings 7:6)*

Overjoyed, the lepers ran back to Samaria to tell the people. Everything the Syrians left behind was theirs for the taking. While the people hid in fear, the Lord used the bravery of four diseased outcasts to bring the good news that the battle was over.

Only the Messiah could have healed leprosy; outside of Miriam's disease departing after her exile (which was before the completion of the Torah), not a single record of any Jew being healed of leprosy took place until Jesus performed His miracles (Naaman, who dipped in the Jordan River seven times in 2 Kings 5, was a Gentile). Leviticus 13–14 even details a temple ritual that should take place in the event of miraculous healing of leprosy; yet as far as we know, these rites never had reason to take place . . . at least not until Jesus healed the leper in Luke 5. Jesus immediately commanded him to go and tell the priest so that the ceremony could be done.

> *And he charged him to tell no man: but go, and shew thyself to the priest, and offer for thy cleansing, according as Moses commanded, for a testimony unto them. (Luke 5:14)*

No doubt the priest was stunned and had no idea what to do. The next verse declares,

> *But so much the more went there a fame abroad of him: and great multitudes came together to hear, and to be healed by him of their infirmities. (Luke 5:15)*

This had never happened in the history of Israel or Judah! Unsurprisingly, the following verse states,

> *And it came to pass on a certain day, as he was teaching, that there were Pharisees and doctors of the law sitting by, which were come out of every town of Galilee, and Judaea, and Jerusalem: and the power of the Lord was present to heal them. (Luke 5:17)*

The Pharisees were now present to investigate what they'd heard.

> *And it shall come to pass if they will not believe thee, neither hearken to the voice of the first sign, that they will believe the voice of the latter sign. And it shall come to pass if they will not believe also these two signs, neither hearken unto thy voice, that thou shalt take of the water of the river, and pour it upon the dry land: and the water which thou takest out of the river shall become blood upon the dry land. (Luke 5:8-9)*

This sign is a little different because God didn't perform any action here; He simply told Moses what to do *in case* the people still didn't believe. Before any plague took place, all Moses had to do was pour water on the ground, and it would become blood before their very eyes. This directly foreshadowed the first plague. Blood is a symbol of both life and death; it is crucial for life, yet its spilling is synonymous with carnage. Water, too, is necessary for all life to exist; the food chain is completely dependent on it, and the Nile itself is the focal point of Egyptian civilization. How interesting that both blood and water spewed forth from Jesus' side when the Roman soldier speared His body.

Strangely, these three signs covered all ten of the plagues that were about to bring Egypt and its Pharaoh to their knees. In Moses' staff becoming a snake, as well as the plagues of frogs, gnats, flies, locusts, and disease to Egypt's livestock, the Lord would demonstrate His mastery over the animals. In the leprous hand, God showed that He is master of the human body, to be reflected as well in the boils and the deaths of all the firstborn. Finally, the water becoming blood showcased His power over the earthly elements; the same would happen to the Nile, which would be followed by fiery hailstorms and darkness.

But Moses *still* had reservations.

EXODUS 4:10-17

> *And Moses said unto the* Lord, *O my* Lord, *I am not eloquent, neither heretofore, nor since thou hast spoken unto thy servant: but I am slow of speech and of a slow tongue. (Exodus 4:10)*

Moses had doubted whether or not the people would accept him when he arrived. Now his doubt shifted to himself. He simply didn't believe he was up to the task.

The meaning of "I am slow of speech and the tongue" isn't exactly clear. Moses had spent the last forty years, now half of his life, away from Egypt. It may be that his Egyptian was a little rusty. Or it could mean that while he was once privileged to dwell in the royal courts of Pharaoh, his exile and subsequent shepherding period had been lessons in humility that took away his courage to stand before world leaders. It could be that he had a genuine stuttering problem. Or, as what I think is most likely, he may have just not wanted to go.

> *And the* Lord *said unto him, Who hath made man's mouth? Or who maketh the dumb, or deaf, or the seeing, or the blind? Have not I the* Lord? *Now therefore go, and I will be with thy mouth, and teach thee what thou shalt say. (Exodus 4:11-12)*

This excuse was truly pitiful, considering to whom he was speaking. The Lord had just demonstrated such awesome power over the human body that He could give a hand leprosy then immediately heal it. Stuttering seemed a small problem in comparison.

Here before the burning bush, God stated, "I will be with thy mouth." Need we any further evidence that this was the Holy Ghost? He is the One who possesses us and speaks through us. But Moses' reasoning was exposed by his next statement: "I stutter" was not a legitimate reason to disobey the Lord, and he knew it.

And he said, O my LORD, send, I pray thee, by the hand of him whom thou wilt send. (Exodus 4:13)

In other words, Moses prayed for God to send someone else. He didn't want to go, and stuttering was a thinly veiled excuse to pass the responsibility on to someone else.

After proving Himself so many times, God had chipped away at each question and proved beyond a shadow of a doubt that the mission was divine. But in doing so, He had exposed the real truth that Moses' heart did not want to accept the calling. Our questions often conceal hidden inner truths.

And the anger of the LORD was kindled against Moses, and he said, Is not Aaron the Levite, thy brother? I know that he can speak well. And also, behold, he cometh forth to meet thee: and when he seeth thee, he will be glad in his heart. (Exodus 4:14)

Why was God angry now, when He had shown so much patience before? Notice the timing. When Moses doubted whether the people would accept him, the Lord understood. When Moses doubted himself, the Lord was patient. But God had made him an offer that the Holy Spirit would take over his tongue to help him fluently speak to Pharaoh and the Israelites, and Moses had rejected it.

THE TIES THAT BIND

Wherefore I say unto you, All manner of sin and blasphemy shall be forgiven unto men: but the blasphemy against the Holy Ghost shall not be forgiven unto men. (Matthew 12:31)

People can shake their fists at the Father if they want. They can spit in Jesus' face and will still find forgiveness. But blaspheming the Holy Ghost is the ultimate unforgivable sin, the one that even Calvary cannot pardon.

Few preachers today will dare mention this controversial topic, but it is biblical. The Holy Spirit is what takes conviction to bring someone to Jesus. Once He has been grieved so greatly that He will never dwell with a person again, God's mercy has run out for them.

Did Moses blaspheme? No. But notice that God did not become angry with him until he rejected the Spirit. The Lord had offered to dwell

THE BURNING BUSH

in his mouth, using his tongue to speak before his enemies. This was a foreshadowing of the power that would fall on the Day of Pentecost: Holy Ghost fire falling on the disciples in the form of other tongues.

We also grieve the Spirit by not wanting Him. The church is firmly entrenched in its commitment to the Father and the Son; but when it comes to the Holy Ghost, the majority of Christians aren't interested. This is why we no longer see the miracles and healings like we once did. It's why the devil seems to keep defeating Christianity over and over again. We lack the true power that the Holy Spirit brings. God is a Trinity that is inseparable; we cannot accept two-thirds of Him.

At this point, had Moses truly walked away from the mountain and resumed his life as a shepherd, God certainly would have been done with him forever and found another deliverer. But fortunately, the Lord was merciful enough to give one more offer. However, in a sense, it was also a punishment. For rejecting the power of the Holy Spirit that had been given, Moses would be denied the priesthood.

> *And thou shalt speak unto him, and put words in his mouth: and I will be with thy mouth, and with his mouth, and will teach you what ye shall do. And he shall be thy spokesman unto the people: and he shall be, even he shall be to thee instead of a mouth, and thou shalt be to him instead of God. (Exodus 4:15-16)*

For every sin Moses committed, a price had to be paid. Later on we'll see that smiting the rock instead of speaking to it robbed him of ever seeing the Promised Land. Likewise, this plea for the Lord to send someone else cost him the chance to be the first priest. Aaron would be the first of an honored lineage. Not only did Moses' apprehension cause him to lose a tremendous blessing, it robbed his children and children's children as well. His own descendants would eventually be lost in the sands of time, but Aaron's descendants would serve as the spiritual leaders for God's people over the ages.

This is the price of disobedience. We fear God's wrath for terrible sins, but do we fear the judgment that comes from questioning His will? What will be the effects on our future generations? Will our children suffer the consequences of our own disobedience?

The irony is that, though this arrangement was set, if the scriptures are to be taken at face value, it never took place. Not once do we read of Moses whispering into Aaron's ear while Aaron speaks the message. Every verse in the story henceforth describes *Moses* boldly proclaiming God's Word to Pharaoh, while his brother seems to just stand back and watch. It seems God gave him the power anyway, indicating perhaps that worst of all, Moses lost his blessing for nothing.

> *And thou shalt take this rod in thine hand, wherewith thou shalt do signs. (Exodus 4:17)*

Something was holy about that staff. God had transformed it into a serpent, then back again. It would bear Moses' weight on the long journey. It would be used to usher in many of the plagues that smote Egypt. It would be a symbol of his authority as he led the way to Canaan. At one time just a piece of wood; now it had become one with the finger of God. The Lord can work with anything, even bringing life to an inanimate object and making it an everlasting symbol.

EXODUS 4:18–31

The Journey to Egypt

> *And Moses went and returned to Jethro his father in law, and said unto him, Let me go, I pray thee, and return unto my brethren which are in Egypt, and see whether they be yet alive. And Jethro said to Moses, Go in peace. (Exodus 4:18)*

Now that the awe-inspiring encounter at the burning bush was over, Moses returned to his family. But he would never again be a lowly shepherd working for a Midianite patriarch.

But rather than showing us the man springing into a Spirit-led calling, the story takes a rather puzzling turn. Moses almost sheepishly returned to his father-in-law, and instead of boldly proclaiming his intentions, told a partial truth, as if trying to hide his true mission.

Why remains a mystery. Either Moses was afraid that Jethro would say no, or he was still unsure about his calling. But was he actually lying? What he told his father-in-law was technically true, but it concealed his real intentions. He was going to see his brethren in Egypt and would certainly be able to tell if they were alive or not, but he completely left out that he was going to free them. He didn't even mention God.

Despite seeing God Himself, appearing in the burning bush, an honor most people dare not even dream of, Moses was still hesitant. The seeds of the same doubt that would plague the Israelites for the next forty years were taking root in the early ministry of their leader. This was a far cry from the later Moses who would carry such a powerful anointing when he came down from the mountain that the glory of God would shine from his face.

> *And the* LORD *said unto Moses in Midian, Go, return into Egypt: for all the men are dead which sought thy life. (Exodus 4:19)*

Now, finally, here is a clue to Moses' behavior. From the moment he first questioned God at the burning bush, to his flat-out refusal to obey, to his uneasy half-truth to his wife's father, this was a big reveal. From the very get-go, he was afraid men might still live in Egypt who wanted to kill him. Moses had been trying to bury a dark past for four decades. Egypt represented a former life where danger lurked and his wicked deeds could catch up to him. After all, he hadn't just been living a different life; he'd been *hiding*.

THE PRACTICAL APPLICATION

For God hath not given us the spirit of fear; but of power, and of love, and of a sound mind. (1 Timothy 1:7)

Now that some light has been shed on Moses' reasoning, we can address what it means to us. More often than not, the calling of God is a frightening thing. It requires us to step out of our comfort zones.

If God has called you to a great ministry, be it teaching, preaching, or anything, and you are uncertain due to doubt and fear, be of good courage. Even Moses, one of the greatest men in the entire Bible and the most pivotal figure in Jewish history, hesitated to start. Every great preacher had that first sermon. Even if they preach to millions, they started with dozens and were likely terrified the first time they took that podium. The Lord will always provide us the strength we need and will never ask us to do something without giving us the ability. No matter how daunting the task He's put before you, all you need is to trust in Him.

And Moses took his wife and his sons and set them upon an ass, and he returned to the land of Egypt: and Moses took the rod of God in his hand. And the LORD *said unto Moses When thou goest to return into Egypt, see that thou do all those wonders before Pharaoh, which I have put in thine hand: but I will harden his heart, that he shall not let the people go. (Exodus 4:20-21)*

This is the third time the staff of Moses is specifically mentioned. God turned it into a snake and back and then promised it would be an instrument of signs and wonders. This seems like an odd detail to give, as if, in the picture that the scripture paints, it wants to make sure we notice the long wooden rod he carries.

If we can picture Moses leaning on his staff on this long, arduous journey, we can see the cross. God's power emanates from it and gives us strength. It is our staff we lean on through the wilderness of life. Just like Moses' staff, it will bring signs and wonders for the world to see. Moses held up his rod, and the miraculous took place, showing all Egypt who was truly God. Likewise, we hold up the cross of Jesus, and miracles and healings flow from its nail prints for the world to see.

And I, if I be lifted up from the earth, will draw all men unto me. (John 12:32)

> *And thou shalt say unto Pharaoh, Thus saith the* LORD, *Israel is my son, even my firstborn: And I say unto thee, Let my son go, that he may serve me: and if thou refuse to let him go, behold, I will slay thy son, even thy firstborn. (Exodus 4:22-23)*

The Lord specifically gave Israel special status as His "firstborn." He was spelling out the terms and conditions that Moses must lay out before Pharaoh. If he would not release the firstborn of the Lord, and we had been assured he would not, then his own firstborn would be slain. Here, God was already laying out the conclusion to the drama about to unfold. Pharaoh's arrogance would not just be his undoing but would bring death to his family. We think that our sins are between God and us, but we have to stop and consider that they will bring death to our entire household.

It would seem that the stage had been set. But the story took one final, strange turn. Many scholars have debated this next passage, yet none have ever been able to conclude what exactly it means.

GOD SEEKS TO KILL

> *And it came to pass by the way in the inn, that the* LORD *met him, and sought to kill him. Then Zipporah took a sharp stone, and cut off the foreskin of her son, and cast it at his feet, and said, Surely a bloody husband art thou to me. So he let him go: then she said, A bloody husband thou art, because of the circumcision. (Exodus 4:24-26)*

These alarming verses seem to contradict what had come before. Moses was on the verge of obeying his mission when the Lord "met him, and sought to kill him." Why in the world would God seek to kill the man He'd spent years raising up for a divine purpose, right as he was about to accomplish that purpose? And why did Zipporah have to circumcise their son in order to stop it?

First we need to look at the setting. At what point in the journey were they? The only clue we are given is "the inn." They were not in Egypt yet, as the next series of verses (27-28) describe Aaron going out into the wilderness to meet Moses "at the mountain of God." Was this inn at a village along the way? Were they just outside the gates? No more is given.

Secondly, the scripture doesn't specify whom exactly God was seeking to kill. Was it Moses or his son? The impersonal noun *him* doesn't provide a name. The subject of verse 24 remains unclear. Read quickly without much thought, the victim would seem to be Moses, but even if it was his child, this doesn't make much sense. Did lack of circumcision make a child worthy of death?

Looking into this controversy, I found that biblical scholars have never been able to agree on this conclusively; but I can at least offer my take at deciphering these three enigmatic verses.

My first question is, *What was Moses' family doing there in the first place?* If we look back to the burning bush and read over the words of the Lord, at no point did God instruct Moses to take his wife and child with him. Examining other passages to understand the nature of God, it seems more likely He would not want Moses to bring his family along. It sounds harsh, but God often calls us quickly into great ministries and gives no time to say goodbye to loved ones. To serve Jesus, we often have to leave everything behind.

> *For I am come to set a man at variance against his father, and the daughter against her mother, and the daughter in law against her mother in law. And a man's foes shall be they of his household. (Matthew 10:35-36)*

God has to come first, always.

> *He that loveth father or mother more than me is not worthy of me: and he that loveth son or daughter more than me is not worthy of me. And he that taketh not his cross, and followeth after me is not worthy of me. (Matthew 10:37-38)*

Jesus had to deal with people who put family before Him. One man very much wanted to follow Him but made an excuse:

> *Lord, I will follow thee; but let me first bid them farewell, which is at home at my house. And Jesus said unto him, No man, having put his hand to the plow, and looking back, is fit for the kingdom of God. (Luke 9:61-62)*

The fact that Moses had taken them indicated his heart was still not right. Oh, sure, he had decided to obey God. He would go to Egypt and demand that Pharaoh release his people. But he wasn't willing to give up *everything* first, still clinging to what made him feel safe. And God was displeased.

Add up every doubt Moses had from the moment God met him. At the burning bush, he questioned whom he should tell people God was. Then he claimed he had a stuttering problem and doubted whether he would be the right person for the job. After being given three definitive signs, he pleaded with the Lord to send someone else. Then he refused to tell his father-in-law the entire truth about where he was going. Now, finally, he had brought his wife and child with him. Now it's a little clearer to see why the Lord had lost patience with him.

And on top of all that, let's add the fact that apparently his son wasn't even circumcised. Circumcision was a commandment by God to Abraham given many centuries earlier.

> *And the uncircumcised man child whose flesh of his foreskin is not circumcised, that soul shall be cut off from his people; he hath broken my covenant. (Genesis 17:14)*

This was a mark to differentiate His children from the heathens. Since Moses had been circumcised (having been raised from childhood by his Hebrew birth mother), the responsibility fell on him to ensure that his son was as well. It was perhaps a sign of his weak spiritual condition; how could he bear the awesome responsibility of leading the Israelites when he had failed one of the basics of God's commandments for his household?

Later we learn that circumcision had not been taking place when they reached the Promised Land after Moses' death. Joshua would have to order it performed on all the young men preparing for battle.

> *At that time the LORD said unto Joshua, Make thee sharp knives, and circumcise again the children of Israel the second time. And Joshua made him sharp knives and circumcised the children of Israel at the hill of the foreskins. (Joshua 5:2-3)*

For this reason, I would assume the Lord had allowed them to come as far as they did; but now, they could not set foot into Mount Sinai before the flesh had been cut away, symbolizing the final removal of the past life. I almost picture the angel of God standing with a flaming sword outside of the mountain, guarding it like the entrance of Eden, warning Moses that his son would have to be marked before he could enter. In some way, this was really for his good; God would not be with him to fight this battle until he (and his household) were in complete obedience.

But not everyone will be happy for us. People who were part of our former lives will try to keep us in our old mentality. Zipporah despised Moses, calling him a "bloody husband" and casting the foreskin down at his feet. As Jesus said, He came to divide families, and often we have to choose between serving Him and pleasing loved ones.

In any case, the final step had been made, and now it was time for Moses to enter Egypt. From here on, the Lord would take over completely as Moses' resistance to His will faded away.

> *And the LORD said to Aaron, Go into the wilderness to meet Moses. And he went, and met him in the mount of God, and kissed him. And Moses told Aaron all the words of the LORD who had sent him and all the signs which he had commanded him. (Exodus 4:27-28)*

It was important that Aaron met his brother at the "mountain of God" rather than Moses simply knocking on his door one morning. Since Aaron was now an integral part of the plan, he, like Moses, must receive the anointing. He must be separated from his family and people for his calling. We must go on journeys sometimes to find the Lord's will, and it can only be found on the mountain of His glory: Calvary.

And Moses and Aaron went and gathered together all the elders of the children of Israel: And Aaron spake all the words which the LORD had spoken unto Moses, and did the signs in the sight of the people. (Exodus 4:29-30)

Perhaps it was an early indication of the Israelites' infamous struggle with doubt. Since *signs* is plural, we can deduce that more than one had to be shown. Was it all three? Did he have to turn his staff into a snake and back again? Did he have to turn his own hand leprous, then dump a vase of water onto the ground and turn it into blood before their very eyes? The signs had been reserved for *if* the Israelites did not believe him. They obviously didn't.

And the people believed: and when they heard that the LORD had visited the children of Israel, and that he had looked upon their affliction, then they bowed their heads and worshiped. (Exodus 4:31)

The people believed. But did the Lord need this before He could start smiting Egypt with plagues? After all, He is God. He could speak and all Egypt would crumble into oblivion with only the slaves left alive. But the answer, surprisingly, was yes.

THE PRACTICAL APPLICATION

God cannot move with unbelief. Doubt ties His hands because, while He certainly has the *power* to do all things, He is not a dictator and has given men free will. Man chose to live in a degraded world; God is not responsible. Doubt brings death to His children. We'll see its devastating consequences later. The Lord's plan requires faith, always.

But without faith, it is impossible to please him. (Hebrews 11:6)

While it is good that the signs demonstrated that God had truly sent Moses, a dark cloud still hung over this scenario, explained by Matthew:

A wicked and adulterous generation seeketh after a sign. (Matthew 16:4)

We'll see throughout Exodus that it always took the miraculous to convince the Israelites to obey God, and even then, sometimes they would complain. This is why so many of them would die in the desert.

CONCLUSION

Nevertheless, the plan of God was now in motion. He had heard the cries of His people. The first forty years of Moses' life were spent in Egypt, the second in the wilderness as a shepherd. God had His hand on his life from the beginning, spending all these decades patiently molding and making him into the deliverer that he was destined to become. He was now ready to use Moses to perform the greatest series of miracles seen since Creation to demonstrate His power.

For now, all the people had to do was stand back and watch while God's hand moved for them. It would be a wonderful yet terrible sight to behold.

Chapter 5

THE TEN PLAGUES

INTRODUCTION

It is a fearful thing to fall into the hands of the living God. (Hebrews 10:31)

Many Christians don't want to talk about judgment anymore. While love is certainly the heart of Christianity, we do ourselves a disservice by no longer facing the full reality of God; He is just as capable of horrifying death and destruction. But He always gives ample warning.

He warned Adam and Eve that they would be cast out of Eden if they ate the forbidden fruit, but they didn't listen. Before Cain murdered his brother, God saw his jealousy and warned him,

Sin lieth at the door. (Genesis 4:7)

For one hundred twenty years, Noah preached that a flood was coming. Even after God closed the door to the Ark, He extended seven days of mercy to give people one last chance.

And it came to pass after seven days, that the waters of the flood were upon the earth. (Genesis 7:10)

They pounded on the door as the waters came, but it was too late.

People spit in the face of God as He extends mercy to them, then act surprised when judgment comes. Of course, the ten plagues are a perfect example. Studying them reveals much about the nature of both God and man. The Lord had already laid the plan out so thoroughly that He promised Pharaoh's heart would be hardened. But He still gave chance after chance to the Egyptians.

EXODUS 5:1-23

Moses and Aaron Confront Pharaoh

> *And afterward Moses and Aaron went in, and told Pharaoh, Thus saith the* LORD *God of Israel, Let my people go, that they may hold a feast unto me in the wilderness. (Exodus 5:1)*

Moses and Aaron had heard from God, and now the Israelites believed them, so they were extraordinarily confident approaching Pharaoh for the first time. But sometimes, when we obey God's will, things don't start out the way we imagine.

Moses, as a historical figure, is now synonymous with the phrase *let my people go*. It was not a plea but a forceful command. Pharaoh was not too pleased with this lack of respect. Kings traveled from around the world for a mere chance to bow before him. Who was this shepherd who dared approach him on behalf of slaves?

Just like with Jethro earlier, Moses told an intriguing partial truth. Of course, going into the wilderness to hold a feast wasn't the plan at all. Rather than looking at God as deceitful, we should focus on just how merciful He was being. He knew what Pharaoh would say but still gave him an opportunity to reconsider. This wasn't even the last chance Pharaoh would get. It didn't have to play out the way it was going to.

But Moses and Aaron were not prepared for Pharaoh's response.

> *And Pharaoh said, Who is the* LORD, *that I should obey his voice to let Israel go? I know not the* LORD, *neither will I let Israel go. (Exodus 5:2)*

This wasn't what the men of God were expecting, but Pharaoh was right. He did not know the God of Israel. Furthermore, consider the economic implications. For four centuries now, Egypt had relied on free labor. By now, it was a crucial part of their infrastructure. Was Pharaoh going to let the people go and bring possible financial ruin to his kingdom so they could obey a religious sacrament? Hardly. Pharaoh's response, while defiant of God, was perfectly logical from a worldly point of view.

THE PRACTICAL APPLICATION

"Who is the Lord, that I should obey His voice?" (Exodus 5:2) is a common mantra of the world today. It is the cry of the unsaved from their places of worldliness. We try to reach them. We preach the gospel, yet they do not hear. We warn them of God's judgment if this nation doesn't turn back to holiness. We plead with them to give their hearts to Jesus, or hell will be their eternal destiny. We go into the dark places where sin abounds. Our cry reverberates through the bars and drug houses. But so often, the answer that echoes back is this same phrase Pharaoh uttered. It is eleven words of defiance to the Lord, an indication that we are too important to listen to Him. But it was going to bring damnation to Pharaoh.

People today don't think they need God. But their resistance will be their undoing. Pharaoh had no idea the horrors that awaited him once these words escaped his lips.

And they said, The God of the Hebrews hath met with us: let us go, we pray thee, three days' journey into the desert, and sacrifice unto the LORD our God; lest he fall upon us with pestilence, or with the sword. (Exodus 5:3)

Moses' first request to Pharaoh was a stern command, but his tone was now somewhat more like negotiating. Since Pharaoh didn't acknowledge God (yet), Moses made the next petition as almost a plea: "Let us go, we pray thee." He elaborated that God wanted them to make sacrifices and now warned of dire consequences if they failed. He was backpedaling to appeal to Pharaoh's merciful side. He wouldn't want anything to happen to his valuable slave labor, would he? As the Egyptians also believed in gods that brought pestilence or famine when displeased, surely Pharaoh would understand the urgency.

And the king of Egypt said unto them, Wherefore do ye, Moses and Aaron, let the people from their works? Get you unto your burdens. And Pharaoh said, Behold, the people of the land now are many, and ye make them rest from their burdens. (Exodus 5:4-5)

Whether or not their names had been brought to him when they came before him, or if he did, in fact, know who Moses was from his previous life, Pharaoh called them by name. And then he smacked down the very idea of their being in his presence.

This response was condescending. Pharaoh had world leaders and important diplomats to tend to. This was a waste of his valuable time. He even asked Moses and Aaron why *they* weren't working in the slime pits. To add insult to injury, the king decided to remind these slaves just who was in charge. Perhaps he sensed the winds of rebellion blowing through their camp. Now he'd better put that down fast before it grew any stronger.

> *And Pharaoh said, Behold, the people of the land now are many, and ye make them rest from their burdens. And Pharaoh commanded the same day the taskmasters of the people, and their officers, saying, Ye shall no more give the people straw to make brick, as heretofore: let them go and gather straw for themselves. And the tale of the bricks, which they did make heretofore, ye shall lay upon them; ye shall not diminish ought thereof: for they be idle; therefore they cry, saying, Let us go and sacrifice to our God. Let there more work be laid upon the men, that they may labor therein; and let them not regard vain words. (Exodus 5:5-9)*

Not only did Pharaoh deny the request but he inflicted a cruel punishment for even making it. Bricks were made out of mud, but chopped straw was just as important an ingredient. As the straw decayed, it released humic acid, which made the bricks stronger and more pliable once they hardened.[70] Since mixing it in the slime pit was the dirtiest job, these people, considered to be the most inferior, were stuck with it; gathering and chopping straw was provided by their taskmasters.

Pharaoh gave explicit orders that the taskmasters no longer supply the Hebrews with any straw. Now they had to gather and cut it themselves, effectively doubling the workload. And the king was clear that they should not miss their quota by one brick; if this required extra beating as motivation, then so be it.

The king gave the taskmasters a further look into his mindset of extreme cruelty: "For they be idle" (Exodus 5:8). The slaves were less than human to him. They must have rest, but Pharaoh viewed them as lazy and in need of swift discipline to remind them of their place at the bottom of the social ladder.

> *Then the officers of the children of Israel came and cried unto Pharaoh, saying, Wherefore dealest thou thus with thy servants? There is no straw given unto thy servants, and they say to us, Make brick: and, behold, thy servants are beaten, but the fault is in thine own people. (Exodus 5:15-16)*

Moses still had the authority of Almighty God. He had little doubt in the power he had experienced before the burning bush. The representatives, on the other hand, approached Pharaoh, begging for mercy. They were excited to see Moses but not prepared for the backlash.

Clearly their minds were not on the price of freedom, but survival. They were willing to make their overlords happy if it just meant making it to the next day. This made it all the more shocking when they learned why the edict had come.

> *And the officers of the children of Israel did see that they were in evil case after it was said, Ye, shall not minish ought from the bricks of your daily task. And they met Moses and Aaron, who stood in the way, as they*

> *came forth from Pharaoh: And they said unto them, The Lord look upon you, and judge; because ye have made our savor to be abhorred in the eyes of Pharaoh, and in the eyes of his servants, to put a sword in their hand to slay us. (Exodus 5:19-21)*

With wounds still fresh and the psychological damage still raw, the officials of Israel blamed Moses and Aaron. It was clear why it would take years to weed the doubt out of them.

Take a closer look at what they said to the brothers: "The Lord look upon you and judge" indicates not only did they no longer believe the men were sent of God but that they were actively working against His will. They put a curse on Moses and Aaron, hoping that God would punish them for being imposters. They could not possibly see the full plan of God at this point. They expected freedom to come immediately. Unfortunately, with this dramatic setback, Moses couldn't see clearly either.

> *And Moses returned unto the Lord, and said, Lord, wherefore hast thou so evil entreated this people? Why is it that thou hast sent me? For since I came to Pharaoh to speak in thy name, he hath done evil to this people; neither hast thou delivered thy people at all. (Exodus 5:22-23)*

This was the final time Moses would doubt his mission. Now it had run its course. The odds seemed insurmountable. He fully expected Pharaoh to tremble at the name of God. But the backlash was far from what any of them anticipated. Instead of freedom, bondage was now worse than ever.

THE PRACTICAL APPLICATION

We get excited when God calls us and expect people to cheer us on while the gates of hell tremble. But more often than not, our first steps are fraught with peril and sometimes even disaster. It may even seem that God has immediately abandoned us. We also think we'll always have total victory from beginning to end. I would love to meet the Christian that has experienced this. Little do we realize that once we begin the journey, the devil is always going to bombard us with everything he has.

EXODUS 6:1-13

Often the Lord doesn't show up until we're at our lowest points. If this is true for Moses, none of us are immune. The greatest evangelists and preachers who have ever lived can attest to many nights of frustration and feeling abandoned by the Lord. But if Moses had left and given up, the greatest miracles he'd ever seen would never have taken place. Before beginning to smite Egypt, the Lord gave him a message of encouragement.

> *Then the* LORD *said unto Moses, Now shalt thou see what I will do to Pharaoh: for with a strong hand shall he let them go, and with a strong hand shall he drive them out of his land. And God spake unto Moses, and said unto him, I am the* LORD: *And I appeared unto Abraham, unto Isaac, and unto Jacob, by the name of God Almighty, but by my name* JEHOVAH *was I not known to them. (Exodus 6:1-3)*

God declared that Pharaoh would release the people "with a strong hand." Pharaoh refused to budge now, but soon he would force them out as fast as he could.

On Mouth Horeb, when Moses asked who he should tell the people had sent him, the answer was, "I am that I am." This was the revelation of the Lord's sacred name, *Yahweh*. God shared that He had never revealed this name before—not even to Abraham, Isaac, or Jacob (JEHOVAH is the Latin version of YAHWEH).

Then, in verse 2, God gave a new name when He said, "I am the LORD." The Hebrew text calls Him *El-Shaddai*, meaning, "The God Who Is Enough."[71] It's not as powerful as the previous name, but it was just what Moses needed to hear; while "Yahweh" referred to His omnipotence, "El-Shaddai" described Him as the God who meets our earthly needs.

God has different names, each one fitting whatever we need Him to be, accordingly. When Moses needed to know what to tell people, God was *Yahweh, the Great I Am*. But when Moses was at his lowest point of discouragement, He was *the God who was enough*. When we need a friend, He is a friend. When we need a Savior, He is a Savior. Whether we need a warrior, a protector, or a comforter, or whatever we need, *God is*. Moses was now closer to Him than any other previous figure in Bible history.

And in the midst of our greatest disappointments, God is already moving to bring us the greatest victories we've ever seen.

EXODUS 6:14-27

The Heads of the Twelve Tribes

Unexpectedly, right before the final warning and beginning of the ten plagues, the narrative shifts dramatically. We are suddenly given a list of the heads of some of the tribes of Israel at the time (Reuben, Simeon, and Levi), as well as Aaron's wife and children.

> *And Aaron took him Elisheba, daughter of Amminadab, sister of Naashon, to wife; and she bares him Nadab, and Abihu, Eleazar, and Ithamar. (Exodus 6:23)*

Even Aaron's grandchildren are listed and are revealed to be heads of a Levitical tribe.

> *And Eleazar Aaron's son took him one of the daughters of Putiel to wife, and she bare him Phinehas: these are the heads of the fathers of the Levites according to their families. (Exodus 6:25)*

Verses 23-30 conclude chapter 6 by resuming the story—the lead-up to the coming confrontation with Pharaoh.

Genealogy was very important to the Israelites and even plays an important role in the New Testament, which records the family lineage of Jesus. However the placement of this list and the details are unusual. Instead of introducing a particular book, it is briefly mentioned in the middle of a story and only provides us the names of the heads of the three eldest tribes of Israel, including Aaron and Moses as leaders of the Levites. Then the focus shifts back to the story as if nothing happened.

In all likelihood, God was trying to remind Moses of his place as leader of the people in order to encourage him. The Lord's patience was amazing, considering how many times Moses questioned him on Mount Sinai. Now Moses was using the same old excuse as earlier to avoid confronting Pharaoh again. He was probably afraid that if he made any more demands of the already angered king, Pharaoh would just be all that much harder on the Hebrew slaves. This is the sad note upon which chapter 6 concludes. But Moses' doubts would be long gone once he saw firsthand what was about to befall Egypt. From this point forward, he would emerge as the strong leader to bring a faithless people through the wilderness to their homeland.

EXODUS 7:1-13

Egyptian Theology

> *And the LORD said unto Moses, See, I have made thee a god to Pharaoh: and Aaron thy brother shall be thy prophet. Thou shalt speak all that I command thee: and Aaron thy brother shall speak unto Pharaoh, that he send the children of Israel out of his land. And I will harden Pharaoh's heart, and multiply my signs and my wonders in the land of Egypt. But Pharaoh shall not hearken unto you, that I may lay my hand upon Egypt, and bring forth my armies, and my people the children of Israel, out of the land of Egypt by great judgments. And the Egyptians shall know that I am the LORD, when I stretch forth my hand upon Egypt and bring out the children of Israel from among them. (Exodus 7:1-5)*

God revealed to Moses that, whether he realized it or not, he had been made a god in the eyes of Pharaoh. Which leads to the next point—that God was not just doing this to reveal His greatness to the Israelites but also to the Egyptians. Egypt's idols were going to be put on trial and disproven.

> *For the Egyptians buried all their firstborn, which the* LORD *had smitten among them: upon their gods also the* LORD *executed judgments. (Numbers 33:4)*

The Greek philosopher Celsus said of the Egyptians, "If a stranger reaches Egypt, he is struck by the splendid temples and sacred groves that he sees, great and magnificent courts, marvelous temples with pleasant walks about them, imposing and occult ceremonies; but when he had entered into the innermost sanctuary, he finds the god worshiped in the buildings to be a cat, or an ape, or a crocodile, or a he-goat, or a dog."[72]

What made the religion of Egypt stand out was its obsession with animal worship. Many of the gods themselves were depicted with human bodies and animal heads. The human spirit was divided in two; the *Ba* represented the immortal soul, and the *Ka* referred to the guardian spirit that watched after the body. After death, the Ka and the body were united as one. The afterlife in Egypt evolved and changed over the years; in the Old Kingdom, the dead simply lived in their tombs, eating and drinking (which is why food and drink were provided in mummies' tombs), and could occasionally escape to haunt the streets. Over time, they came to believe that a giant ladder existed in the West where the departed souls could ascend to the gods. This eventually came to be known as the realm of Osiris, ruler of the underworld. The dead would have to be judged by Osiris to eventually, one day, become one with him. Perhaps for this reason, the Egyptians are one of few ancient cultures to never engage in ancestor worship.[73]

The sun god, Ra, was synonymous with Pharaoh himself, who was a patron deity over all Egypt. We can identify at least one Egyptian god with each plague:

1. The Nile was the source of life for Egypt and considered the lifeblood of Osiris. Its *turning to blood* would have been detrimental to belief in Khnum (creator of water and life) or Hapi (god of the Nile).

2. The plague of *frogs* was directed at Hekket, goddess of fertility, portrayed as a frog.

3. The third and fourth plagues of *lice* and *flies* would have disputed Khepri, god of the earth, who had the head of a fly.

4. Hathor was the sky goddess, whose head was a cow's, and would have been the target of the *dead livestock*. The Israelites would later attempt to resurrect Hathor worship at the foot of Mount Sinai.

5. Isis, the goddess of medicine and peace, was powerless to save the Egyptians from the sixth plague, *boils*.

6. The Egyptians would have also cried out to Seth, god of storms, to stop the *hailstorms mingled with fire*.
7. They would have begged Min, protector of the crops, to save them from the plague of *locusts*.
8. Ra, the sun god, was powerless when the Lord brought *darkness* over Egypt.
9. The god of the dead, Osiris, was also of no use when the angel of death took *all the firstborn*.[74]

Moses Performs a Miracle Before Pharaoh

And Moses and Aaron went in unto Pharaoh, and they did so as the Lord had commanded: and Aaron cast down his rod before Pharaoh, and before his servants, and it became a serpent. Then Pharaoh also called the wise men and the sorcerers: now the magicians of Egypt, they also did in like manner with their enchantments. For they cast down every man his rod, and they became serpents: but Aaron's rod swallowed up their rods. (Exodus 7:10-12)

The *uraeus* was an image of a small coiled serpent, usually a rearing cobra, worn on the headdresses of Pharaohs. From an Egyptian word meaning "risen one," they were symbols of royal authority[75] and are almost always found on mummies' sarcophaguses. The uraeus was thought to have been created by Isis as a gift for Osiris as he ascended to the throne, and to wear it around one's head was to ensure divine approval and protection over Egypt.

This is why the Lord chose to turn Moses' staff into a serpent. He knew the magicians would be able to replicate the trick. But they were simply using magic or illusionism; the power of God was in Moses' staff. God was demonstrating His power over not just the serpent (He created snakes, not Isis) but also His authority over Pharaoh. The serpent of Moses devouring the magicians' serpents was an omen of what was to come.

But it still didn't make a believer out of Pharaoh.

And he hardened Pharaoh's heart, that he hearkened not unto them; as the Lord had said. (Exodus 7:13)

THE TIES THAT BIND

Earlier I referenced blasphemy of the Holy Ghost when Moses angered God on Mount Sinai. Pharaoh ultimately made the wrong decision. This was the first moment when his heart was hardened. This was the moment he blasphemed.

Verily I say unto you, All sins shall be forgiven unto the sons of men, and blasphemies wherewith so ever they shall blaspheme: But he that shall

> *blaspheme against the Holy Ghost hath never forgiveness, but is in danger of eternal damnation. (Mark 3:28-29)*

Blaspheming the Holy Spirit is real and does happen.

Why? Let's consider what was happening when Jesus said this. In Matthew 12, Jesus had just cast devils out of a man. But the Pharisees, who often criticized His miracles from afar, went too far when,

> *. . . they said, This fellow doth not cast out devils but by Beelzebub the prince of the devils. (Matthew 12:24)*

The Holy Spirit was the source of Jesus' power (as evidenced by the fact that Jesus received Him after being baptized by John the Baptist). It was through the Spirit that Jesus was able to cast out devils and heal. Therefore the Pharisees were calling the power of the Holy Ghost the power of the devil. And this caused them to commit the unforgivable sin.

It takes the Holy Ghost to convict people to Calvary. If one grieves the Holy Ghost so badly that He departs from that person to never dwell with them again, there is no hope for them. Jesus and the Spirit work together in perfection, and without one, the other can't bring you to the Father. It's why David wrote in Psalm 51:11,

> *Cast me not away from thy presence, and take not thy holy spirit from me.*

It's the most dangerous sin to commit. And it is increasingly common in this hour; we are living in the age of great blasphemy. It's in the news, the government, the media, the schools, everywhere.

Did blaspheming the Holy Ghost take place in Old Testament days? Absolutely. King Saul committed it once, as the scriptures state:

> *But the Spirit of the Lord departed from Saul, and an evil spirit from the Lord troubled him. (1 Samuel 16:4)*

God was so done with him that He even told the prophet Samuel to stop mourning.

> *And the Lord said unto Samuel, How long wilt thou mourn for Saul, seeing I have rejected him from reigning over Israel? (1 Samuel 16:1)*

Notice the change that took place in Saul after this point; study how devil-possessed he became, and you will get the complete picture of what blasphemy does to someone.

Perhaps the most terrifying example of blasphemy is in Revelation.

> *And he [the antichrist] causeth all, both small and great, rich and poor, free and bond, to receive a mark in their right hand, or in their foreheads:*

> *And that no man might buy or sell, save he that had the mark, or the name of the beast, or the number of his name. Here is wisdom. Let him that hath understanding count the number of the beast: for it is the number of a man; and his number is Six hundred threescore and six. (Revelation 13:16-18)*

Without the mark, you won't be able to buy or sell; but to take it means eternal damnation.

> *If any man worship the beast and his image, and receive his mark in his forehead, or in his hand, The same shall drink of the wine of the wrath of God, which is poured out without mixture into the cup of his indignation; and he shall be tormented with fire and brimstone in the presence of the holy angels and in the presence of the Lamb. (Revelation 14:9-10)*

Look at how Saul changed into a madman, intent on killing David for no reason. That same demonic spirit will take over those with the mark, giving them an unquenchable desire to butcher the children of God.

> *And he had power to give life unto the image of the beast, that the image of the beast should both speak, and cause that as many as would not worship the image of the beast should be killed. (Revelation 13:15)*

Devil-possessed lunatics take guns and massacre schools full of children. Around the world, terrorists without emotions torture and behead Christians. It's as if they've already taken the mark. We shudder in horror at what is only going to grow more prevalent in this last hour; the stage is being set for the mark of the beast to take over.

Throughout the ten plagues, Pharaoh went through a cycle of claiming he would let the Israelites go, then changing his mind. Biblical scholars have debated this throughout the years, but my take is that by examining it through the lens of blasphemy, his actions make much more sense. God was merely using him to bring judgment on a sinful nation.

EXODUS 7:14-19

> *And the LORD said unto Moses, Pharaoh's heart is hardened, he refuseth to let the people go. Get thee unto Pharaoh in the morning; lo, he goeth out unto the water; and thou shalt stand by the river's brink against he come; and the rod which was turned to a serpent shalt thou take in thine hand. And thou shalt say unto him, The LORD God of the Hebrews hath sent me unto thee, saying, Let my people go, that they may serve me in the wilderness: and, behold, hitherto thou wouldest not hear. Thus saith the LORD, In this thou shalt know that I am the LORD: behold, I will smite with the rod that is in mine hand upon the waters which are in the river, and they shall be turned to*

blood. And the fish that is in the river shall die, and the river shall stink, and the Egyptians shall loathe to drink of the water of the river. And the LORD *spake unto Moses, Say unto Aaron, Take thy rod, and stretch out thine hand upon the waters of Egypt, upon their streams, upon their rivers, and upon their ponds, and upon all their pools of water, that they may become blood; and that there may be blood throughout all the land of Egypt, both in vessels of wood, and in vessels of stone. (Exodus 7:14-19)*

MIDDLE KINGDOM DYNAMICS

For years archaeologists have claimed that there is no evidence of ten plagues striking Egypt. But again, this has been based on the assertion that Ramses was the Exodus Pharaoh, placing the events towards the middle of the New Kingdom era.

If we search through artifacts of the late Middle Kingdom, we come across an intriguing document. Translated by Sir Alan Gardiner and given the name "The Admonitions of Ipuwer," the papyrus was dated in 1966 to have been written sometime in the Middle Bronze Age, probably towards the end of the thirteenth dynasty (placing it within the timeframe to coincide with our new date for the Exodus).[76] We established earlier that a series of disasters struck Egypt during the reign of Dudimose II, weakening the nation and exposing it to invasion by the Hyksos. Ipuwer, an Egyptian sage, seems to be an eyewitness to these events, describing the horror in an urgent letter to the Pharaoh. Was he describing the ten plagues? Let's compare excerpts from his work with the book of Exodus.

> *... that thou shalt take of the water of the river, and pour it upon the dry land: and the water which thou takest out of the river shall become blood upon the dry land. (Exodus 4:9)*

> Ipuwer: Behold, Egypt has fallen into the pouring water. And he who poured water on the ground seizes the mighty in misery.

> *And Moses and Aaron did so, as the* LORD *commanded; and he lifted up the rod, and smote the waters that were in the river, in the sight of Pharaoh, and in the sight of his servants; and all the waters that were in the river were turned to blood. And the fish that was in the river died and the river stank, and the Egyptians could not drink of the water of the river, and there was blood throughout all the land of Egypt. (Exodus 7:20-21)*

> Ipuwer: The river is blood! As you drink of it, you lose your humanity and thirst for water.

*And the L*ORD *did that thing on the morrow, and all the cattle of Egypt died: but of the cattle of the children of Israel died not one. . . . And the flax and the barley was smitten: for the barley was in the ear, and the flax was bolled. . . . And the locust went up over all the land of Egypt, and rested in all the coasts of Egypt: very grievous were they; before them, there were no such locusts as they, neither after them shall be such. For they covered the face of the whole earth, so that the land was darkened, and they did eat every herb of the land, and all the fruit of the trees which the hail had left: and there remained not any green thing in the trees, or in the herbs of the field, through all the land of Egypt. (Exodus 9:6, 31; 10:14-15)*

Ipuwer: Gone is the grain of abundance. Food supplies are running short. The nobles hunger and are suffering. Upper Egypt has become a wasteland. Grain is lacking on every side. The storehouse is bare. Women say, "Oh that we had something to eat!"

And Moses stretched forth his hand toward heaven, and there was a thick darkness in all the land of Egypt three days. (Exodus 10:22)

Ipuwer: Those who had shelter are now in the dark of the storm. The whole of the delta cannot be seen.

*And it came to pass, that at midnight the L*ORD *smote all the firstborn in the land of Egypt, from the firstborn of Pharaoh that sat on his throne unto the firstborn of the captive that was in the dungeon; and all the firstborn of cattle. And Pharaoh rose up in the night, he, and all his servants, and all the Egyptians; and there was a great cry in Egypt; for there was not a house where there was not one dead. (Exodus 12:29-30)*

Ipuwer: Behold, plague sweeps the land; blood is everywhere with no shortage of the dead. Children are dashed against the walls. The funeral shroud calls out to you before you come near. Woe is me for the grief of this time. He who buries his brother in the ground is everywhere . . . wailing is throughout the land mingled with lamentations.

*And the children of Israel did according to the word of Moses, and they borrowed of the Egyptians jewels of silver, and jewels of gold, and raiment: And the L*ORD *gave the people favor in the sight of the Egyptians, so that they lent unto them such things as they required. And they spoiled the Egyptians. (Exodus 12:35-36)*

Ipuwer: The slave takes what he finds. What belongs to the place has been stripped. Gold, lapis lazuli, silver, and turquoise are strung on the necks of female slaves. See how the poor of the land have become rich while the man of property is a pauper.

As if these writings weren't enough, Ipuwer also lays blame on a certain people for the calamities befalling Egypt, wishing a previous Pharaoh had wiped them out.

> Ipuwer: There is fire in their hearts! If only he [Amenemhat?] had perceived their nature in the first generation! Then he would have smitten the evil, stretched out his arm against it. He would have destroyed their seed and their heritage.

EXODUS 7–11:10

The River Turns to Blood

The Nile was Egypt, and Egypt was the Nile. The great river was the source of life for the kingdom, providing water for drink and crops and fish for food (ancient civilizations were often built around sources of water). This first plague was already going to be catastrophic.

THE TIES THAT BIND

As we'll explore further later, the ten plagues also seem to have intriguing parallels with the horrible judgments in Revelation. In the latter half of the Tribulation, after the antichrist has required all people to take his mark, persecution against Christians will reach a fever pitch. God will begin to avenge the saints by bringing two rounds of seven judgments—fourteen total. The first seven are brought by angels blowing trumpets, the latter seven by pouring vials of judgment.

The second trumpet judgment calls a meteor that crashes into the sea, turning a third of it into blood and decimating marine life.

> *And the second angel sounded, and as it were a great mountain burning with fire was cast into the sea: and the third part of the sea became blood; And the third part of the creatures which were in the sea, and had life, died; and the third part of the ships were destroyed. (Revelation 8:8-9)*

This is followed by another meteor, given the biblical name "wormwood," which strikes the remaining freshwater and renders it undrinkable.

> *And the third angel sounded, and there fell a great star from heaven, burning as it were a lamp, and it fell upon the third part of the rivers, and upon the fountains of waters; And the name of the star is called Wormwood: and the third part of the waters became wormwood; and many men died of the waters, because they were made bitter. (Revelation 8:10-11)*

"Wormwood" appears only this time in the New Testament but is used eight other times in the Old Testament. In Jewish tradition, it refers to a bitter herb that could ruin the taste of food or water.

This will have catastrophic effects on the planet, but each successive plague will only get worse. During the second round, the vials of judgment will finish the job.

> *And the second angel poured out his vial upon the sea, and it became as the blood of a dead man: and every living soul died in the sea. And the third angel poured out his vial upon the rivers and fountains of waters, and they became blood. (Revelation 16:3-4)*

The last judgments had destroyed a third of both the oceans and fresh waters. Now, all of the sea and drinking water in the world will be blood. The angels will rejoice as God punishes the wicked.

> *And I heard the angel of the waters say, Thou art righteous, O Lord, which art, and wast, and shalt be because thou hast judged thus. For they have shed the blood of saints and prophets, and thou hast given them blood to drink; for they are worthy. (Revelation 16:5-6)*

The Egyptians cried out to their false gods during the ten plagues. So too will those with the mark cry out to the antichrist to save them from the judgment of the Almighty. But just like the Egyptians, their screams will fall on deaf ears. Because false gods can't save you.

> *And the magicians of Egypt did so with their enchantments: and Pharaoh's heart was hardened, neither did he hearken unto them; as the Lord had said. And Pharaoh turned and went into his house, neither did he set his heart to this also. And all the Egyptians dug round about the river for water to drink; for they could not drink of the water of the river. And seven days were fulfilled, after that the Lord had smitten the river. (Exodus 7:22-25)*

Once again, the priests could copy the miracles. However, in every instance, the Lord God was able to demonstrate a power greater than what they could conjure. The snake from the staff devoured their snakes. They could transform some water into blood—but not at the same level. Nevertheless, it was still enough to convince Pharaoh that it all had been a cheap parlor trick. He was unmoved.

The Plague of Frogs

> *And the LORD spake unto Moses, Go unto Pharaoh, and say unto him, Thus saith the LORD, Let my people go, that they may serve me. And if thou refuse to let them go, behold, I will smite all thy borders with frogs: And*

*the river shall bring forth frogs abundantly, which shall go up and come into thine house, and into thy bedchamber, and upon thy bed, and into the house of thy servants, and upon thy people, and into thine ovens, and into thy kneading-troughs: And the frogs shall come up both on thee, and upon thy people, and upon all thy servants. And the L*ORD *spake unto Moses, Say unto Aaron, Stretch forth thine hand with thy rod over the streams, over the rivers, and over the ponds, and cause frogs to come up upon the land of Egypt. (Exodus 8:1-5)*

THE NATURALIST THEORY

For years, people have tried to come up with scientific explanations for the ten plagues, and the order of the chain of events is intriguing.

The water turning red is an occasional real-life phenomenon, caused by varieties of events. Unusually high rainfall from the Ethiopian highlands could have caused a surge in algae.[77] This undrinkable red water would have killed most marine life and driven the frogs from the river to infest Egyptian homes. With the water tainted by anthrax, the frogs would have died within a few days, and the heaps of decaying creatures would unleash viruses, killing livestock. Logically, insect infestations (flies, mosquitos, and locusts) would come next.

A variation of this theory was first proposed in 1985, citing a volcanic eruption on the Mediterranean island of Thera at around 1450 BC (very close to our date for the Exodus).[78] Rather than algae, volcanic ash would have turned the Nile red (due to increased levels of iron oxide) and would have rained down fireballs on Egypt (explaining the hailstones mingled with fire). Pyroclastic clouds of volcanic dust could have caused boils (which have accompanied eruptions in the past) as well as the darkness over the land.

However, while naturalist theories on the ten plagues are interesting, they all fall short on one important point. How do we explain the deaths of all the firstborn throughout Egypt? Though a major plague would have broken out as a consequence of the natural disaster, it still doesn't explain why only the firstborn would have been targeted. When the volcano theory was first proposed, it included the idea that in desperation to stop the catastrophes rocking their kingdom, the Egyptians resorted to human sacrifice of their own firstborn to the gods.

This would seem to offer a satisfying explanation when one is trying to take God out of the equation. But human sacrifice goes against everything we know about Egyptian culture, and it's very unlikely they would stoop to this, even in extreme circumstances. As we'll see later, it is also weakened by real-life evidence: Egyptian death pits indicating a terrible plague did in fact take the lives of men, women, and children everywhere.

> *And Aaron stretched out his hand over the waters of Egypt, and the frogs came up, and covered the land of Egypt. And the magicians did so with their enchantments and brought up frogs upon the land of Egypt. Then Pharaoh called for Moses and Aaron, and said, Intreat the LORD, that he may take away the frogs from me, and from my people; and I will let the people go, that they may do sacrifice unto the LORD. . . . And Moses and Aaron went out from Pharaoh: and Moses cried unto the LORD because of the frogs which he had brought against Pharaoh. And the LORD did according to the word of Moses; and the frogs died out of the houses, out of the villages, and out of the fields. And they gathered them together upon heaps: and the land stank. But when Pharaoh saw that there was a respite, he hardened his heart and hearkened not unto them; as the LORD had said. (Exodus 8:6-15)*

The first four plagues were inconveniences for the Egyptians. They could work around the water turning to blood by digging wells. The plague of frogs was repulsive, but the frogs themselves were harmless (unless you count the impending disease). The third and fourth plagues, lice and flies, continue this trend. But notice that each plague was getting increasingly catastrophic.

The Plagues of Lice and Flies

> *And the LORD said unto Moses, Say unto Aaron, Stretch out thy rod, and smite the dust of the land, that it may become lice throughout all the land of Egypt. And they did so; for Aaron stretched out his hand with his rod, and smote the dust of the earth, and it became lice in man and in beast; all the dust of the land became lice throughout all the land of Egypt. (Exodus 8:16-17)*

The word *lice* more accurately translates to "gnats."[79] I grew up in Georgia, and one of our jokes was that the state bird is the gnat. In the summertime, the cloud of gnats in our backyard would make playing outside almost unbearable. I've had plenty of them buzz in my ears, fly into my eye, or go up my nose. I can understand how a plague of them would certainly drive anyone crazy. But this was still only the beginning.

> *And the magicians did so with their enchantments to bring forth lice, but they could not: so there were lice upon man, and upon beast. Then the magicians said unto Pharaoh, This is the finger of God: and Pharaoh's heart was hardened, and he hearkened not unto them; as the LORD had said. (Exodus 8:18-19)*

Up until now, the magicians had been able to replicate the miracles of God. But now, for the first time, they were helpless. When the magicians declared, "this is the finger of God," they acknowledged for the first time that their idols were powerless to stop what was happening.

If the leaders of idol worship acknowledged that only God could save them, how much more so were the people of Egypt realizing it? Had they repented, would God have stopped the plagues? It may be a bit controversial, but I think so. And to demonstrate this, I defer to another story in the Bible.

THE TIES THAT BIND

Now the word of the LORD came unto Jonah the son of Amittai, saying, Arise, go to Nineveh, that great city, and cry against it; for their wickedness is come up before me. (Jonah 1:1-2)

Nineveh was the capital of Assyria, one of the most notorious kingdoms in the ancient world and one of Israel's arch-enemies. The Assyrians were legendary for their brutality; it is said that they would skin their enemies alive and decorate the city walls with the flesh. No wonder Jonah hated them and didn't want to go on the mission.

We all know the rest of the story very well. Jonah runs from the will of God, and the Lord has him cast into the sea and swallowed by a fish. Three days later, the humbled prophet is vomited onto the shore and travels to Nineveh, where he goes to preach that judgment is coming.

And Jonah began to enter into the city a day's journey, and he cried, and said Yet forty days, and Nineveh shall be overthrown. (Jonah 3:4)

Jonah's message contained no love or mercy but was still effective. The city repents, and God spares them.

So the people of Nineveh believed God, and proclaimed a fast, and put on sackcloth, from the greatest of them even to the least of them. (Jonah 3:5)

And God saw their works, that they turned from their evil way; and God repented of the evil, that he had said that he would do unto them; and he did it not. (Jonah 3:10)

Now, contrast Nineveh with Egypt. God forgave a nation that had done far more wicked and terrible things than Egypt ever had. But the Egyptians received the fullness of His wrath. Why?

I'm using this story to illustrate an important point: God is merciful to those who repent, no matter the wickedness they've committed. Even more so, it proves the Lord *could* have spared Egypt. If they had forsaken their idols, He possibly would have softened Pharaoh's heart and stopped the plagues.

Even more disturbing—the fact that the priests acknowledged that their idols couldn't stop the wrath of the one true God shows just how close Egypt was to repenting. If even the leaders of idolatry acknowledged this, how much closer were the people? But they still experienced the fullness of all ten plagues. Because "close" isn't good enough.

Many will be in hell who *almost* made it to heaven. The Tribulation period will be filled with people who *almost* made the Rapture. Don't let yourself be one of them.

> *And the* LORD *said unto Moses, Rise early in the morning, and stand before Pharaoh; lo, he cometh forth to the water; and say unto him, Thus saith the* LORD, *Let my people go, that they may serve me. Else, if thou wilt not let my people go, behold, I will send swarms of flies upon thee, and upon thy servants, and upon thy people, and into thy houses: and the houses of the Egyptians shall be full of swarms of flies, and also the ground whereon they are. And I will sever in that day the land of Goshen, in which my people dwell, that no swarms of flies shall be there; to the end, thou mayest know that I am the* LORD *in the midst of the earth. And I will put a division between my people and thy people: to morrow shall this sign be. (Exodus 8:20-23)*

Our God is a God of completion, and we can take Him at His word on this statement. I don't believe that a single fly crossed over from the Egyptian territory into the Israelite camp.

> *And Pharaoh called for Moses and Aaron, and said, Go ye, sacrifice to your God in the land. (Exodus 8:25)*

Before and during the last three plagues, Pharaoh was adamant that the people would not be allowed to leave. This was the first time he showed signs of breaking. He attempted to compromise with Aaron and Moses, granting them the original request (to go and sacrifice in the wilderness). But one doesn't bargain with God. So many try to do just that today, claiming there are many ways to heaven and that each person can come up with their path. But God makes the decisions, not man. And sending His own Son was the supreme sacrifice. If Calvary can't get you there, nothing can.

> *And Moses said, It is not meet so to do; for we shall sacrifice the abomination of the Egyptians to the* LORD *our God: lo, shall we sacrifice the abomination of the Egyptians before their eyes, and will they not stone us? We will go three days' journey into the wilderness, and sacrifice to the* LORD *our God, as he shall command us. (Exodus 8:26-27)*

Pharaoh had not mentioned *where* the children of Israel should sacrifice, and Moses showed a willingness to negotiate. He requested that they travel three days into the wilderness to perform the task. In verses 28-29, Pharaoh agreed to the terms and conditions, and Moses promised that the flies would leave.

But it was a ruse. God knew Pharaoh would break the agreement, and the plan was still in motion.

> *And Moses went out from Pharaoh, and entreated the* Lord. *And the* Lord *did according to the word of Moses; and he removed the swarms of flies from Pharaoh, from his servants, and from his people; there remained not one. And Pharaoh hardened his heart at this time also, neither would he let the people go. (Exodus 8:30-32)*

The Plague Against the Cattle

> *Then the* Lord *said unto Moses, Go in unto Pharaoh, and tell him, Thus saith the* Lord *God of the Hebrews, Let my people go, that they may serve me. For if thou refuse to let them go, and wilt hold them still, Behold, the hand of the* Lord *is upon they cattle which is in the field, upon the horses, upon the asses, upon the camels, upon the oxen, and upon the sheep: there shall be a very grievous murrain. (Exodus 9:1-3)*

The flood season of Egypt was from May to December, when cattle were kept in stables. In January, they would be released to pasture to graze on freshly growing grass from flooded plains (giving us an idea of when this plague struck). With some probably coming in contact with piles of still-rotting dead frogs, and others being bit by the swarms of lice and flies, a plague among Egypt's livestock was inevitable.[80] The cattle would then spread it like wildfire to the horses, donkeys, camels, oxen, and sheep.

The Plague of Boils

> *And the* Lord *said unto Moses and unto Aaron, Take to you handfuls of ashes of the furnace, and let Moses sprinkle it toward the heaven in the sight of Pharaoh. And it shall become small dust in all the land of Egypt, and shall be a boil breaking forth with blains upon man, and upon beast, throughout all the land of Egypt. And they took ashes of the furnace, and stood before Pharaoh, and Moses sprinkled it up toward heaven; and it became a boil breaking forth with blains upon man, and upon beast. And the magicians could not stand before Moses because of the boils; for the boil was upon the magicians and upon all the Egyptians. And the* Lord *hardened the heart of Pharaoh, and he hearkened not unto them; as the* Lord *had spoken unto Moses. (Exodus 9:8-12)*

The situation kept getting worse for the Egyptians; the previous plagues had struck their water, crops, and livestock. But now it was striking *them*. The priests of the idols had once been able to emulate each plague. Now they were struck with boils they couldn't get rid of.

The Plague of Hail

> *And the* Lord *said unto Moses, Rise early in the morning, and stand before Pharaoh, and say unto him, Thus saith the* Lord *God of the Hebrews,*

Let my people go, that they may serve me. For I will at this time send all my plagues upon thine heart, and upon thy servants, and upon they people; that thou mayest know that there is none like me in all the earth. Behold, to morrow about this time I will cause it to rain a very grievous hail, such as hath not been in Egypt since the foundation thereof even until now. (Exodus 9:13-14, 18)

A hailstorm was about to strike Egypt, the likes of which it had never seen. God promised that anything in its path would be destroyed, and not just because of the size of the hailstones; this was no ordinary storm. Exodus 9:24 tells us that hail mingled with fire would rain on Egypt, killing every man and beast in sight and obliterating crops and grass:

So there was hail, and fire mingled with the hail, very grievous, such as there was none like it in all the land of Egypt since it became a nation. (Exodus 9:24)

Fear of the one true God had swept through the courts of Pharaoh; after so many plagues, many were ready to do whatever God said.

He that feared the word of the LORD among the servants of Pharaoh made his servants and his cattle flee into the houses: And he that regarded not the word of the LORD left his servants and his cattle in the field. (Exodus 9:20-21)

Here we see a microcosm of a sad reality throughout the Bible that is still true today: some will heed the warnings of God, others will not. And those who don't will pay the price.

And Moses stretched forth his rod toward heaven: and the LORD sent thunder and hail, and the fire ran along upon the ground, and the LORD rained hail upon the land of Egypt. So there was hail, and fire mingled with the hail, very grievous, such as there was none like it in all the land of Egypt since it became a nation. And the hail smote throughout all the land of Egypt all that was in the field, both man and beast; and the hail smote every herb of the field, and brake every tree of the field. (Exodus 9:23-25)

Once again, only the Israelites were spared. Only in the land of Goshen, where the children of Israel were, was there no hail (Exodus 9:26).

If a volcanic eruption was responsible for this plague (and darkness), it would explain why the hailstones were "mingled with fire." The scene in Egypt was becoming apocalyptic. And like the first plague, this also coincides with another terrible plague from Revelation that will strike the whole earth.

And there fell upon men a great hail out of heaven, every stone about the weight of a talent: and men blasphemed God because of the plague of the hail; for the plague thereof was exceeding great. (Revelation 16:21)

The Plague of Locusts

> *And the LORD said unto Moses, Go in unto Pharaoh: for I have hardened his heart, and the heart of his servants, that I might shew these my signs before him: And that thou mayest tell in the ears of thy son, and of thy son's son, what things I have wrought in Egypt, and my signs which I have done among them; that ye may know how that I am the LORD. (Exodus 10:1-2)*

A new aspect of the plan of God was brought to light. Not only were the plagues meant to punish Egypt and disprove their gods but also to serve as a sign of God's delivering power for future generations. Later, the Lord would instruct Joshua to erect stone monuments as permanent reminders to Israel's descendants.

> *That this may be a sign among you, that when your children ask their fathers in time to come, saying, What mean ye by these stones? Then ye shall answer them, That the waters of Jordan were cut off before the ark of the covenant of the LORD; when it passed over Jordan, the waters of Jordan were cut off: and these stones shall be for a memorial unto the children of Israel forever. (Joshua 4:6-7)*

What about you? Will you be able to tell your children and grandchildren about all the times God brought you out of something? About how He saved you, sanctified you, filled you with the Holy Ghost, and healed you of your sicknesses and diseases? Think of how your testimony could ring forth throughout the generations, continuing to bring your descendants to Jesus throughout the ages.

> *And Moses and Aaron were brought again unto Pharaoh: and he said unto them, Go, serve the LORD your God: but who are they that shall go? And Moses said, We will go with our young and with our old, with our sons and with our daughters, with our flocks and with our herds will we go; for we must hold a feast unto the LORD. (Exodus 10:8-9)*

Pharaoh's servants had now pressed him into letting the children of Israel go. But ultimately, his heart was still, and would always be, hardened. Moses made it clear that *all* of the people must go—young, old, sons, and daughters. But Pharaoh was attempting to manipulate him into only allowing the men to go make sacrifices in the desert.

> *And he said unto them, Let the LORD be so with you, as I will let you go, and your little ones: look to it; for evil is before you. Not so: go now ye that are men, and serve the LORD; for that ye did desire. And they were driven out from Pharaoh's presence. (Exodus 10:10-11)*

Pharaoh's possibly sinister plan was to separate the Israelite men from the women and children. Who knew what he had in store? Perhaps this was an attempt to punish the slaves for all the horrors their God had brought upon Egypt. We'll never know. Fortunately, Moses saw through it. They simply left Pharaoh's presence, signifying the arrival of the next plague.

> *And Moses stretched forth his rod over the land of Egypt, and the LORD brought an east wind upon the land all that day, and all that night; and when it was morning, the east wind brought the locusts. And the locust went up over all the land of Egypt, and rested in all the coasts of Egypt: very grievous were they; before them, there were no such locusts as they, neither after them shall be such. For they covered the face of the whole earth so that the land was darkened; and they did eat every herb of the land, and all the fruit of the trees which the hail had left: and there remained not any green thing in the trees, or in the herbs of the field, through all the land of Egypt. (Exodus 10:13-15)*

Locusts are devastating to agriculture. They come swiftly like a dark cloud, envelop the land, and are gone as quickly as they arrive, leaving all the grass and vegetation stripped bare. This, after the hail and fire had already destroyed most of Egypt's crops, brought a swift famine.

THE TIES THAT BIND

The Bible says that this plague of locusts was the worst the world had ever seen up until that point. But a global plague is coming that will make this one seem mild by comparison. It is the fifth of the seven trumpet judgments during the Tribulation period.

> *And the fifth angel sounded, and I saw a star fall from heaven unto the earth: and to him was given the key of the bottomless pit. And he opened the bottomless pit; and there arose smoke out of the pit, as the smoke of a great furnace; and the sun and the air were darkened by reason of the smoke of the pit. And there came out of the smoke locusts upon the earth: and unto them was given power, as the scorpions of the earth have power. (Revelation 9:1-3)*

But these are no ordinary locusts.

> *And it was commanded them that they should not hurt the grass of the earth, neither any green thing, neither any tree; but only those men who have not the seal of God in their foreheads [those with the mark of the beast]. And to them it was given that they should not kill them, but that they should be tormented five months: and their torment was as the torment of a scorpion when he striketh a man. And in those days shall men seek death, and shall not find it; and shall desire to die, and death shall flee from them. (Revelation 9:4-6)*

> *And the shapes of the locusts were like unto horses prepared unto battle, and on their heads were as it were crowns like gold, and their faces were as the faces of men. And they had hair as the hair of women, and their teeth were as the teeth of lions. And they had breastplates, as it were breastplates of iron; and the sound of their wings was as the sound of chariots of many horses running to battle. And they had tails like unto scorpions, and there were stings in their tails: and their power was to hurt men five months. (Revelation 9:7-10)*

These hideous, demonic creatures will come out of the pits of hell to torment those with the mark of the beast. For five months after the trumpet sounds, the locusts will have the power to deliver painful stings to the followers of the antichrist. Just like God protected the children of Israel, the Tribulation saints will be safe from any danger. God will stop all death on the earth for this brief period. The wicked will try to kill themselves to end their suffering, but the Lord will not let them off that easy. And they're getting exactly what they deserve for the cruelty they've shown His people.

> *Then Pharaoh called for Moses and Aaron in haste; and he said, I have sinned against the LORD your God, and against you. Now therefore forgive, I pray thee, my sin only this once, and entreat the LORD your God, that he may take away from me this death only. And he went out from Pharaoh and entreated in the LORD . And the LORD turned a mighty strong west wind, which took away the locusts, and cast them into the Red sea; there remained not one locust in all the coasts of Egypt. But the LORD hardened Pharaoh's heart so that he would not let the children of Israel go. (Exodus 10:16-20)*

The Plague of Darkness

> *And the LORD said unto Moses, Stretch out thine hand toward heaven, that there may be darkness over the land of Egypt, even darkness which may be felt. And Moses stretched forth his hand toward heaven, and there was a thick darkness in all the land of Egypt three days: They saw not one another, neither rose any from his place for three days: but all the children of Israel had light in there dwellings. (Exodus 10:21-23)*

Pharaoh was not given a chance this time. God bypassed even sending Moses to ask him. The next plague came like a steamroller. Darkness covered the land, and once again, Pharaoh offered to let them go but was secretly trying to set another trap.

> *And Pharaoh called unto Moses, and said, Go ye, serve the LORD; only let your flocks and your herds stay: let your little ones also go with you. And Moses said, Thou must give us also sacrifices and*

burnt offerings, that we may sacrifice unto the LORD *our God. (Exodus 10:24-25)*

Pharaoh had attempted to get the men out of the camp to separate them from the women and children, possibly to kill them. This time, he tried to manipulate Moses into taking everyone out into the wilderness while leaving all their livestock behind. In all likelihood, the people would come back to find their livelihoods destroyed. Moses reminded Pharaoh that they could not make sacrifices without livestock. Pharaoh became enraged and made a vow: he would never see his enemy face-to-face again. This was an ominous sign for the king of Egypt; the final plague was approaching.

But the LORD *hardened Pharaoh's heart, and he would not let them go. And Pharaoh said unto him, Get thee from me, take heed to thyself, see my face no more; for in that day thou seest my face thou shalt die. (Exodus 10:27-28)*

EXODUS 11:1-10

And the LORD *said unto Moses, Yet will I bring one plague more upon Pharaoh, and upon Egypt; afterward he will let you go hence: when he shall let you go, he shall surely thrust you out hence altogether. Speak now in the ears of the people, and let every man borrow of his neighbor, and every woman of her neighbor, jewels of silver and jewels of gold. And the* LORD *gave the people favor in the sight of the Egyptians. Moreover, the man Moses was very great in the land of Egypt, in the sight of Pharaoh's servants, and in the sight of the people. (Exodus 11:1-3)*

God was getting ready to take His people out, and they were instructed to ask for jewels, gold, and silver from the Egyptians. Just like us today, anticipating the return of Jesus, they needed to get ready in advance. The order to leave could happen at any time, but the signs were all in place. Since Moses was apparently still very well respected in the land of Egypt (or maybe due to abject fear of his God, who had already decimated them), the people willingly handed over whatever the Israelites wanted.

The victory for God's people had been so tremendous that the Egyptians were glad to hand over all their treasures, as long as they would take it and leave. What possession of yours does the devil have in bondage? Your children? Your family? Your finances? Your loved ones? We can have such great victory over him that, just like the Egyptians, he will gladly hand it all over and say "Here, take it, and leave!"

And all the firstborn in the land of Egypt shall die, from the firstborn of Pharaoh that sitteth upon his throne, even unto the firstborn of the maidservant that is behind the mill; and all the firstborn of beasts. And

> *there shall be a great cry throughout all the land of Egypt, such as there was none like it, nor shall be like it any more. (Exodus 11:5-6)*

One Wednesday night when I taught a class on the ten plagues, a sister approached me afterward and asked, "Why did the firstborn of the animals have to die too?" I didn't know the answer offhand, but immediately the Holy Spirit fell on me and answered, "Because the Egyptians worshiped animals like gods. Look at their idols; most of them have animal heads. The Lord had to show them that He was master over all the animals as well." It's amazing how God can give you profound revelations right on the spot like that!

EXODUS 12:1-22

The Passover

The Passover is the heart of the Exodus story. It is still one of the most important celebrations in Judaism. Like Hanukkah, it represents more than just a yearly observance of God's delivering power. It is about the resolve of the people and how reliance on Him has brought them out of unimaginable situations. The same God who freed them from Pharaoh's slavery would free them from the wicked king Antiochus a millennium later. They continue to survive despite the many efforts to wipe them out. Pharaoh couldn't do it. Haman couldn't do it. Antiochus couldn't do it. Neither could Hitler. None of the Islamic nations will do it. God will always honor His covenant with Abraham to bless those who bless His descendants and curse those who curse them.

> *And the LORD spake unto Moses and Aaron in the land of Egypt saying, This month shall be unto you the beginning of months: it shall be the first month of the year to you. (Exodus 12:1-2)*

Passover is an eight-day celebration from the fifteenth through the twenty-second of Nissan (roughly April). The first night symbolizes the night of the final plague, when the death angel passed over the homes of the Hebrew slaves who had painted lamb's blood on their doorposts. The final night commemorates the crossing of the Red Sea.

> *And this day shall be unto you for a memorial, and ye shall keep it a feast to the LORD throughout your generations; ye shall keep it a feast by an ordinance forever. (Exodus 12:14)*

It coincides with the Christian celebrations of Lent and Easter (since Jesus was crucified and arose during the Passover gathering in Jerusalem).

THE TEN PLAGUES

In studying the details of the Passover in-depth, we can find remarkable comparisons to the crucifixion and resurrection of Christ.

> *Speak ye unto all the congregation of Israel, saying, In the tenth day of this month they shall take to them every man a lamb, according to the house of their fathers, a lamb for an house: And if the household be too little for the lamb, let him and his neighbour next unto his house take it according to the number of the souls; every man according to his eating shall make your count for the lamb. (Exodus 12:3-4)*

After Adam and Eve ate the forbidden fruit, all people were born into sin.

> *For the wages of sin is death; but the gift of God is eternal life through Jesus Christ our Lord. (Romans 6:23)*

From the beginning, death was the punishment. A sacrificial lamb, the most innocent of all creatures, was a substitute to atone for sin.

> *And almost all things are by the law purged with blood; and without shedding of blood is no remission. (Hebrews 9:22)*

But even in those days, God always despised animal sacrifice.

> *For thou desirest not sacrifice; else would I give it: thou delightest not in burnt offering. (Psalm 51:16)*

It wasn't very effective, either, never truly curing God's people of idolatry.

> *But this man, after he had offered one sacrifice for sins for ever, sat down on the right hand of God. (Hebrews 10:12)*

Jesus came to be the sacrificial Lamb. We experience our own Passover when His blood washes our sins away. Then the death angel (hell) passes us over as we receive eternal life.

> *Your lamb shall be without blemish, a male of the first year: ye shall take it out from the sheep, or from the goats: . . . And they shall take of the blood, and strike it on the two side posts and on the upper door post of the houses, wherein they shall eat it. (Exodus 12:5, 7)*

Like Jesus, who had no sin, the lamb had to be spotless. Impure creatures were not allowed.

> *For I will pass through the land of Egypt this night, and will smite all the firstborn in the land of Egypt, both man and beast; and against all the gods of Egypt I will execute judgment: I am the LORD. And the blood shall be to you for a token upon the houses where ye are: and when I see the blood, I will pass over you, and the plague shall not be upon you to destroy you when I smite the land of Egypt. (Exodus 12:12-13)*

THE TIES THAT BIND

And they shall eat the flesh in that night, roast with fire, and unleavened bread; and with bitter herbs they shall eat it. (Exodus 12:8)

The traditions of the first night of Passover coincide with the events of the Last Supper. First, the patriarch leads in a blessing over the food, then breaks bread and passes it around. Each family member dips his piece in "salt water mixed with bitter herbs." This intentionally tastes terrible, serving as a reminder of the suffering the Israelite slaves had to endure.

Seven days shall ye eat unleavened bread; even the first day ye shall put away leaven out of your houses: for whosoever eateth leavened bread from the first day until the seventh day, that soul shall be cut off from Israel. . . . Seven days shall there be no leaven found in your houses: for whosoever eateth that which is leavened, even that soul shall be cut off from the congregation of Israel, whether he be a stranger, or born in the land. (Exodus 12:15, 19)

Coinciding with Passover is the Feast of Unleavened Bread. According to the Bible, the Israelites had to leave behind any yeast when fleeing Egypt.

And the Egyptians were urgent upon the people, that they might send them out of the land in haste; for they said, We are all dead men. And the people took their dough before it was leavened, their kneading-troughs being bound up in their clothes upon their shoulders. (Exodus 12:33-34)

During Passover, they are not allowed to consume any product containing yeast. The only bread they can eat (and what Jesus and the disciples ate at the Last Supper) is matzah. This is so serious that Jews will spend the two weeks before Passover diligently removing every trace of yeast from their homes.[81] God has the same attitude towards sin, and would that we were so diligent in removing even the specks of disobedience from our lives! We labor under the delusion that God is OK with little sins, excusing our imperfections. But so many will give their usual excuses on Judgment Day and will be caught off guard when He casts them from His presence.

Many will say to me in that day, Lord, Lord, have we not prophesied in thy name? and in thy name have cast out devils? and in thy name done many wonderful works? And then will I profess unto them, I never knew you: depart from me, ye that work iniquity. (Matthew 7:22-23)

And ye shall take a bunch of hyssop, and dip it in the blood that is in the bason, and strike the lintel and the two side posts with the blood that is in the basin; and none of you shall go out at the door of his house until the morning. . . . In one house shall it be eaten; thou shalt not carry forth ought of the flesh abroad out of the house; neither shall ye break a bone thereof. (Exodus 12:22, 46)

THE TIES THAT BIND

Two important points here foreshadow the crucifixion. First, the lamb's bones could not be broken during the ceremony; Jesus' bones were not broken while He hung on the cross, unlike the other two criminals, which fulfills a Messianic prophecy in Psalm 34:20:

He keepeth all his bones: not one of them is broken.

Crucifixion was a slow and agonizing death but could be sped up by breaking the legs (the legs were all that held the body up; so once broken, the victim would suffocate). But He was already dead by the time the Roman soldiers reached Him.

Then came the soldiers, and brake the legs of the first, and of the other which was crucified with him. But when they came to Jesus and saw that he was dead already, they brake not his legs. (John 19:32-33)

The second point involves the hyssop. During the crucifixion, we find a peculiar incident mentioned twice, each time seemingly contradicting the other.

They gave him vinegar to drink mingled with gall: and when he had tasted thereof, he would not drink. (Matthew 27:34)

While Jesus was hanging on the cross, the Roman soldiers offered him a drink of "gall," which He refused.
John's account is a little different:

After this, Jesus knowing that all things were now accomplished, that the scripture might be fulfilled, saith, I thirst. Now there was set a vessel full of vinegar: and they filled a spunge with vinegar, and put it upon hyssop, and put it to his mouth. When Jesus therefore had received the vinegar, he said, It is finished: and he bowed his head, and gave up the ghost. (John 19:28-30)

A sponge was filled with vinegar, placed at the end of a long stick, and held up to His lips. Matthew says that Jesus refused the liquid, but John seems to say that He was given it after complaining of thirst and did indeed drink.

We are reading two separate incidents here. In Matthew, the drink was offered before Jesus was nailed to the cross. He tasted the bitter substance and realized that it was a form of pain-killing poison. This was actually a last act of mercy common in Roman executions. With the prisoner about to suffer an agonizing death, soldiers would offer a mix of bitter herbs to numb the pain and put them out of their misery quicker.

Jesus had already suffered severe dehydration from massive blood loss after being whipped and beaten. Anyone else in the same circumstance would have gladly drunk the poison to hasten their demise. But Jesus still had not finished the plan. He had to endure it *all* to bear the burden of every sin ever committed. There could be no easy way out.

Why then, did He take of the drink in John's account? This was right before His death. At this point, He knew He was about to die and informed the soldiers He was thirsty. They poured the drink on a sponge and attached it to a hyssop, a plant of Egyptian origin with a six-foot hairy stem ideal for holding water.[82] Jesus had already suffered the amount of pain necessary. In dying for our sins, Jesus had to endure the same rituals of atonement enacted upon the sacrificial lamb of Passover.

> *And ye shall take a bunch of hyssop, and dip it in the blood that is in the basin, and strike the lintel and the two side posts with the blood that is in the basin; and none of you shall go out at the door of his house until the morning. (Exodus 12:22)*

The hyssop played an important role in the Passover, and that's why it was required to play a part in the crucifixion. And now the blood is applied to the doorposts of our hearts. Once we stand before God, our sins will be laid out before us; but when He sees the blood, we will be granted eternal life.

> *And whosoever was not found written in the book of life was cast into the lake of fire. (Revelation 20:15)*

Passover and the Last Supper

In Jesus' time, it was customary to travel to Jerusalem to observe Passover; Jesus' own family made the yearly trip from Galilee while He was growing up. This is why they had been in Jerusalem when accidentally leaving Him behind at age twelve in Luke 2.

During this feast, the population of Jerusalem swelled to overcapacity. However it was still a private event held in households among families. This made small inns a booming business this time of year (but every night, the streets were almost empty). Since Jesus and the twelve disciples had left their families behind in ministry, they celebrated together as a family.

Most inns and households contained spare rooms for travelers to celebrate Passover. The furnishings were very simple. Only the very rich could afford simple things like tables and chairs. In most homes, the families ate together, sitting on the floor on goatskin pillows with straw mats for tables.[83]

Luke 22 gives us some details of the upper room. It mentions that this room contained "furnishings," a luxury only the wealthy could afford. Even this, however, would have been humble by our standards. Jews were not known for extravagance. A rich person's spare room would probably contain only a chest of drawers in the corner and a very low table, meaning Da Vinci's painting is extraordinarily inaccurate.

Washing feet is not mentioned in the first Passover; because of unsanitary conditions and feet soiled from walking in the desert all day, it eventually became a necessity and was a full-fledged ritual by Jesus' time.

In Jewish households, the family hierarchy is very important. The patriarch (father or grandfather) sits at the head of the table and conducts the ceremony, leading the prayers and re-reading the story of the final plague. Jesus took this role at the Last Supper. At the time, children would wash the feet of their parents and grandparents before the feast began, then each other's. It was unheard of for the parental figures to do this lowly task; this is why the disciples were so shocked when Jesus washed their feet.

After the Passover story is read, four cups of wine (called "the cups of blessing") are passed around for each family member to share. The sweetness of the drink overpowers the terrible taste of matzah and dip, symbolizing the newfound freedom the Israelites had won from years of slavery. Jesus, however, gave it a new meaning when He explained to the disciples that the bread represented how His body was the bread to be broken and the wine His blood bringing freedom from sin.

In between the second, third, and fourth rounds of cup passing, the family sings Psalms 115, 118, and 136 in Hebrew. Matthew 26:30 mentions that Jesus and the disciples "sang a hymn" before departing. The climax of the meal is roasted lamb, but the Gospels never mention if they finished the meal before leaving for the garden of Gethsemane.

In Luke 22:19, Jesus instructs His followers,

This do in remembrance of Me.

This is why His disciples reenacted the event after He was gone. Paul addresses it in 1 Corinthians 11. The church in Corinth had desecrated the celebration, using it as a time to gather and make merry, even getting drunk (verses 20-22)! In verses 23-29, he declares that this is a celebration that should continue every year until the Lord returns.

EXODUS 12:28-32

The Tenth Plague

And the children of Israel went away, and did as the LORD *had commanded Moses and Aaron, so did they. And it came to pass, that at midnight the*

> LORD *smote all the firstborn in the land of Egypt, from the firstborn of Pharaoh that sat on his throne unto the firstborn of the captive that was in the dungeon; and all the firstborn of cattle. And Pharaoh rose up in the night, he, and all his servants, and all the Egyptians; and there was a great cry in Egypt; for there was not a house where there was not one dead. And he called for Moses and Aaron by night, and said, Rise up, and get you forth from among my people, both ye and the children of Israel; and go, serve the* LORD, *as ye have said. Also take your flocks and your herds, as ye have said, and be gone; and bless me also. (Exodus 12:28-32)*

MIDDLE KINGDOM DYNAMICS

The tenth plague is the darkest moment of the Exodus tale. But did it really happen?

Let's go back to the ruins of Avaris. At a particular moment in history, we can find evidence of a terrible calamity. The "death pits of Avaris," located just outside at the end of Tell ed-Daba, are a series of mass graves from an apparent plague that struck Egypt during the late Middle Bronze Age. The Egyptians were known for their care and reverence for the dead, so for them to bury people in any method other than with elegant caskets and artifacts to accompany them into the afterlife is unheard of. But in this rare case, the thirty-five-hundred-year-old skeletons are twisted and piled on top of one another.[84]

You may be wondering why, if Avaris was the Israelite settlement, mass graves of victims of the tenth plague would be located here. Doesn't the Bible clearly state that the death angel skipped the land of Goshen on its way to Egypt?

Remember that shortly after the death of all the firstborn, the Exodus occurred. So the city was soon abandoned. Perhaps out of spite, necessity, or a little of both, the Egyptians had used the newly evacuated settlement as a quick makeshift cemetery to bury their dead.

Interestingly enough, this horrible disaster is referred to in papyrus documents from the thirteenth dynasty and is described as the "Asiatic plague," something that was clearly viewed as being blamed on the population of Semitic immigrants.[85]

CONCLUSION

The Exodus Occurs

> *And the* LORD *gave the people favour in the sight of the Egyptians, so that they lent unto them such things as they required. And they spoiled the Egyptians. And the children of Israel journeyed from Rameses to Succoth, about six hundred thousand on foot that were men, beside children. And*

> *a mixed multitude went up also with them; and flocks, and herds, even very much cattle. (Exodus 12:36-38)*

In most movies, the Exodus itself is depicted as a grand and ceremonious event. Music plays while the happy Jewish crowds gather at the gates of Egypt. Egyptian soldiers watch in disgust. Moses stands over the crowd solemnly, looking up to heaven and praying that God will give him the strength to lead them. They leave singing.

But the Bible isn't clear on the details. In Exodus 12:37, it only announces that they traveled from "Rameses to Succoth." The closest thing resembling any ceremony is the Lord's strict instructions to Moses that the Israelites observe this event every year. This would serve as a reminder to their children, children's children, and all future generations, how God delivered them at this moment.

> *It is a night to be much observed unto the LORD for bringing them out from the land of Egypt: this is that night of the LORD to be observed of all the children of Israel in their generations. (Exodus 12:42)*

All of chapter 13 is devoted to this.

Personally, I can't help but picture the moment a little differently. It's late at night. Screams of terror echo through the Nile delta. Moses and Aaron are summoned quickly to Pharaoh's court. The grief-stricken king, holding his dead child, tells them to leave. The word comes suddenly: it's time to leave! The night is chaotic as the Israelites abandon their homes and gather together, groping for some kind of leadership. Moses hurriedly shepherds them into the black wilderness. Behind them, the howls of mourning are turning into cries for blood. The Egyptians want revenge against the escaping slaves and their God.

The next morning, the sun rises to bring sweltering heat over the encampment of Succoth. Still exhausted, the escaped slaves can now line up, reunite with families, and make a final headcount before heading into the foreboding desert.

How Many Israelites Were There?

According to Exodus 12:37, the entirety of the nation of Israel, including all twelve tribes, numbered at about six hundred thousand. In the book of Numbers, the figure is 601,730. When added with women and children, estimates arrive at about two to three million total people.

Historians have debated this figure for many years. In four hundred thirty years since the sojourn of seventy people at the Avaris settlement, each family would have had to produce at least eight children to arrive at this number.[86] Furthermore, such a staggering figure would have outweighed the population of the Middle Kingdom Egypt itself. It hardly seems likely that a slave race, especially one that had survived an attempted genocide, would have arrived at such a high population in such short order.

Of course, this serves as more ammunition for Bible critics who claim the story is a fairy tale. However another possibility has been proposed that involves re-examining the exact meaning of Hebrew words here. Let's look at a specific example:

> *Those that were numbered of them, even of the tribe of Reuben, were forty and six thousand and five hundred. (Numbers 1:21)*

The ancient word *aleph* does indeed mean "thousand" but also has the duel meaning of "tribal leader" or "clan head" (note the similarity to the phrase "alpha male").[87] It's easy to literally interpret this verse as "the entire tribe of Reuben was forty-six thousand, five hundred." But change the meaning of "thousand" to "clan head," and we arrive at "the entire tribe of Reuben was forty-six tribal leaders, five hundred able-bodied men."

Don't worry about recalculating the entire population of Israel with this figure in mind; I've done that for you. Adding up all the tribes of Israel, we arrive at approximately thirty-five thousand total leaving Egypt, a much more manageable and realistic number.

I am completely aware that some readers might be furious at me for what seems to be disputing the literal English translation of the Bible, but I promise that is not my intention. This, along with the crossing of the Red Sea in the next chapter, represents divisive issues among people who believe in the Bible but also want to investigate the real historical evidence behind it.

Either way, when I arrive at such quandaries, I usually prefer to present both sides of the issue and leave it to my students or readers to decide for themselves.

At the end of the day, the exact number of Israelites leaving Egypt doesn't matter; it does, however, lead us to a more pressing issue.

Did It Really Happen?

Let's review Bietak's fascinating discoveries at Avaris. What had started as a small settlement of seventy Asiatic immigrants blossomed into a wealthy metropolis, until sudden poverty and harsh living conditions were imposed. Then, some centuries later, towards the end of the thirteenth dynasty and just before the Hyksos invasion (and perfectly in line with our new date for the Exodus, according to the New Chronology), the city was suddenly abandoned. Clearly this was a ghost town when the Egyptians dug mass graves after a catastrophic plague brought the kingdom to its knees.

If you search for Avaris in an encyclopedia, the entry will likely describe it as "the capital of Egypt during the reign of the Hyksos."

Remember what I said earlier, that Dudimose II was the last Pharaoh before the end of the thirteenth dynasty, when the Hyksos suddenly invaded Egypt and ruled as conquerors? The evidence we've looked at so far overwhelmingly supports that the events of the Exodus were what weakened Egypt so severely as to be easily invaded by an outside tribe.

However there was no actual single group of people called "the Hyksos." The name actually comes from the Egyptian word *hykau*, indicating that they were rulers from a faraway northern hill-country.[88] Archaeologists lump them under one name (which comes from Egyptian *priest* and historian *Manetho*) for simplicity's sake, but they were actually a band of disparate warrior-tribes from the wilderness. When the most powerful kingdom in the world was suddenly weakened by plagues and a drowned army, they saw a perfect opportunity and united together to launch an invasion. After a brutal conquest, they reoccupied the city that had been recently abandoned by the fleeing Israelites and established it as a place to rule Egypt with an iron fist. The Pharaoh was driven out, and the Egyptians were placed in the same kind of slavery they had imposed on the children of Israel for four hundred thirty years.

An exciting clue from chapter 17 will help us solve another brain teaser from the Bible; but we'll address that later. For now, we can safely conclude that this story is not a myth or fairytale invented by a people creating their own history, but an actual, provable event. Whether people want to accept that or not is beside the point; the evidence cannot be denied. The Exodus was real.

Chapter 6

THE RED SEA

INTRODUCTION

The crossing of the Red Sea is the most iconic scene in Exodus. The two are intrinsically linked in our collective psyche; say "Exodus" and the first image that comes to mind is a dramatic picture of Moses standing over the split waters as his people dash across, Pharaoh's army in hot pursuit. If Exodus just ended with the Israelites slipping quietly into the night, the story would be an intriguing but somewhat less memorable biblical event.

But the crossing is more than just a symbolic moment in the national identity of the Jewish people. It also contains important lessons for Christians. In this chapter, I want to put a fresh take on one of the Bible's most infamous stories.

MIDDLE KINGDOM DYNAMICS

Trying to find the exact spot where the crossing took place is an irresistible puzzle, but years of expeditions have offered few clues. However one man made a bold proclamation and published a series of discoveries that is still stirring controversy to this day.

Let's start by tracing the steps of the Israelites from the land of Goshen to the Red Sea. Take another look at Exodus 12:37:

And the children of Israel journeyed from Rameses to Succoth, about six hundred thousand on foot that were men, beside children.

Next, we skip to chapter 13, verse 20:

And they took their journey from Succoth, and encamped in Etham, in the edge of the wilderness.

Chapter 14, verse 2 gives us the third and final encampment before they reach the edges of the water:

Speak unto the children of Israel, that they turn and encamp before Pihahiroth, between Migdol and the sea, over against Baalzephon: before it shall ye encamp by the sea.

The Hebrew word *sukkot* means "temporary dwellings," or "booths,"[89] indicating that a large campsite was located here. The place still contains some importance in Jewish lore: the seven-day feast of Sukkot, celebrated in September–October, commemorates the first taste of freedom.

Ye shall dwell in booths seven days; all that are Israelites born shall dwell in booths: That your generations may know that I made the children of Israel to dwell in booths, when I brought them out of the land of Egypt: I am the LORD your God. (Leviticus 23:42-43)

According to some archaeologists, the ghostly desert ruins in modern Tell el-Maskhuta serve as the most likely campsite for the fleeing Israelites.

The next stop was Etham, which the Bible describes as being "on the edge of the wilderness." The name may have origins in the Egyptian word *khetem*, meaning "border fortress."[90] During the Middle Bronze Age, an ancient worker city called Kahun was located in this vicinity.[91] Nearby Lake Timsa, "Crocodile Lake," would have served as a perfect temporary campground in the harsh desert climate. The route from here to the Promised Land, called the "Way of Shur," is the same path Abraham took from Egypt many years ago. As they traveled, the Lord sent a cloud to lead them during the day and a pillar of fire by night.

And the LORD went before them by day in a pillar of a cloud, to lead them the way; and by night in a pillar of fire, to give them light; to go by day and night: He took not away the pillar of the cloud by day, nor the pillar of fire by night, from before the people. (Exodus 13:21-22)

The third destination, however, indicates that the people suddenly and inexplicably turned a different direction. Bible historians attempting to trace the route have struggled to understand why, but recent discoveries have shed new light on this. According to Middle Kingdom papyri, on the other side of Lake Timsa was an unexpected two-hundred-thirty-foot-wide manmade canal dotted with fortresses manned by hostile Egyptian militia.[92] The canal connected Crocodile Lake with the Bitter lakes to the south. Word may not have reached these kingdom guards yet that Pharaoh had agreed to let the slaves go, so Moses had to think fast and find an alternate route to Canaan. The Spirit led them to Pihahiroth, "between Midgol and the sea."

Once again, by placing the Exodus in its proper time period, we see how the ancient topography of Egypt helps make sense out of a mystery from the story and continues to support its historical accuracy.

The Israelites had been traveling southeast from Avaris, but now had to swing north around the series of canals, lakes, and swampy marshlands. While technically free, they were still in Egyptian territory, and the Pharaoh could have changed his mind at a moment's notice. Before long, they found themselves trapped, while the faint figures of hostile forces began to appear on the horizon.

THE NUWEIBA CROSSING THEORY

I was somewhat more gullible new when I first heard of the Nuweiba crossing theory. Ready to believe everything supporting my beliefs, I excitedly described it to my Wednesday night Bible class and proclaimed that archaeologists had found conclusive proof that the Exodus was real. But years of hard-earned experience has taught me to be more cautious about new discoveries.

First, let me provide some background information. In the early 1960s, a young anesthetic nurse named Ron Wyatt managed to come up with the funds to go on an expedition to the Middle East. Wyatt had seen the discovery by the Turkish army of a football-shaped mound on the side of a mountain called Judi Dagh and was intrigued. His first trip was a disaster, as he and his two young sons were chased away by local thieves. But he vowed to return.[93]

After some three decades and countless expeditions, each one armed with a better equipped team of experts, Wyatt went public with the claim that he had discovered Noah's Ark. For a brief period in the late 80s, his excavations garnered appearances on nightly news. The Turkish government even joined him in a ceremony officially determining that the mysterious mound on Judi Dagh was in fact the legendary ship.

Public interest has since faded, but Wyatt was bolstered by his discovery and became a bit of a Christian folk hero. Wyatt Archaeological Research continues to honor his legacy. (He passed away in 1999.)

Over the decades, Wyatt claimed to have made numerous groundbreaking discoveries, including the Ark of the Covenant, a piece of Jesus' cross, and the Holy Grail. Most archaeologists don't take him seriously, but if you read my blog on the subject, you'll find that for a variety of reasons, I think it's plausible he discovered the ruins of Noah's Ark.

The Ark mound on Judi Dagh is probably still his most infamous discovery, with Nuweiba a close second. In the early 90s, Wyatt began publishing a series of photographs from underwater expeditions in the Gulf of Aqaba and claimed he had found the site where God parted the waters for the children of Israel to cross. According to him, the site was at a beach near the Middle Eastern city of Nuweiba. Let's examine them one-by-one.

First, the Red Sea is extraordinarily deep. Even if the waters were parted, the bottom would be like trying to walk across the Grand Canyon. Deep abysses and jagged rocks would await you, rendering the crossing impossible (unless God also raised up the ocean floor, a detail the Bible doesn't mention). At the beach of Nuweiba, though, is an underwater "saddle" where the treacherous sea floor rises up into what appears to be a shallow path that theoretically could be crossed.[94]

In 1978 Wyatt's team did their first undersea exploration of this rocky strip and discovered coral-encrusted chariot wheels. Confirming that they were in fact Egyptian, the team went on several more dives, eventually finding more broken wheels and a fossilized human bone.[95] These seem to provide solid evidence that Pharaoh's army was drowned at this location, as the walls of water came crashing down.

Jutting out of the beach on either side are two matching ancient pillars containing Hebrew inscriptions and names and were allegedly erected by Solomon as a monument to the Exodus.[96] *Nuweiba* actually means "waters of Moses opening."[97]

Journey a little farther into the Arabian wilderness on the other side of the gulf and you'll come across a giant rock split nearly cleanly in half. This is allegedly the rock that Moses struck to bring forth water for the Israelites. Nearby, in eastern Midian, is Gebel el-Lawz, a mountain whose blackened summit looks dramatically burned. Could this be the biblical Mount Sinai, where the fire of God gave Moses the Ten Commandments?[98]

Added up, this looks very impressive. Seeing the colorful pictures on Wyatt's website of the split rock, underwater chariot wheels, and ancient pillar were enough to get me excited that proof of one of the most famous miracles in the Bible existed in the Middle Eastern deserts! With so much overwhelming evidence, how could anyone still deny that this is the definitive site of the Red Sea crossing?

But now let's take a closer look at the problems.

The first hole is perhaps the most fatal: Nuweiba is in the wrong place.

If you look at a map of the Middle East, you'll see that the Red Sea is split at the top, forming a "V" shape. The triangle-shaped land in the middle forms the Sinai Peninsula, the traditional site of the forty years of wandering. The Eastern body of water is the Gulf of Aqaba, where Nuweiba is located, over two hundred miles away from where the Exodus took place. At an estimated rate of twenty-two miles a day,[99] it would have taken the Israelites about nine days (with no water) to reach the site. Certainly more campsites would have been necessary in such a long grueling journey, but the Bible only records the three we've already mentioned. It's also unlikely that the Egyptian chariots would have been able to chase them that far through such inhospitable terrain!

So for the Nuweiba crossing theory to hold up, its proponents have to shift the entire geographic location of the Exodus. On the other side of the Gulf of Aqaba was the wilderness of Midian (modern Saudi Arabia), the proposed "new location" for the forty years of wandering. They cite the aforementioned discoveries and even point to scriptural evidence in the New Testament:

For this Agar is mount Sinai in Arabia, and answereth to Jerusalem which now is, and is in bondage with her children. (Galatians 4:25)

First off, this verse in Galatians needs to be put in proper context. In Paul's time, "Arabia" was not the modern kingdom of the Saudis but a vast untamed land that did include the Sinai Peninsula. So nothing in the New Testament can be used to support the Midian theory.

Secondly, let's look at the so-called "new" Mount Sinai. Gebel el-Lawz contains a peculiar blackened summit, almost resembling burn marks. It's tantalizing to label this Mount Sinai, but that shows a lack of understanding of what caused its peculiar color. Its summit consists of basalt and granite, which together, combined with centuries of sun exposure, naturally darken.[100] It is difficult to not notice the dramatic difference between the summit and the rest of the mountain, but it is not the result of fire and smoke.

The split rock poses even more problems. The giant boulder is impressive, jutting high out of a pile of rocks on the desert floor with a giant separation almost evenly down its middle. But this cleft was likely the result of years of wind and erosion, and plenty of other unique patterns can be found all across the Middle Eastern deserts. Furthermore, I defer back to the New Testament:

Moreover, brethren, I would not that ye should be ignorant, how that all our fathers were under the cloud, and all passed through the sea; And were all baptized unto Moses in the cloud and in the sea; And did all eat the same spiritual meat; And did all drink the same spiritual drink: for they drank of that spiritual Rock that followed them: and that Rock was Christ. (1 Corinthians 10:4)

In his letter to the Corinthians, Paul uses the story of Moses leading the Israelites through the desert to illustrate a point and informs us that the rock actually continued to follow them through the wilderness to provide water. This means that, according to the Bible, it wouldn't be found in its original resting place anyway.

This leads us back to the crossing site of Nuweiba itself. Doesn't it seem coincidental that the land bridge is strewn with ancient chariots and human remains?

The problem is that if God had parted the waters here, despite the so-called "underwater land bridge," it still would have been too steep for the Israelites to cross. The walk would have started off with a precipitous drop of 863 feet, followed by a steady decline, then another plunge into 2,500-foot depths.[101] By the time the fleeing people would have reached the middle, assuming they had survived, they would have found themselves trapped. It's an equally treacherous climb back up the other side! If all the water in the Gulf of Aqaba were to suddenly disappear, no human being could reasonably make it across in one night—and certainly not an entire tribe of nomads with all their goods and livestock in tow!

What, then, of the ancient Egyptian chariot wheels and human remains resting at the bottom? As far as I can tell, Wyatt Archaeological Research's stance is that the Exodus took place during the New Kingdom, and they have excitedly identified the pattern on the wheels as belonging to the eighteenth dynasty, probably from the time of the infamous young Pharaoh Tutankhamen.[102] If you've read this far into my book, by now you've seen the amount of evidence placing the Exodus farther back in time, at the tail end of the thirteenth dynasty.

This itself opens up a whole new can of worms. I am confident in the Middle Kingdom date. However, reconsidering any New Kingdom theory leads back to the original puzzle of identifying the Exodus Pharaoh; and this is where many claims get bizarre. Some even go as far as to claim that legendary Egyptian vizier Imhotep, who helped Old Kingdom Pharaoh Djoser construct the step pyramid and later was immortalized as god of medicine, was the biblical Joseph.[103] If the chariot remains Wyatt discovered are from the time of Tutankhamen, some have concluded Akhenaten is the logical Exodus Pharaoh. But this runs into even more problems.

Akhenaten was originally Amenhotep IV, who according to the traditional chronology ruled Egypt from 1377–1360 BC.[104] He is one of history's most controversial Pharaohs. Egypt wasn't known for embracing change, which is reflected in the fact that so many statues of Pharaohs bear bland expressionless features. The sun rose and set every day, and the people prayed to the gods that it would never end. Amenhotep IV, however, was a man of radical reform. Upon taking the throne, he moved the capital two hundred fifty miles north to El Amarna,[105] then inexplicably banished all gods except Aten, a lesser-known deity of midday light (the name "Akhenaten" means "agreeable to Aten").[106]

As if that weren't enough, Akhenaten turned the Egyptian art world upside down. His statues are easy to recognize among other Pharaohs: tall, grotesque, with protruding lips and a potbelly. The depictions look so deformed that some theories over the years have speculated that he might have had physical handicaps—or was even an alien.

Akhenaten's queen was the mysterious Nefertiti, and his successor was his younger brother, nine-year-old Pharaoh Tutankhamen.[107] Most of us are familiar with the fact that King Tut had a very short rule before dying suddenly at the age of eighteen. Why is still a mystery, but his well-preserved mummy indicates wide feminine hips and clubbed feet (a plethora of canes was found in his tomb), leading to speculation that he may have been plagued with health problems resulting from inbreeding.[108]

King Tut, like Ramses, is synonymous with "Pharaoh" in our minds. In grammar school, he's often the first king of Egypt we ever learn about. However this is somewhat of a historical misconception. His reign was short and quickly forgotten by the Egyptians after his sudden death. While most Pharaohs have magnificent burial pyramids, his was a small shoddy mound.

The reason King Tut is so famous today is even more ironic. Grave robbers were a huge problem in ancient Egypt (thieves were primarily interested in the massive treasure troves buried with the kings). By the early twentieth century, most tombs in the Valley of the Kings had been picked clean. When Howard Carter accidentally discovered the crypt of Tutankhamen in 1922, he was amazed at how well-preserved it was; but this is for no other reason than that no robber had suspected King Tut's burial mound to be worth the trouble. As a result, the relatively small burial site was one of the most perfectly preserved ever discovered. King Tut quickly became a household name, as artifacts were placed in museums around the world.

So according to the theory that makes Akhenaten the Exodus Pharaoh, he converted to monotheism once he realized the Israelites worshiped the one true God. His firstborn son, Tutankhamen, was the unfortunate victim of the tenth plague.

This theory is full of holes. For one, no record of anything resembling the Exodus event exists during the reign of either Akhenaten or Tutankhamen, and certainly not on the same level as the aforementioned Ipuwer papyrus. Despite the seismic changes he brought, his reign seemed to be relatively stable, with no major cataclysmic events akin to the ten plagues. King Tut was the younger brother of Akhenaten, not his son, and became Pharaoh after his death. The idea that his death, which occurred nine years later, had anything to do with the tenth plague simply doesn't fit. The usual excuse by New Kingdom theorists for this lack of documentation is that "the Egyptians were too embarrassed to make record of the Exodus,"[109] which I frankly find absurd.

This is why I can't accept that the chariot wheels at the bottom of the Gulf of Aqaba are in any way connected to the crossing of the Red Sea. As I've mentioned earlier, our tendency to jump to conclusions too fast leads us to match famous historical figures with unnamed characters in the Bible. It's why people will quickly name Ramses or Akhenaten as the Exodus Pharaoh and King Tut as the firstborn victim of the tenth plague, even when the evidence is flimsy at best.

But when observed under the new chronology and placed in his proper time period, Akhenaten does still have an intriguing connection with the Bible. The newly proposed date places his reign from 1023–1007 BC and actually makes him a contemporary of King Saul.[110] The logic of the "heretic Pharaoh's" sudden move to monotheism and cultish devotion to the light-god Aten was clearly a political maneuver against the priesthood, as well as a reform back to "pure worship," when Egypt had deified the sun, from which all other gods had sprung.

When Akhenaten was growing up in the court of Pharaoh, still under the name Amenhotep IV, we find that he was greatly schooled and influenced by a royal tutor named Abd-El. If you haven't noticed by now, many great figures in the Bible have an "El" in their names somewhere, as it is one of the original Hebrew titles for God. Samu-El (Samuel), for example, means "offspring of El."[111] We can then conclude that this mysterious figure in the court of Pharaoh, whose name means "servant of El," was actually a foreign Israelite who worshiped Yahweh and may have had the sway that made the Pharaoh embrace monotheism as an adult.

So to conclude, I am not entirely persuaded by the Nuweiba crossing theory, for all of the aforementioned reasons. However in this chapter's endnotes I've included the links to Wyatt Archaeological Research's website, where you can see pictures of their discoveries and read their case to decide for yourself.

But of course, this still leaves us with the original question: Where did the crossing take place?

The first thing we have to address is one of the most common misnomers in the Bible. Typically the name "Red Sea" refers to the large body of water that stretches from the Gulf of Aden, splitting Africa from the Middle East. But after a little investigation, we find that the original phrase for "Red Sea" in ancient Hebrew was *yam suph*, which actually means "sea of reeds."[112] The Septuagint first presented the "yam suph" as *Erythra Thalassa*, or "Red Sea." This became embedded in most Bible translations afterwards, finding its way into almost all the versions we read today.[113]

All this means is that the crossing took place in a body of water that contained reeds, which doesn't give us much to go by.

Just north of the Red Sea's tip is a small cluster of lakes known as the Bitter Lakes. We've already traced the Israelites' journey from Succoth to Etham, followed by a dramatic swing north to Piharoth. We've determined that they ran into a canal dotted with armed Egyptian fortresses connected to the lakes and decided to take a safe passage to get out of the Pharaoh's territory. But the farther they went, the grimmer the situation looked. Then they slammed into a dead end. But if you travel there today (the Kantara region around the Suez Canal), you won't be able to see what used to be a large expanse of freshwater lakes connected to the Mediterranean known as the Balla Lakes. The ancient Egyptians knew the area as *pa-Tjuf*, which means "the reeds" (note the similarities between the Hebrew *suph* and Egyptian *Tjuf*).[114]

Let's take a second look at Exodus 10:19:

> *And the* LORD *turned a mighty strong west wind, which took away the locusts, and cast them into the Red sea; there remained not one locust in all the coasts of Egypt.*

If the Lord drove the insects from Egypt with a mighty wind into the Red Sea (sea of reeds), the Balla Lakes is directly west of Avaris, making it the most logical destination.

Unfortunately, finding any archaeological evidence of the Red Sea crossing proves impossible, since the Balla Lakes were drained by the Egyptian government in the 1860s to build the nearby Suez Canal. All that remains of the pa-Tjuf is a vast flat landscape baking in the sun.

When I say, "shallow lakes," I can already hear many Christians up in arms. They probably think I'm selling out to the secular notion that Moses just reached a swampy marshland when the tide receded, allowing the Israelites safe passage. But this is not the case at all. Obviously, the water still had to be deep enough for Pharaoh's army to drown here. We don't really know how deep the Balla Lakes were, but we do have historical testimony from British Officer Sir Alexander Tulloch while inspecting the Suez Canal a few years after its completion that the waters there were deep enough for fishing boats to pass through.[115]

After researching it, I personally think this is the most likely spot for one of the most pivotal moments in human history. I still refer to the crossing site as "the Red Sea" merely out of tradition, which is also perfectly valid. But at the end of the day, it doesn't really matter *where* the crossing took place so much as *that* it took place, and we apply the lessons from the story to our own lives.

EXODUS 14:5-31

> *And it was told the king of Egypt that the people fled: and the heart of Pharaoh and of his servants was turned against the people, and they said, Why have we done this, that we have let Israel go from serving us? (Exodus 14:5)*

After all Egypt had been through, they should have been quivering in fear of the Almighty. But losing his firstborn wasn't enough to soften Pharaoh's heart. His servants, who, during the plagues, begged the king to release the Israelites, whispered into his hear that it was a mistake. He geared up for battle.

> *But the Egyptians pursued after them, all the horses and chariots of Pharaoh, and his horsemen, and his army, and overtook them encamping by the sea, beside Pihahiroth, before Baalzephon. (Exodus 14:9)*

Remember that Pihahiroth was the third encampment of the Israelites before crossing the sea (Baalzephon refers to the other side). As they desperately searched for an exit, an army of Egyptian chariots appeared on the horizon. Like so many times before, the situation looked hopeless. But they couldn't see the entire plan of God, which was not yet finished. He was about to complete the judgment on Egypt.

> *And when Pharaoh drew nigh, the children of Israel lifted up their eyes, and, behold, the Egyptians marched after them; and they were sore afraid: and the children of Israel cried out unto the LORD. And they said unto Moses, Because there were no graves in Egypt, hast thou taken us away to die in the wilderness? wherefore hast thou dealt thus with us, to carry us forth out of Egypt? Is not this the word that we did tell thee in Egypt, saying, Let us alone, that we may serve the Egyptians? For it had been better for us to serve the Egyptians, than that we should die in the wilderness. (Exodus 14:10-12)*

The Israelites were not able to see with supernatural eyes. But this statement was not just an insult to Moses; it was a slap in the face to the God who had brought them this far. Not only did they claim that they were content to be left alone by Moses and continue lives in slavery, but they actually claimed it would have been better to die at the hands of the Egyptian task masters.

THE PRACTICAL APPLICATION

One of the devil's craftier tricks was on display here. Sin, for the most part, is a miserable experience. Addiction fuels us to seek happiness we can never find. Coming to Jesus is finding true freedom. But a Christian's life is not going to be perfect, as Psalm 34:19 assures us:

Many are the afflictions of the righteous.

Somehow, when the going gets tough, Satan will bring a skewed memory of sin to our minds. He can make us miss the drugs, alcohol, or pornography. Just like the children of Israel, we can so easily forget what bondage it really was. Now that God had answered their cries for freedom, they were remembering the past differently.

> *And Moses said unto the people, Fear ye not, stand still, and see the salvation of the LORD, which he will shew to you to day: for the Egyptians whom ye have seen to day, ye shall see them again no more for ever. . . . And the LORD said unto Moses, Wherefore criest thou unto me? speak unto the children of Israel, that they go forward: But lift thou up thy rod, and stretch out thine hand over the sea, and divide it: and the children of Israel shall go on dry ground through the midst of the sea. (Exodus 14:13, 15-16)*

The Lord's answer was brutally honest and can be summed up as follows: "Why are you wasting time crying to Me? Just walk towards the water!" It's tempting to condemn them for being hesitant. But with any Bible story, it's always helpful to put ourselves in the same situation and ask how different we would act. In a worldly mindset, walking into water leads to drowning. If that sounds difficult to comprehend after all the miraculous things God had done for them, picture yourself standing on the ledge of the roof of a high building. Now imagine the voice of God telling you to step forward and trust in Him. Even if you knew beyond a shadow of a doubt that it was the Lord, you would still hesitate.

> *And the angel of God, which went before the camp of Israel, removed and went behind them; and the pillar of the cloud went from before their face, and stood behind them: And it came between the camp of the Egyptians and the camp of Israel; and it was a cloud and darkness to them, but it gave light by night to these: so that the one came not near the other all the night. (Exodus 14:19-20)*

THE TIES THAT BIND

As they walked forward, first a cloud followed by a pillar of fire came down from the sky between them and Pharaoh's army. This was the same cloud that filled the temple at Solomon's dedication.

> *And it came to pass, when the priests were come out of the holy place, that the cloud filled the house of the LORD, So that the priests could not stand to minister because of the cloud: for the glory of the LORD had filled the house of the LORD. (1 Kings 8:10-11)*

It was the cloud that filled the Holiest of Holies when the priest went to offer atonement for the people every year. And that same cloud fills your prayer chamber when you kneel before God every day.

But there's a difference between that glory cloud in the Old and New Testaments. Israel had to follow the cloud from a distance. They couldn't be inside it. Today, however, the glory of God fills our churches. It doesn't hover above the steeples every Sunday morning. We are *in* the cloud, carried by God across the wilderness in this final hour.

And we aren't alone. In Matthew 17:5, right after Peter, James, and John saw Jesus in His glorified state on top of the Mount of Transfiguration,

> *While he yet spake, behold, a bright cloud overshadowed them: and behold a voice out of the cloud, which said, This is my beloved Son, in whom I am well pleased; hear ye him. (Matthew 17:5)*

The Father Himself dwells with us in the cloud.

> *And it came to pass, that in the morning watch the L*ORD *looked unto the host of the Egyptians through the pillar of fire and of the cloud, and troubled the host of the Egyptians. (Exodus 14:24)*

THE PRACTICAL APPLICATION

After the cloud came a pillar of fire. The Bible is very specific in verse 20 that "it was a cloud and darkness to them, but it gave light by night to these." In ancient times, a common military practice involved using fire at night to confuse the enemy. They didn't have light pollution like we have today. Nighttime in the ancient world, even around populated areas, was much blacker. An unsuspecting army would have enlarged pupils adjusted to the darkness. Their opponents would step forward and, a few feet behind, light a sudden gigantic fire. Anyone looking in that direction would be completely blinded. But for the attackers, the flame behind them would illuminate the darkness, exposing their helpless enemy. Then it was time to move in for the ambush.

The Lord here did the exact same thing. As His people moved toward the water, He sent a pillar of fire behind them that lit the way. But Pharaoh's pursuing army, facing towards the flame, was temporarily blinded and helpless while the Israelites hurried to safety.

I made an earlier point that fire, oil, or a dove in the Old Testament always symbolized the Holy Ghost. If the Father was in the cloud, the Spirit was in the pillar of fire. The Third Person of the Trinity was also in the burning bush. The same fire would later carve the Ten Commandments on the tablets of Mount Sinai and would appear in the form of a chariot to take Elijah to heaven.

As crucial as this is for Judaism, the Day of Pentecost should be even more important for Christians. Speaking in tongues is the New Testament era manifestation of the Holy Ghost and the initial evidence of His baptism.

The crossing of the Red Sea took place in the darkest of night at the moment things seemed most futile. But when God sent the fire, it lit the way to safety. It showed the children of Israel where the water was split. This hour, leading up to the Rapture and the Great Tribulation, is the darkest we've ever seen. But the tongue of fire is a torch for God's children, urging us forward with the cry, "Just a few more steps!"

Jesus' story of ten virgins waiting on the bridegroom also illustrates this point. In ancient times, Jewish ritual was that after an engagement, the groom-to-be would disappear to build a house for his new bride. He could return for her at any moment, so she had to be ready at all times. It could even be in the middle of the night, so she had to be well dressed and constantly surrounded by her bridesmaids.

> *Then shall the kingdom of heaven be likened unto ten virgins, which took their lamps, and went forth to meet the bridegroom. And five of them were wise, and five were foolish. They that were foolish took their lamps, and took no oil with them: But the wise took oil in their vessels with their lamps. (Matthew 25:1-4)*

The bridesmaids had to be ready with lamps to light the way when the groom came to take her away.

> *And at midnight there was a cry made, Behold, the bridegroom cometh; go ye out to meet him. (Matthew 25:6)*

The five wise virgins got to accompany the bride and groom while the five foolish were left behind.

The night is dark. But with the Holy Ghost, we have a torch to light the way for us. Without the pillar of fire, Pharaoh's army would have slaughtered the Israelites before they even reached the parted waters. Likewise, without the Holy Ghost, you'll be lost in the darkness, and the devil will destroy you before you make it to the Rapture. The crossing is just ahead.

> *And Moses stretched out his hand over the sea; and the LORD caused the sea to go back by a strong east wind all that night, and made the sea dry land, and the waters were divided. And the children of Israel went into the midst of the sea upon the dry ground: and the waters were a wall unto them on their right hand, and on their left. (Exodus 14:21-22)*

Like other examples I've already mentioned, researching the Exodus has made me rethink how I picture the story. The popular depiction of this event has been akin to the flight from Egypt itself: The Israelites watched in awe as Moses raised his staff and shouted, "Behold His mighty hand!" Dramatic music swelled as the Red Sea split apart. Then they marched forward in a musical procession, gazing at hundred-foot walls of water at either side. A fish was visible, swimming by. Children pointed in wonder as their parents, livestock in tow, hurried them along. Once they reached the other end, they solemnly turned back to see the water crashing down on the pursuing Egyptians. Then songs of praise began.

Very sentimental, but I have trouble seeing it realistically that way. The chaos and confusion of the departure probably pales in comparison to the crossing. Up until the end, when Pharaoh's army was clearly no longer a threat, this night would be the most terrifying ordeal of their lives: The sky was black, and the scene chaotic. Screams of terror and panic rushed throughout the trapped Israelites as Pharaoh's army approached. Trying to keep calm, Moses instructed them to have faith in God and walk towards the lake water. A pillar of fire did indeed light up the night and keep the Egyptians at bay. A powerful wind probably added to the confusion and panic . . . at first.

Moses stood perched on a high rock, his staff pointing towards the lake. Someone had to be the first to notice that the howling wind seemed to be driving back the waters, forming what just might have been a path of escape. A quick decision had to be made; it was now or never. Some brave souls ventured into the division. Others worked up the nerve to follow. Before long, all twelve tribes scurried across.

Imagine crossing the perilous path that night. You desperately hold onto your children, family, and possessions, keeping your head down in the monstrous wind, dark walls of water surrounding you on either side. Like passing through a trembling underground tunnel, screams reverberate all around. At any moment, the wind could die down. The shimmering waters are like a nervous cluster of angry hornets that could strike at a sudden movement.

Little by little, the fleeing Israelites emerge from the sand bar to safety on the other side. Maybe there were young, able-bodied men helping people, taking the hands of the elderly to help them from the watery divide. You had made it to safety, but now all around you, women and children are still shaking and crying. Just like the immediate aftermath of narrowly missing a terrible car accident, the reality of what just happened settles in, and the body starts to tense up with panic.

What if the waters hadn't held?

The sense of time was gone. What may have only been a few hours seemed like an eternity for some, a few minutes for others. Off in the distance, the pillar of fire cast an eerie glow like a torch in the night, illuminating the awaiting Egyptian soldiers.

Then the glow faded out. The pillar was gone. The wind had still kept the waters apart. People pointed and screamed, "Here they come!" The ominous thunders of chariots and horses accompanied Pharaoh's army, venturing into the wind-driven sand bar. But screams would soon turn to cheers.

THE RED SEA

> *And the Egyptians pursued, and went in after them to the midst of the sea, even all Pharaoh's horses, his chariots, and his horsemen. And it came to pass, that in the morning watch the L*ORD *looked unto the host of the Egyptians through the pillar of fire and of the cloud, and troubled the host of the Egyptians, And took off their chariot wheels, that they drave them heavily: so that the Egyptians said, Let us flee from the face of Israel; for the L*ORD *fighteth for them against the Egyptians. (Exodus 14:23-25)*

As Pharaoh's army approached, the powerful wind began to wane. The sand bar turned to mud, then quicksand. Horses screeched as chariot wheels got stuck. The once-formidable army started to look helpless as they were stopped dead in their tracks. The Bible assures us that at this point, they knew they had opposed the one true God. But it was too late. They had been led into a trap.

This is the ultimate fate for all those who fight God. Just like the Egyptian charioteers desperately trying to turn back, knowing that the waters would soon close in on them, those who end up in hell will forever try to escape. Imagine the torture of all eternity, trying to climb out of the burning pits, only to always be pushed back in by hideous demons.

> *And the L*ORD *said unto Moses, Stretch out thine hand over the sea, that the waters may come again upon the Egyptians, upon their chariots, and upon their horsemen. And Moses stretched forth his hand over the sea, and the sea returned to his strength when the morning appeared; and the Egyptians fled against it; and the L*ORD *overthrew the Egyptians in the midst of the sea. And the waters returned, and covered the chariots, and the horsemen, and all the host of Pharaoh that came into the sea after them; there remained not so much as one of them. (Exodus 14:26-28)*

As the army ground to a halt, Moses stepped up and raised his hand again. Suddenly, the waters receded back. Bloodcurdling screams of death filled the air as the Egyptians and their horses were trapped. The waters enclosed over them, snuffing out their shrieks one-by-one. A few were seen struggling and splashing. But soon, the night was quiet. None had survived. Then mangled, lifeless bodies washed up ashore.

> *Thus the L*ORD *saved Israel that day out of the hand of the Egyptians; and Israel saw the Egyptians dead upon the sea shore. (Exodus 14:30)*

What a change of tone! The most terrifying night of their lives had now become the most exhilarating. Laughing fathers hugged their wives and children. Dancing and music filled the air. God had shown them the most incredible thing they had ever seen.

> *And Israel saw that great work which the L*ORD *did upon the Egyptians: and the people feared the L*ORD*, and believed the L*ORD*, and his servant Moses. (Exodus 14:31)*

MIDDLE KINGDOM DYNAMICS
Did Pharaoh Drown with His Army?

Exodus is unclear on Pharaoh's fate. The king whose heart was hardened so many times is never mentioned again. Cleverly, most film depictions show Pharaoh parking his horse at a distance, exposing what a true coward he was. It sets him up to watch in horror as his magnificent army is crushed by avalanches of water and left standing alone, the only survivor to deal with the lifelong consequences of opposing the God of Moses.

Assuming Dudimose II was the Exodus Pharaoh, we are left with the conundrum of knowing very little about him. We do, however, have some clues to follow. Since the king of Egypt in the tale lost his firstborn in the tenth plague, we can assume that Khonsuemwaset, his son, was next in line. Ancient reliefs do show engravings of this Egyptian prince, sitting beside his wife with objects underneath. Under her is a mirror and jewelry box; he is typically portrayed with a pair of gloves, symbols that specifically identify charioteers. This son of Pharaoh was probably an important captain leading the Egyptian army into battle.[116] It is within reason, then, that Khonsuemwaset was unfortunate enough to be the first trapped in the sea of reeds as the waters came crashing down, especially considering that there is no record of him ever becoming Pharaoh. Dudimose, having just lost his firstborn, now watched as his prince and army, pride of Egypt, were lost to a watery grave.

CONCLUSION

The crossing of the Red Sea is a seminal moment for the Israelite people. In a way, it symbolizes baptism, a transformation by going down into water and emerging victorious. They went into the Red Sea a frightened band of escaped slaves but emerged on the other side a new nation forged by God's delivering power.

In Genesis, when the Holy Spirit moved upon the waters, the light came forth, setting the creation of the world in motion.

> *And the earth was without form, and void; and darkness was upon the face of the deep. And the Spirit of God moved upon the face of the waters. And God said, Let there be light: and there was light. (Genesis 1:2-3)*

In Exodus, when the Spirit moved upon the waters, it brought forth God's chosen people on the earth. As the waters returned to normal, the chaotic night broke into songs of praise. The book of Exodus records two songs: a song of Moses and a song of Miriam. Moses led the people in a delivering hymnal first, in Exodus 15:1-19:

THE RED SEA

Then sang Moses and the children of Israel this song unto the LORD, *and spake, saying, I will sing unto the* LORD, *for he hath triumphed gloriously: the horse and his rider hath he thrown into the sea.*

The LORD *is my strength and song, and he is become my salvation: he is my God, and I will prepare him an habitation; my father's God, and I will exalt him.*

The LORD *is a man of war: the* LORD *is his name.*

Pharaoh's chariots and his host hath he cast into the sea: his chosen captains also are drowned in the Red sea.

The depths have covered them: they sank into the bottom as a stone.

Thy right hand, O LORD, *is become glorious in power: thy right hand, O* LORD, *hath dashed in pieces the enemy.*

And in the greatness of thine excellency thou hast overthrown them that rose up against thee: thou sentest forth thy wrath, which consumed them as stubble.

And with the blast of thy nostrils the waters were gathered together, the floods stood upright as an heap, and the depths were congealed in the heart of the sea.

The enemy said, I will pursue, I will overtake, I will divide the spoil; my lust shall be satisfied upon them; I will draw my sword, my hand shall destroy them.

Thou didst blow with thy wind, the sea covered them: they sank as lead in the mighty waters.

Who is like unto thee, O LORD, *among the gods? who is like thee, glorious in holiness, fearful in praises, doing wonders?*

Thou stretchedst out thy right hand, the earth swallowed them.

Thou in thy mercy hast led forth the people which thou hast redeemed: thou hast guided them in thy strength unto thy holy habitation.

The people shall hear, and be afraid: sorrow shall take hold on the inhabitants of Palestina.

Then the dukes of Edom shall be amazed; the mighty men of Moab, trembling shall take hold upon them; all the inhabitants of Canaan shall melt away.

Fear and dread shall fall upon them; by the greatness of thine arm they shall be as still as a stone; till thy people pass over, O LORD, *till the people pass over, which thou hast purchased.*

> *Thou shalt bring them in, and plant them in the mountain of thine inheritance, in the place, O LORD, which thou hast made for thee to dwell in, in the Sanctuary, O LORD, which thy hands have established.*
>
> *The LORD shall reign for ever and ever.*
>
> *For the horse of Pharaoh went in with his chariots and with his horsemen into the sea, and the LORD brought again the waters of the sea upon them; but the children of Israel went on dry land in the midst of the sea.*

Then, in verses 20-21, his sister Miriam leads the women with timbrels in another song of praise:

> *And Miriam the prophetess, the sister of Aaron, took a timbrel in her hand; and all the women went out after her with timbrels and with dances.*
>
> *And Miriam answered them, Sing ye to the LORD, for he hath triumphed gloriously; the horse and his rider hath he thrown into the sea.*

Unfortunately, as we've seen all too often for the children of Israel, it's easy to praise God right after such a great deliverance. But it wasn't to last. Literally in the next verse, the grumbling and complaining began. The Israelites were about to learn that it wouldn't be an easy road to freedom. It was going to take forty years in the hellish desert before the Lord would refine and purify them to be worthy of taking the Promised Land.

Chapter 7

NOW WHAT?

INTRODUCTION

Imagine yourself traveling back in time to July 4, 1776. Word sweeps over the American colonies that the Declaration has been signed. We are now independent of British rule. Celebrations abound. Fireworks light up the night as bands play and people dance in the streets. At the pinnacle of such joy, few could realize that a brutal eight-year war was ahead.

And the war was just the beginning. A hard-fought victory against the British would only leave an uncertain future. The ratification of the Constitution was years away, the way paved by the failed Articles of Confederation and the near collapse of the newly formed government.

And the British didn't let the colonies go easily. Assuming they would come crawling back, warships would harass American merchant ships over the coming decades, eventually leading to the War of 1812 (what some historians call the second war for independence). After a crushing defeat at the hands of General Andrew Jackson during the battle of New Orleans, the British Empire finally retreated and left the newly founded nation alone.

But the price for Constitutional rights for all was even more bloodshed, as a horrible Civil War tore the nation apart. And for the freed slaves, who no doubt celebrated with the same vigor as the colonists had just before the Revolution, years of oppression and segregation lie ahead.

"Freedom is not free," while true, is a bit of a cliché. What we tend to overlook is the universal question of what happens immediately after achieving liberty: *What next?* The answer is not so easy.

In the aftermath of great triumph, difficult times were already upon the Israelites. Once the sun rose the next day, food and water quickly ran out as they were faced with the unbearable heat of the desert.

EXODUS 15:22–16:1

> *So Moses brought Israel from the Red sea, and they went out into the wilderness of Shur; and they went three days in the wilderness, and found no water. And when they came to Marah, they could not drink of the waters of Marah, for they were bitter: therefore the name of it was called Marah. And the people murmured against Moses, saying, What shall we drink? (Exodus 15:22-24)*

Marah was the first stop after the Red Sea. They just saw God send a pillar of fire from heaven to drive back their enemies before parting the waters. But only two verses later, doubt was taking hold.

"The wilderness of Shur," where Marah ("bitterness") is located, is given a different name in the book of Numbers: "the wilderness of Etham."

> *And they departed from before Pihahiroth, and passed through the midst of the sea into the wilderness, and went three days' journey in the wilderness of Etham, and pitched in Marah. (Numbers 33:8)*

Tracing the route of the journey through the Sinai wilderness, scholars generally agree that this first encampment is an area about sixty-three miles south from what used to be the Balla Lakes. We can confidently place it at the eastern end of the Wadi Tumilat, just beyond the modern city of Ismaliya.[117] The difference is likely that "Shur" represents the greater wilderness, while "Etham" was a local name. At the average rate of traveling nomads, it would have taken about three days to reach. Just east of the Gulf of Suez (the western side of the Red Sea split), is a water well named *Bir el-Mura*, Arabic for "Bitter Well."[118]

> *And he cried unto the LORD; and the LORD shewed him a tree, which when he had cast into the waters, the waters were made sweet: there he made for them a statute and an ordinance, and there he proved them, . . . (Exodus 15:25)*

Here, Moses performed the first miracle of supply, casting a piece of wood into bitter water and making it sweet. As I mentioned earlier, any time wood is referenced in the Old Testament can be interpreted as a symbol of the cross. When we read of the branch making water drinkable, we can't help but think of the cross of Calvary being cast into the bitter waters of our souls, to make them sweet before the Lord.

> *. . . And said, If thou wilt diligently hearken to the voice of the LORD thy God, and wilt do that which is right in his sight, and wilt give ear to his commandments, and keep all his statutes, I will put none of these diseases upon thee, which I have brought upon the Egyptians: for I am the LORD that healeth thee. (Exodus 15:26)*

The wilderness would be a great killing ground as God's vengeance was enacted on a grumbling and complaining people. But it wasn't always that way. The Lord reaffirmed a promise here; if they would submit to His will and do what was right in His sight, He would protect them. At the first step, God was patient with the complainers.

He made this same covenant with us; but just like the children of Israel, we're often all-too-willing to abuse His mercy, assuming it will last forever. But the Lord has a breaking point, as the Israelites will have to learn the hard way.

> *And they came to Elim, where were twelve wells of water, and threescore and ten palm trees: and they encamped there by the waters. (Exodus 15:27)*

The Bible doesn't give the number of days from Marah to Elim, indicating a short journey. If Bir el-Mura is the site of the biblical Marah, then the most logical site for Elim (Hebrew for "trees") is Ayun Musa (Arabic for "Springs of Moses"), nine miles to the south (a distance the Israelites could have walked in less than a day). Exodus describes the oasis as having twelve wells and seventy palm trees, and Ayun Musa still contains springs of fresh water from underground artesian wells and dozens of palm date trees.[119]

At this point, the Israelites were still traveling on the outer edge of the Sinai Peninsula, just outside of Egyptian territory. How long they were there is unclear, but Exodus 16:1 gives us a clue:

> *And they took their journey from Elim, and all the congregation of the children of Israel came unto the wilderness of Sin, which is between Elim and Sinai, on the fifteenth day of the second month after their departing out of the land of Egypt. (Exodus 16:1)*

In other words, their departure from Elim, really venturing into the foreboding wilderness of Sin (Sinai) for the first time, took place fifteen days into the second month after the actual Exodus. Since the Hebrew calendar was based on the lunar month, this amounts to four weeks total. Personally, I estimate two weeks from the departure of Avaris to the arrival at Elim and one week's journey from Elim to Sin, leaving us with about a week stationed at the desert oasis.

EXODUS 16:2-36

Manna

> Then said the LORD unto Moses, Behold, I will rain bread from heaven for you; and the people shall go out and gather a certain rate every day, that I may prove them, whether they will walk in my law, or no. . . . And when the dew that lay was gone up, behold, upon the face of the wilderness there lay a small round thing, as small as the hoar frost on the ground. (Exodus 16:4, 14)

The next morning, as the dew evaporated, the ground was covered with a small, edible frost-like substance. The people were given strict instruction to eat it as they found it; any attempt to store it would prove fruitless, as it rotted and filled with worms.

> And Moses said, Let no man leave of it till the morning. Notwithstanding they hearkened not unto Moses; but some of them left of it until the morning, and it bred worms, and stank: and Moses was wroth with them. (Exodus 16:19-20)

THE NATURALIST THEORY

One way historians can verify the accuracy of an ancient text is if it contains subtle details clueing the reader in on a specific date or location, and this is further evidence that the wandering took place in the Sinai Peninsula and not the Midianite wilderness.

Unique to Sinai is a phenomenon where every spring, plant lice infest the stems of tamarisk tree branches. After sucking out the carbohydrate-rich sap, they excrete small white globules. These sweet edible frosts covering the morning ground dry up very quickly, and if not harvested, will be consumed by insects and worms.[120] This can be essential food for traveling nomads and, since the wilderness produces about five hundred pounds worth every year, has even been commercially gathered and sold around the world as biblical manna since the fifteenth century.

> And when the children of Israel saw it, they said one to another, It is manna: for they wist not what it was. And Moses said unto them, This is the bread which the LORD hath given you to eat. (Exodus 16:15)

THE TIES THAT BIND

Manna is a quintessential Bible term, immediately conjuring images of miraculous blessings falling from heaven. Anyone like me who was raised on Southern Gospel has probably heard it in countless songs. But do we know what it really means?

The children of Israel didn't. The word *manna* literally means "what is it?" Rather than praising God, they looked at this food with puzzlement. This was the same reaction people often had when meeting Jesus for the first time. Even His most devout followers were often perplexed when they first encountered Him.

> *Then saith the woman of Samaria unto him, How is it that thou, being a Jew, askest drink of me, which am a woman of Samaria? for the Jews have no dealings with the Samaritans. (John 4:9)*

His own disciples uttered their own version of "manna" when He calmed the raging seas:

> *But the men marvelled, saying, What manner of man is this, that even the winds and the sea obey him! (Matthew 8:27)*

If manna is likened unto "bread" (Exodus 16:4), then it was the "bread of life" that sustained the Israelites for the next forty years. Jesus likened Himself to it at the Last Supper.

> *Then Jesus said unto them, Verily, verily, I say unto you, Moses gave you not that bread from heaven; but my Father giveth you the true bread from heaven. For the bread of God is he which cometh down from heaven, and giveth life unto the world. And Jesus said unto them, I am the bread of life: he that cometh to me shall never hunger; and he that believeth on me shall never thirst. (John 6:32-33, 35)*

Christ is the manna that God has prepared to sustain His people through the wilderness of this hour.
But be warned.

> *I am the way, the truth, and the life: no man cometh unto the Father, but by me. (John 14:6)*

Jesus isn't just *the* bread; He's the *only* bread. The Israelites would pay a heavy price to learn this lesson.
According to Exodus 16:13, the Lord met their desire for meat with quail. This time, there was no retribution. But years later, lack of satisfaction with what He had provided would come back to haunt them.

> *And the mixt multitude that was among them fell a lusting: and the children of Israel also wept again, and said, Who shall give us flesh to eat? We remember the fish, which we did eat in Egypt freely; the cucumbers, and the melons, and the leeks, and the onions, and the garlick. (Numbers 11:4-5)*

It wasn't enough that they didn't want manna anymore, but they specifically yearned for the "abundance" of Egypt. The enemy will do everything he can to bring you away from manna (Christ) back to the exotic foods of Egypt (sin).

God's anger was so great that He would use the very thing they wanted to bring judgment.

> *Ye shall not eat one day, nor two days, nor five days, neither ten days, nor twenty days; But even a whole month, until it come out at your nostrils, and it be loathsome unto you. (Numbers 11:19-20)*

By this point, He was far beyond the patient and forgiving God of Exodus 16.

> *And there went forth a wind from the LORD, and brought quails from the sea, and let them fall by the camp, as it were a day's journey on this side, and as it were a day's journey on the other side, round about the camp, and as it were two cubits high upon the face of the earth. (Numbers 11:31)*

The dead quail were piled so high that it took all day to gather them all. But death came to those who ate.

> *And while the flesh was yet between their teeth, ere it was chewed, the wrath of the LORD was kindled against the people, and the LORD smote the people with a very great plague. (Numbers 11:33)*

Once again, a natural explanation can help us determine that the story took place in the Sinai desert and nowhere else. Every fall, huge flocks of quail migrate from Europe to Central Africa and then return north for the spring. On their way, many are so exhausted that they simply lose strength and fall out of the sky, crashing to their deaths on the ground below. The northern coastline of Egypt and Sinai are sometimes covered with mass heaps of dead quail, providing an overwhelming feast for traveling Bedouins.[121]

But that does nothing to undermine the divine aspect of the story. Mount Sinai, or at least the prime candidate we're going to discuss later, is too far south for the birds to have reached. But look closer and you'll see that God "sent a wind" that carried the tainted quail their way.

> *And they laid it up till the morning, as Moses bade: and it did not stink, neither was there any worm therein. And Moses said, Eat that to day; for to day is a sabbath unto the LORD: to day ye shall not find it in the field. (Exodus 16:24-25)*

God commanded the people to gather manna and eat for six days; but on the Sabbath, they were to rest and trust that He would supply. But they couldn't even pass this simple test. Here, for the first time, we see the Lord's patience wearing thin.

> *And it came to pass, that there went out some of the people on the seventh day for to gather, and they found none. And the LORD said unto Moses,*

How long refuse ye to keep my commandments and my laws? So the people rested on the seventh day. (Exodus 16:27-28, 30)

And the children of Israel did eat manna forty years, until they came to a land inhabited; they did eat manna, until they came unto the borders of the land of Canaan. (Exodus 16:35)

Manna would be the primary source of their diet for the remaining forty years.

EXODUS 17:1-7

Water from the Rock

And all the congregation of the children of Israel journeyed from the wilderness of Sin, after their journeys, according to the commandment of the LORD, and pitched in Rephidim: and there was no water for the people to drink. (Exodus 17:1)

Rephidim, the next encampment, is Hebrew for "resting places." Notice that it is plural.[122] This is from the *im* at the ending; the original name of this location is likely *Rephid*. Scholars have assumed that this stopping point was at the lush valley of Wadi-Feiran, but this makes no sense. This fertile oasis would not be a place where travelers would thirst for water. A much more likely candidate is a place known in Arabic as the Wadi-Refayid, with its dry, open, flat terrain (notice the similarities between the words *Rephid* and *Refayid*).[123] And since a battle would soon take place here, an open desert plain is a more logical site than a large fertile valley in between a large wilderness gorge.

And the people thirsted there for water; and the people murmured against Moses, and said, Wherefore is this that thou hast brought us up out of Egypt, to kill us and our children and our cattle with thirst? And Moses cried unto the LORD, saying, What shall I do unto this people? they be almost ready to stone me. (Exodus 17:3-4)

Once again, God hadn't run out of patience yet. He was ready to provide another miracle of supply. But Moses was beginning to get exasperated. Despite the Lord providing for them miraculously over and over, they still couldn't seem to walk in faith. Their lack of divine vision blinded them from seeing past their own thirst and hunger. Moses asked God to do with these people, and verse 2 shows him cracking under the pressure when he cries,

Why chide ye with me? wherefore do ye tempt the LORD? (Exodus 17:2)

Behold, I will stand before thee there upon the rock in Horeb; and thou shalt smite the rock, and there shall come water out of it, that the people may drink. And Moses did so in the sight of the elders of Israel. (Exodus 17:6)

Moses was instructed to strike the rock, and water would come out. Like the previous story, this would be reflected again later in Numbers. After decades of wandering, the same people were still making the same complaints.

> *And why have ye brought up the congregation of the LORD into this wilderness, that we and our cattle should die there? (Numbers 20:4)*

God instructed Moses to speak to a rock, and water would come forward.

> *And the LORD spake unto Moses, saying, Take the rod, and gather thou the assembly together, thou, and Aaron thy brother, and speak ye unto the rock before their eyes; and it shall give forth his water, and thou shalt bring forth to them water out of the rock: so thou shalt give the congregation and their beasts drink. (Numbers 20:7-8)*

However Moses wouldn't accomplish this the way God wanted.

> *And Moses and Aaron gathered the congregation together before the rock, and he said unto them, Hear now, ye rebels; must we fetch you water out of this rock? And Moses lifted up his hand, and with his rod he smote the rock twice: and the water came out abundantly, and the congregation drank, and their beasts also. (Numbers 20:10-11)*

Years earlier, he had struck the rock; but this time, he was instructed to speak to it. God was so angry over this that He sentenced a terrible punishment on the leader of the Israelites.

> *And the LORD spake unto Moses and Aaron, Because ye believed me not, to sanctify me in the eyes of the children of Israel, therefore ye shall not bring this congregation into the land which I have given them. (Numbers 20:12)*

He would never be allowed to enter the Promised Land.

THE NATURALIST THEORY

Along with manna, this story contains yet another detail to identify the Sinai Peninsula as the unique setting for years of wandering. Throughout this great wilderness, one can find rocks with strange-looking holes on them, almost like eyes. These windows, called *tafuni* by locals, are caused by humidity in the air that slowly, over the course of thousands of years, gets trapped inside the rock and dissolves it from the inside. The rock may appear big and sturdy, but one tap can reveal the water-filled cavity inside.[124]

This sounds like it would produce a tiny trickle at best. But consider this report from Major C. S. Jarvis, British governor over Sinai in the 1930s:

> Several men of the Sinai Camel Corps had halted in a dry wadi and were in the process of digging about in the rough sand that had accumulated at the foot of the rock-face. They were trying to get at the water that was trickling slowly out of the limestone rock. The men were taking their time about it and Besh Shawish, the color sergeant, said: "Here, give it to me!" He took the spade off one of the men and began digging furiously in the manner of NCOs the world over who want to show their men how to do things but have no intention of keeping it up for more than a couple of minutes. One of his violent blows hit the rock by mistake. The smooth hard crust which always forms on weathered limestone split open and fell away. The soft stone underneath was thereby exposed and out of its apertures shot a powerful stream of water. The Sudanese, who are well up in the activities of the prophets but do not treat them with a vast amount of respect, overwhelmed their sergeant with cries of: "Look at him! The prophet Moses!"[125]

This gives us a satisfactory explanation for why water came from the rock when Moses struck it but also helps answer another big question: A natural occurrence doesn't require much faith to believe in, but speaking to the rock to bring out water would defy explanation. The Israelites would know for sure that God had done it.

By striking the rock, Moses was taking away the glory God was supposed to receive. Notice in Numbers 20:12 that there's no record of anyone praising God; they immediately scrambled to the geyser and drank. The Lord was furious with Moses for allowing his anger to take away the praise that had rightfully been His.

EXODUS 17:8-16
The Battle with the Amalekites

Then came Amalek, and fought with Israel in Rephidim. (Exodus 17:8)

Another famous story from the Exodus began immediately near where the rock gave water. At this moment, for unexplained reasons, the traveling nomads found themselves in a hostile confrontation with another tribe. The ensuing battle contained not just one of the most teachable moments in the entire book but one of the biggest puzzle pieces at our disposal in placing the tale in its proper historical timeline.

Amalek was the grandson of Esau, child of his son Eliphaz to a concubine named Timna (Genesis 36:12). Tribes related to God's chosen people roamed the ancient world, but many of them were hostile. For example, once they inherited the Promised Land, Moab and Ammon would be thorns in their sides for years to come.

But the Amalekites would play a very special role in this story.

> *And Moses said unto Joshua, Choose us out men, and go out, fight with Amalek: to morrow I will stand on the top of the hill with the rod of God in mine hand. (Exodus 17:9)*

We can deduce that the Amalekites attacked first from Deuteronomy 25:17-18:

> *Remember what Amalek did unto thee by the way, when ye were come forth out of Egypt; How he met thee by the way, and smote the hindmost of thee, even all that were feeble behind thee, when thou wast faint and weary; and he feared not God.*

This was clearly a sneak attack that specially targeted the women, children, and elderly. Moses and Joshua (who appeared for the first time in the story here) planned retaliation in the morning.

Along the route in the Sinai wilderness, a few areas emerge as candidates for the site of this famous battle. In my opinion, the most likely spot is a large, sandy plain with a rocky hill jutting out of its center near the Wadi Islaf. On the summit of the hill, marking the spot where Moses would lift up his hands overlooking the battle, is a Muslim shrine called Sheik Abu Taleb.[126]

> *So Joshua did as Moses had said to him, and fought with Amalek: and Moses, Aaron, and Hur went up to the top of the hill. And it came to pass, when Moses held up his hand, that Israel prevailed: and when he let down his hand, Amalek prevailed. But Moses hands were heavy; and they took a stone, and put it under him, and he sat thereon; and Aaron and Hur stayed up his hands, the one on the one side, and the other on the other side; and his hands were steady until the going down of the sun. (Exodus 17:10-12)*

THE PRACTICAL APPLICATION

Overlooking the battle, Moses raised his hands, and the Israelites started to win the battle. But if he lowered them, the tide turned. Usually victories are exhausting. But here, Joshua proved himself as second-in-command and future leader. He was willing to take on the burden to hold Moses' arms up. The aides got a stone for him to sit on, then beared the weight of his arms themselves long enough for the Israelites to defeat Amalek.

This is a mindset missing from so much of the church today, which is part of why we're failing so badly in our mission to win the lost. So many Christians would look at Moses and say, "Let him lift up his own arms!" We want our pastors and church leadership to do all the work while we sit back and enjoy the service for ourselves. We want them to go out and preach the gospel while we selfishly receive blessings for all their work. We come to church with a "me! me! me!" mindset but never seek to make our pastors' jobs easier.

Our outlook on church is wrong. It isn't about going just to hear a great sermon or be blessed by a good anointing. It's about working for the Lord. Every ministry we take on, no matter how small, holds up our leaders' arms. The church will thrive if more Christians will step out of their comfort zones. It wasn't Christ's commandment for us to preach great sermons or play good music; it was to make disciples.

> *And Joshua discomfited Amalek and his people with the edge of the sword. And the LORD said unto Moses, Write this for a memorial in a book, and rehearse it in the ears of Joshua: for I will utterly put out the remembrance of Amalek from under heaven. And Moses built an altar, and called the name of it Jehovahnissi: For he said, Because the LORD hath sworn that the LORD will have war with Amalek from generation to generation. (Exodus 17:13-16)*

The victory had been won, and Moses built the first altar in the desert as a memorial to the triumph of their God over a vicious enemy. *Jehovah Nissi*, or *YAHWEH NISSI* literally means "God is my banner."[127] Moses' raised arms acted as a banner to inspire the Israelites to defeat the Amalekites. When we lift up our hands in praise, we think of it as submission to God, as it well is. But we should also look at it as a symbol of war. We are at war with the devil, and raising up our hands before God in worship is how we can defeat him in battle every time.

> *But thou art holy, O thou that inhabitest the praises of Israel. (Psalm 22:3)*

Furthermore, in Moses' hands stretched out before the heavens, we should see the symbol of Christ hanging on the cross; His arms spread out before us, blood running from His nailed hands, is the symbol of victory we can always look to, no matter how vicious the devil gets in his attacks against us.

MIDDLE KINGDOM DYNAMICS

Whenever a legal case is presented before a jury, all sides have to be reviewed. A defendant can appear certainly guilty due to one eyewitness testimony. But witnesses can put that first one, as well as the other factors, in a new light. We can be certain we've arrived at the truth when all the facts eventually fit snugly together.

After all I've done to build up support for the Middle Kingdom theory, I think now is a good time to put the final piece together and watch how beautifully archaeological history and the Bible line up. The Amalekites don't seem to play an important role in the story, only appearing in a few verses towards the end of Exodus 17. But they help us see the big picture in its entirety and can also help us solve a separate mystery from later in the Bible.

Let me rewind and review a little bit. If the Exodus took place towards the end of the thirteenth dynasty, it explains why Egypt collapsed shortly thereafter. The ten plagues (chronicled by Ipuwer) ravaged Egypt, and their army was destroyed in the Red Sea, leaving them weak and helpless. This would attract the attention of hostile invaders. Shortly after the end of Pharaoh Dudimose, Egypt was conquered by a group of foreign raiders called the Hyksos. These brutal rulers inhabited the recently abandoned Avaris settlement (still with freshly dug mass graves from the tenth plague), plunging Egypt into darkness and ending the second Intermediate period. Many years would pass before the Egyptians would overthrow and drive out the Hyksos, rebuilding their nation and ushering in the New Kingdom era, which would see Egypt ascend to the height of its power and produce legendary Pharaohs such as Ramses.

Perhaps our most important source of Egyptian history is the priest and historian Manetho, who lived in the timeframe of 300 BC. Manetho had compiled a detailed list of the kings of Egypt and chronicled what happened during their reigns. Unfortunately his original writings have never been found, but they were preserved and translated by other ancient historians such as Josephus, Africanus, Eusebius, and Syncellus. These secondhand accounts contain many contradictions but are generally acknowledged as vital insights into ancient Egypt.[128]

Via Josephus, a crucial excerpt from Manetho helps support the Middle Kingdom theory:

> Tutimaus [Dudimose]: in his reign, for what cause I know not, a blast of God [the plagues] smote us. And unexpectedly, from the regions of the east, invaders of an obscure race [the Hyksos] marched in confidence of victory against our land. By main force they easily seized it without striking a blow [the Egyptian army was drowned in the Red Sea]; and having overpowered the rulers of the land, they then ruthlessly burned our cities, razed to the ground the temples of the gods, and treated all the natives with a cruel hostility, massacring some and leading into slavery the wives and children of others. Finally, they appointed as king one of their number whose name was Salitis. He had his seat at Memphis, levying tribute from Upper and Lower Egypt, and always leaving garrisons behind in the most advantageous positions. . . . In the Saite nome, he founded a city very favourably situated on the east of the Buastite branch of the Nile, and called it Auaris [Avaris] after an ancient religious tradition.[129]

Now let's tie this in with the story at hand. The Israelites were fleeing Egypt but ran into a hostile army, the Amalekites, traveling in the opposite direction (towards Egypt). They were viciously attacked, and a victorious defensive battle ensued. The Amalekites were beaten, but their aim was not to defeat the Israelites. The ravaged and weakened Egypt was in their crosshairs.

We can now conclude that the biblical Amalekites were part of the Hyksos who invaded Egypt at the end of the Middle Kingdom era. Some New Kingdom theorists, who have their dating wrong, have assumed that the Hyksos themselves were the Israelites—that their invasion coincided with Joseph's sojourn and their departure in the Exodus; but this writing from Manetho should completely dispel that notion.[130]

The skeptical reader might next point out that the Amalekites had just been beaten in battle by desperate, fleeing nomads, indicating that they were in no shape to decisively conquer Egypt. But remember that the Hyksos were not a single tribe but a large confederation of invading forces. The Amalekites, a small piece of the greater army, were likely on the way to join the others to begin the bloody conquest.

Joshua 12 lists the different cities and kings that were conquered by the Israelite army. One that is conspicuously absent is the people who were legendary as Israel's arch-enemies: the Philistines. Moses never mentioned them in Deuteronomy either. This is because the Philistines didn't exist at the time. One of the unspoken riddles of the Bible is that the greatest thorn in the side of God's children seemed to magically appear out of nowhere between Jericho and King Saul. Where did they come from?

By identifying the Amalekites as the Hyksos, I believe we've found the answer. When Saul was at war with the Philistines, God gave him an interesting commandment to destroy the Amalekites as punishment for the attack at Rephidim so many centuries earlier.

Thus saith the LORD of hosts, I remember that which Amalek did to Israel, how he laid wait for him in the way, when he came up from Egypt. (1 Samuel 15:2)

Saul was ordered to destroy them all, even the livestock. But he failed to do so, sparing King Agag and saving the sheep and cattle for sacrifice. This disobedience angered God and caused Samuel to utter an infamous phrase from the Bible:

To obey is better than sacrifice. (1 Samuel 15:22)

From this point onward, Saul was rejected as king.

Here, then, is the connection. The Amalekites were part of the group of people constituting the Philistines. After years of oppressive rule, the Hyksos were defeated and driven out of Egypt by Ahmose II, first Pharaoh of the New Kingdom. In our new timeline, this was roughly when the Philistines appeared. These disparate bands dispersed in the wilderness with nowhere to go. Many of them, including the Amalekites, settled in the coastal plains of Philistia, sandwiched between Israel and the sea, and built communities. The Amalekites *were* the Hyksos, who were also the biblical Philistines.

EXODUS 18:1-27

Seventy Elders

> *When Jethro, the priest of Midian, Moses' father in law, heard of all that God had done for Moses, and for Israel his people, and that the* LORD *had brought Israel out of Egypt; Then Jethro, Moses' father in law, took Zipporah, Moses' wife, after he had sent her back, . . . And he said unto Moses, I thy father in law Jethro am come unto thee, and thy wife, and her two sons with her. (Exodus 18:1-2, 6)*

Jethro had heard of all the wonders God had worked through Moses, destroying Egypt and setting the Israelites free. While Moses tried to get the affairs of Israel in order, Zipporah, at some point, had been sent back home with her two sons.

> *And Moses went out to meet his father in law, and did obeisance, and kissed him; and they asked each other of their welfare; and they came into the tent. (Exodus 18:7)*

Moses was clearly thrilled and relieved to see his family again. He greeted his father-in-law and, in the tent, shared a firsthand account of the incredible story so far. Jethro was pleased to hear about all that God had done through his son-in-law.

> *And Jethro rejoiced for all the goodness which the* LORD *had done to Israel, whom he had delivered out of the hand of the Egyptians. (Exodus 18:9)*

They joined together with Aaron and his sons to make a sacrifice and worship the Lord. But the next morning, Jethro noticed a problem.

> *And it came to pass on the morrow, that Moses sat to judge the people: and the people stood by Moses from the morning unto the evening. (Exodus 18:13)*

I already discussed earlier the controversy over the number of Israelites. Bible purists insist that Exodus accurately gives a population of two-to-three million. Others would point out the aforementioned evidence for a Hebrew recalculation arriving at about thirty-five thousand. Either way, this is a gargantuan number of people to be leading through the wilderness. And at the moment, Moses was their sole judge, which was proving to be a tremendous burden. He should have been concerned with the bigger issue of charting a safe path to their homeland and preparing them for the ensuing war. Clearly he was getting bogged down with micromanaging every minutiae of their lives.

> *And Moses' father in law said unto him, The thing that thou doest is not good. Thou wilt surely wear away, both thou, and this people that is with*

NOW WHAT?

> *thee: for this thing is too heavy for thee; thou art not able to perform it thyself alone. . . . Moreover thou shalt provide out of all the people able men, such as fear God, men of truth, hating covetousness; and place such over them, to be rulers of thousands, and rulers of hundreds, rulers of fifties, and rulers of tens: And let them judge the people at all seasons: and it shall be, that every great matter they shall bring unto thee, but every small matter they shall judge: so shall it be easier for thyself, and they shall bear the burden with thee. (Exodus 18:17-18, 21-22)*

Jethro had the idea to appoint elders over each of the twelve tribes of Israel. This would free up Moses' time to focus on the long journey ahead, as well as start the great work of compiling a detailed account of the events that had taken place—what would eventually become the first five books of the Bible. Furthermore, the elders would have a very distinct hierarchy, divided by power over the size of groups they would oversee (tens, hundreds, then thousands). Moses, however, would serve as the final say in every decision.

> *And Moses chose able men out of all Israel, and made them heads over the people, rulers of thousands, rulers of hundreds, rulers of fifties, and rulers of tens. And they judged the people at all seasons: the hard causes they brought unto Moses, but every small matter they judged themselves. (Exodus 18:25-26)*

A careless reading of the text has led to the misconception that seventy elders total were appointed over Israel. This is due to confusion with a later passage in Numbers 11. After Moses prayed for death after being unable to tolerate the complaining Israelites, God instructed him to . . .

> *Gather unto me seventy men of the elders of Israel, whom thou knowest to be the elders of the people, and officers over them; and bring them unto the tabernacle of the congregation, that they may stand there with thee. (Numbers 11:16)*

As we've seen from Exodus 18, elders had already been appointed over Israel, though the number is never given. To ease Moses' burden further, God asked him to appoint seventy *from* the group of elders to be anointed leaders.

All well and good, but I can't help but wonder if Moses' anointing was ever as strong afterwards.

> *And Moses let his father in law depart; and he went his way into his own land. (Exodus 18:27)*

This was the last Moses would ever see his father-in-law. The one who rescued him from the desert, taught him about the God of Abraham, and gave him a home, job, and wife, now exited the story forever.

But what about Moses' wife, Zipporah? A common belief is that he divorced her somewhere at this point and remarried a Cushite woman, based on Numbers 12:1:

> *And Miriam and Aaron spake against Moses because of the Ethiopian woman whom he had married: for he had married an Ethiopian woman.*

The implication seems clear that he had wedded an African woman sometime after leaving Jethro at Midian; coincidentally, Zipporah was never mentioned again.

There's no mention of a divorce in scripture, however, and this Ethiopian woman *could* have been a second marriage. On the other hand, here's a more interesting theory: could the Ethiopian woman have actually been Zipporah herself? The Hebrew *kush* referred to the African descendants of Ham, translated by the Greek Septuagint as *Aithiopiai*.[131] However the Midianites were known as a darker-skinned people as well, indicating that this is either a mistranslation or a slur against Zipporah by Miriam and Aaron.[132] If this is the case, why they say it is a mystery; it simply could be that they didn't like her and had a certain prejudice against the color of her skin (after all, the Midianites weren't technically part of the same tribe). Interestingly enough, God punished Miriam's insult by smiting her with leprosy, a disease that often renders skin snow-white and rotten.

If true, this would also explain away the strange idea of Moses marrying an Ethiopian woman, even though the wandering Israelites never came anywhere near the African continent in their journeys.

CONCLUSION

The situation immediately following the Red Sea was a grim indicator of what was to come. Israel wasn't ready for independence. Generations of living in Egyptian slavery had made them used to dependence on overlords for survival, a mindset that couldn't be shed in just a few weeks.

It would ultimately take forty years of wandering through the wilderness, sprinkled with mass death from God's judgment due to disobedience, to purge them of wickedness. It sounds cruel, but the crueler thing would have been God allowing them to attack Canaan without being ready. They all would have died at the walls surrounding Jericho.

The stepping stone from slavery to independence wasn't just the few weeks from the Red Sea to Sinai. It would be the grueling decades ahead. Ultimately a generation that had lived its entire life in the wilderness, groomed to be entirely dependent on God for survival, would be required to take the Promised Land. They've showed promise by winning the battle against the Amalekites at Rephidim, but they were about to commit the biggest failure—and lead to possibly the greatest tragedy imaginable—at the foot of God's holy mountain.

Chapter 8

MOUNT SINAI

INTRODUCTION

Just like the Red Sea or burning bush, Moses descending from Mount Sinai carrying the Ten Commandments is one of the most indelible images from the Bible. But in our ongoing mission to demonstrate the reality of these events, we now have to tackle one final gigantic puzzle: is Mount Sinai an actual place or something mythical along the lines of Mount Olympus?

Some would say it's beside the point. After all, does it matter so much where Mount Sinai was located, so long as the symbolism remains? Metaphorically, the mountain stands as an intersection where God and man meet. As such, the Ten Commandments being carved from its stone reflects the Word eternally imprinted on our minds.

This is indeed true; however, my purpose for this book is to bring the Exodus to life, which requires me to sort through the different possible scenarios to bring the reader the facts so that we can experience together just what it was like for the people who lived through this amazing story. Mount Sinai plays a crucial role in that.

With enough research, I feel comfortable in at least whittling it down to what is most likely. But to do so, I have to spend some more time on Ron Wyatt's Midianite Exodus theory, closely re-examining the Exodus route to arrive at the logical candidate for the mountain of God.

To review briefly: The traditional path of the Israelites places the crossing of the Red Sea just east of the land of Goshen and the route to Mount Sinai along the southern coast of the Sinai Peninsula. The Midianite Exodus theory, however, places the Red Sea crossing two hundred miles away at the Gulf of Aqaba and suggests that the forty years of wandering took place in what is today Saudi Arabia. It cites all the aforementioned evidence: chariot wheels and bones at the bottom of a natural land bridge across the Nuweiba coastline as well as a burnt-topped mountain called Gebel el-Lawz on the other side. A giant split boulder is found in the region surrounding Gebel el-Lawz (proposed as the site of Rephidim) as well as twelve ancient stone structures, which are said to be the ghostly ruins of altars the people built (including ancient depictions of a calf-like god).

At least twenty-two mountains have been proposed as candidates for Mount Sinai,[133] but I would narrow it down to either Gebel el-Lawz or Gebel Musa. There are too many theories for me to detail them all, so I'm going to focus solely on these two (and I will argue, ultimately, that the Gebel Musa is the most likely true site for Sinai).

Gebel Musa (Arabic for "the mountain of Moses") has a fascinating history all its own. While I've tried to change people's classic mental images of the events in Exodus, this mountain looks exactly how one would picture the biblical Mount Sinai. Large, bold, and terrifying, it is one of the highest mountains in the region, with an almost hidden summit nestled among its dramatic peaks that requires a treacherous hike up an ancient pathway some call the "trail of Moses."

One of the world's oldest churches is located here. In the fourth century, Constantine ruled as one of the last great emperors of Rome. He was the first to legalize Christianity, even adopting it as the official state religion. His mother, Helena, first began construction on a shelter for monks on pilgrimages to the Middle East. This monastery eventually was dedicated to the Virgin Mary but was named "The Monastery of the Burning Bush," as local tradition held that the burning bush had been located in its vicinity. Many centuries later, in about 1,000 AD, a devout saint named Catherine was offered marriage by Emperor Maximinus, but she refused due to devotion to God and celibacy and was beheaded, with her remains dumped somewhere nearby. Holy relics of her were supposed to have healed the sick, and her spirit is said to have appeared to Joan of Arc. The church, now Greek Orthodox, was renamed in her honor.[134]

Saint Catherine's Monastery contains a large bramble bush that its monks claim is the long descendant of the actual burning bush.[135] It was also the site of the discovery of the world's oldest complete copy of the New Testament, the Codex Sinaiticus, a Greek translation that can be dated to about the early fourth century.[136]

This rich history, however, is precisely what Midianite proponents target in dismissing any possibility that Gebel Musa might be the true location of Sinai. Their claim accompanies the writings of Danish explorers from the 1700s that rejected this as the possible site.[137]

MOUNT SINAI

As you may have gathered, the traditional route I support doesn't seem very logical. Instead of going straight to the Promised Land, Moses turned them south along the Gulf of Suez and headed straight in the opposite direction. But this served a two-fold purpose: Mount Sinai was where he first encountered the burning bush. It was clear to Moses that this was a holy mountain, and before the Israelites could be worthy to take Canaan, they must first make a pilgrimage here to offer sacrifices to God.

But getting there wasn't a straight journey. Moses had intimate knowledge of the land; and with the leading of the Holy Spirit, he directed the people along the path where there were enough oases with springs to keep them traveling onward. The presence of water was a very simple and clear explanation of why the Israelites seemed to be traveling so far out of their way from the ultimate destination.

The Midianite theory has to rearrange more than just the route of the Exodus, however. It also places Moses' original flight from Egypt to the other end of the Gulf of Aqaba. The claim is that the entire Sinai Peninsula was Egyptian territory, and Moses would have had to travel all this way to hide from armed Egyptian soldiers. Furthermore, the forty years of wandering is placed in the desert of Saudi Arabia to stay out of Pharaoh's jurisdiction.

But this is based on a fundamental misunderstanding of the ancient world and assumes modern nation-boundaries were the same then as they are now. The whole Sinai Peninsula was never part of Egyptian territory until it was annexed from the Ottoman Empire in 1906.[138] There are ruins of ancient Egyptian turquoise mines located on the other side of the Gulf of Suez, but this is hardly evidence that armed soldiers were stationed in strategic locations to trap the escaping Israelites. In fact, the maps proponents use to place the "land of Midian" east of the Gulf of Aqaba are themselves too modern to be considered reliable depictions of the ancient world (the oldest dating to 1654).[139]

In Moses' time, the Midianites were a tribe of wandering nomads, so it's perfectly reasonable to assume they were shepherding in the Sinai Peninsula when he first met his wife and father-in-law. I want to rewind a little and point to Exodus 4:27:

> *And the* LORD *said to Aaron, Go into the wilderness to meet Moses. And he went, and met him in the mount of God, and kissed him.*

This clearly indicates that Aaron left Egypt and traveled east to Sinai to meet Moses, who had to travel west. This places the mountain between Midian and Egypt, making the Sinai Peninsula the only logical location for it. Gebel el-Lawz is east of the capital of Midian, in the exact opposite direction![140]

But what of all the evidence? In any book I've read on the Midianite theory, the entire case is built on the overwhelming number of finds supporting that the events of the Exodus took place here. But a closer look will knock those down one-by-one.

I've already mentioned that the land bridge connecting Nuweiba to Arabia is too deep to be where the Israelites crossed. A question that came to mind, and perhaps to yours, was, *Yes, but is it as deep today as it was back then?* Maybe thirty-five-hundred years of erosion could have naturally chiseled it away to its current levels. But a quick Google search reveals the exact opposite to be the case: the erosion of sand and debris from the surrounding mountains has built up the land bridge itself, meaning that it was likely *deeper* at the time of Moses.[141] You simply can't accept this theory if you believe the Bible when it states that an eastern wind (which would be from the wrong direction at Nuweiba) is what separated the Red Sea.

But what about the coral-crusted chariot wheels and human skeletons lying across the bottom of the Gulf of Aqaba?

As a general rule of archaeology (and most other sciences), the more outlandish the claim, the more evidence needed to support it. In the course of his journeys, Ron Wyatt would develop a notorious reputation for making big claims without producing sufficient evidence. For example, he would later declare that he had discovered the Ark of the Covenant hidden in a cave in Israel, but an angel told him not to share its location (a secret he would take to his deathbed). He even recounted finding the blood of Christ on it, which he then sent to a laboratory for DNA analysis but never publicized any results.[142]

Although Wyatt did in fact orchestrate a dive to the bottom of the Nuweiba sand bar, for the size of the claim he made, the evidence he produced is actually sparse. One photograph of an underwater structure is clearly a chariot wheel, and the four-spoke design does help identify it as a product of eighteenth dynasty Egypt.[143] The rest, however, are so covered with coral that identifying them as the remains of ancient chariots could well be a case of seeing something we want to be there.

The skeletal remains reflect this as well. At least one human bone was extracted from the dive; what is unquestionably a petrified human femur is currently in the possession of Dr. Lennart Moller, who assisted Wyatt in his research.[144] The other only hard evidence pulled from the dive is, oddly enough, a piece of an ox bone.[145] As for the rest of the skeletons, all that is presented is another photograph taken by one of the divers, this one showing a cluster of coral outgrowths.[146] However, just like the chariot structures, they appear to be simple natural coral that we're imagining bones onto. Until we can actually take apart the reef and examine it, we can't say with any certainty what it actually is.

So when we step back and look at the hard evidence, we're left with one chariot wheel, one human femur, and part of an ox thighbone. Everything else is purely speculative. Evidence of human activity can be found even in the most remote places. Numerous ruins of settlements and even human remains can be found at the bottom of seas around the world. When put together, this isn't proof we can build a rock-solid scientific case on.

Getting back to the Mount Sinai issue, much is made of Gebel el-Lawz having what appears to be a semi-circle of twelve stone pillars at its base, as well as a nearby strange, long "corridor" of stone.[147] This would seem to coincide with Exodus 24:4:

> *And Moses wrote all the words of the* LORD, *and rose up early in the morning, and builded an altar under the hill, and twelve pillars, according to the twelve tribes of Israel.*

However, unlike most of the findings at the bottom of the Gulf of Aqaba, these can clearly be examined to determine whether or not they could have been set in place by the Israelites. They are actually marble columns from a long-gone ancient structure, but not as ancient as the time of Moses. Sherds of nearby pottery can actually verify that the building was likely Nabatean, from the time of the Roman Empire.[148] The "corridor" and marble columns are made out of hewn and chiseled stone, which would violate the Mosaic laws requiring all altars to Yahweh be constructed from natural stones not touched by tools.

> *And if thou wilt make me an altar of stone, thou shalt not build it of hewn stone: for if thou lift up thy tool upon it, thou hast polluted it. (Exodus 20:25)*

The ruins at the base of Gebel el-Lawz are probably from a marble quarry where workers mined stone to be sent to Arabia for construction.

There is also ancient rock art in the vicinity of Gebel el-Lawz depicting cattle and feet, which, according to Midianite theorists, indicates that the golden calf was located here. The feet would represent a marker where Moses had to remove his shoes before the burning bush.[149] Again, however, this needs a closer look. If the marble quarry are dated too late to be part of any events from the 1400s BC, this rock art is in the opposite direction, being products of the Neolithic sub-pluvial period (thousands of years before the Exodus), when wild cattle still roamed the region.[150] Literally thousands of rock art of cows and feet can be found across the Middle East and North Africa, so this is hardly unique to Gebel el-Lawz.

If it sounds like I'm being too hard on Ron Wyatt, I actually still retain respect for the man. Science is about presenting different hypotheses and then testing them through deductive reasoning to arrive at the truth. Wyatt thought outside the box and for the most part presented us with things we can test.

EXODUS 19:1-25

The People Fear God

> *In the third month, when the children of Israel were gone forth out of the land of Egypt, the same day came they into the wilderness of Sinai. . . .*

> *And Moses went up unto God, and the L*ORD *called unto him out of the mountain, saying, Thus shalt thou say to the house of Jacob, and tell the children of Israel; . . . Now therefore, if ye will obey my voice indeed, and keep my covenant, then ye shall be a peculiar treasure unto me above all people: for all the earth is mine: And ye shall be unto me a kingdom of priests, and an holy nation. These are the words which thou shalt speak unto the children of Israel. (Exodus 19:1, 3, 5-6)*

The people had arrived at Mount Sinai, where God had called them, in order to sanctify them and give them the law. They were to be a peculiar people on the earth, holy and separated from the other nations. The Lord gave Moses specific instructions: they would be privileged to hear from God just like he did. But what followed was a poignant story demonstrating how unprepared the Israelites were.

> *And Moses came and called for the elders of the people, and laid before their faces all these words which the L*ORD *commanded him. And all the people answered together, and said, All that the L*ORD *hath spoken we will do. And Moses returned the words of the people unto the L*ORD*. (Exodus 19:7-8)*

This point is crucial to the story. Pay very careful attention to the wording: "All that the LORD hath spoken we will do." This was a pretty bold statement. It's also the attitude many Christians have at first. We proudly announce that we'll obey God no matter what He says. But like Peter, who swore up and down to Jesus that he would never forsake Him, our words can end up tripping us up. In this case, they were going to be privileged to actually be in God's presence, an honor given to a precious few since the Garden of Eden.

> *And the L*ORD *said unto Moses, Lo, I come unto thee in a thick cloud, that the people may hear when I speak with thee, and believe thee for ever. And Moses told the words of the people unto the L*ORD*. (Exodus 19:9)*

No one could see the face of God; but He would appear in a cloud (akin to the one leading them through the wilderness) and speak to them directly. But great preparation had to be made for this momentous event.

> *And the L*ORD *said unto Moses, Go unto the people, and sanctify them to day and to morrow, and let them wash their clothes, And be ready against the third day: for the third day the L*ORD *will come down in the sight of all the people upon mount Sinai. (Exodus 19:10-11)*

The people had three days. First, they had to wash their garments to be counted pure and spotless before Him. Our orders today are to be holy and ready for Christ's return.

> *That he might present it to himself a glorious church, not having spot, or wrinkle, or any such thing; but that it should be holy and without blemish. (Ephesians 5:27)*

> *And thou shalt set bounds unto the people round about, saying, Take heed to yourselves, that ye go not up into the mount, or touch the border of it: whosoever toucheth the mount shall be surely put to death. (Exodus 19:12)*

Similar to the veil in the tabernacle separating the Holiest of Holies from the rest of the building, ropes had to be tied all around the base of the mountain as partitions between God and man. When He descended, the ground would be so holy that anyone who touched it would die. These are the Old Testament times still, and not just anyone could enter into His presence.

On the third day, the people gathered around. Ropes were set up. They were washed clean and were expecting His appearance. But from the outset, something was clearly wrong.

> *And it came to pass on the third day in the morning, that there were thunders and lightnings, and a thick cloud upon the mount, and the voice of the trumpet exceeding loud; so that all the people that was in the camp trembled. (Exodus 19:16)*

The earth trembled at God's presence when He descended upon the mountain. There was a thick cloud, with lightning, thunder, and earthquakes. A terrifying trumpet blared through the world (Christ's return will also be accompanied by a trumpet). The Israelites, who thought they were ready to see God, trembled in fear. This was more frightening than they expected.

> *And mount Sinai was altogether on a smoke, because the LORD descended upon it in fire: and the smoke thereof ascended as the smoke of a furnace, and the whole mount quaked greatly. (Exodus 19:18)*

But Moses wasn't afraid. And because of that, he alone was counted worthy to tread his feet on holy ground and ascend God's mountain.

> *And when the voice of the trumpet sounded long, and waxed louder and louder, Moses spake, and God answered him by a voice. And the LORD came down upon mount Sinai, on the top of the mount: and the LORD called Moses up to the top of the mount; and Moses went up. And the LORD said unto Moses, Go down, charge the people, lest they break through unto the LORD to gaze, and many of them perish. (Exodus 19:19-21)*

Before he could climb the mountain and disappear into the glory, Moses had to warn the people not to try to break the boundaries and follow him, or they would die. All the work that went into washing and setting up boundaries still hadn't made them worthy of His presence. It was very telling that they would later beg Moses not to allow God to speak to them again.

> *And they said unto Moses, Speak thou with us, and we will hear: but let not God speak with us, lest we die. (Exodus 20:19)*

THE TIES THAT BIND

This all-too-familiar pattern repeats itself throughout the Bible. Mankind has an inherent yearning to be in the presence of his Creator. And yet when the Lord appears, those who claim they were waiting for His arrival reject Him.

There's no reason why the Jews shouldn't have recognized Jesus as their Messiah. Everything in the Old Testament pointed to it. The place of His birth had been foretold in Micah 5:2:

> *But thou, Bethlehem Ephratah, though thou be little among the thousands of Judah, yet out of thee shall he come forth unto me that is to be ruler in Israel; whose goings forth have been from of old, from everlasting.*

The time had been prophesied in Daniel 9:25:

> *Know therefore and understand, that from the going forth of the commandment to restore and to build Jerusalem unto the Messiah the Prince shall be seven weeks, and threescore and two weeks: the street shall be built again, and the wall, even in troublous times.*

During the darkest days of the Roman Empire, Judah yearned for its freedom. The people desperately longed for their Savior to arrive. But once He showed up, they despised and rejected Him.

> *Is not this the carpenter, the son of Mary, the brother of James, and Joses, and of Juda, and Simon? and are not his sisters here with us? And they were offended at him. (Mark 6:3)*

Later, the disciples promised Jesus they would wait for Him in Gethsemane.

> *Then cometh Jesus with them unto a place called Gethsemane, and saith unto the disciples, Sit ye here, while I go and pray yonder. (Matthew 26:36)*

Luke 21:41 tells us He was only a stone's throw away. They knew He was coming back, and He was so close to them they could likely hear Him, but they still fell asleep.

> *And he cometh unto the disciples, and findeth them asleep, and saith unto Peter, What, could ye not watch with me one hour? (Matthew 26:40)*

We Christians need to be very careful, or we too will be caught unaware. We preach, teach, and sing about the Rapture. We tell God every day that we can't wait to see Jesus. But when He actually does appear, how many will truly be ready? No wonder Jesus asked in Luke 18:8,

Nevertheless when the Son of man cometh, shall he find faith on the earth?

Many Christians have experienced God in so many miraculous ways. They have seen Him answer prayers. But I have a terrible feeling that very few will actually be worthy to ascend into His presence. The rest will be spewed out of the mouth of God, into Great Tribulation.

Therefore be ye also ready: for in such an hour as ye think not the Son of man cometh. (Matthew 24:44)

EXODUS 20:1-17

The Ten Commandments

"The Ten Commandments" is another iconic image synonymous with the word *Exodus*. Movies have portrayed a long-bearded Moses carrying down two perfectly-shaped tablets, five inscriptions on each. This isn't precisely accurate, though. The law is not confined to ten and actually takes up thirteen verses in Exodus 20. The first starts with a preamble:

I am the LORD thy God, which have brought thee out of the land of Egypt, out of the house of bondage. (Exodus 20:2)

Most of us know the first ten by heart, but God then gives Moses a long and detailed list of specific instructions. Was all of this written on two stone tablets? We could assume not, but the Bible really doesn't say.

We can, however, study in depth the first set, which clearly do constitute "ten commandments" that provide the foundation of one of the world's oldest religions.

Thou shalt have no other gods before me.

Thou shalt not make unto thee any graven image, or any likeness of any thing that is in heaven above, or that is in the earth beneath, or that is in the water under the earth. . . .

Thou shalt not take the name of the LORD thy God in vain; for the LORD will not hold him guiltless that taketh his name in vain.

Remember the sabbath day, to keep it holy. Six days shalt thou labour, and do all thy work: . . .

> *For in six days the L*ORD *made heaven and earth, the sea, and all that in them is, and rested the seventh day: wherefore the L*ORD *blessed the sabbath day, and hallowed it. (Exodus 20:3-4, 7-9, 11)*

The first four laws instruct us how to interact with God. Do not have any other gods before Him, do not take His name in vain, and remember the Sabbath day. Most Protestant denominations are unique in considering verses 3 and 4 as two separate commandments.[151]

Idolatry would be a major problem for Israel before this story was even over and would continue to haunt them for centuries. Today we look down on ancient idol worship, as if it's something we don't struggle with today, but we forget exactly what it means. "Thou shalt have no other gods before me" refers to *anything* you put before God. Nobody, not even the most hardcore atheist, worships nothing. We all worship something. Whether it's your family, your marriage, your job, your children, your television, social media, or your cell phone, if it gets in the way of your prayer time, it has become an idol, and you need to change your priorities.

> *Honour thy father and thy mother: that thy days may be long upon the land which the Lord thy God giveth thee.*
>
> *Thou shalt not kill.*
>
> *Thou shalt not commit adultery.*
>
> *Thou shalt not steal.*
>
> *Thou shalt not bear false witness against thy neighbour.*
>
> *Thou shalt not covet thy neighbour's house, thou shalt not covet thy neighbour's wife, nor his manservant, nor his maidservant, nor his ox, nor his ass, nor any thing that is thy neighbour's. (Exodus 20:12-17)*

The latter six commandments order us to honor our parents and not to kill, commit adultery, steal, or covet our neighbor's possessions. These dictate how we should act towards one another. But what is interesting is that there are more of these than laws demanding we honor God (four versus six). It's just a subtle enough hint to remind us that the Lord is slightly less concerned with His own glory than He is how we treat others. I've often said in my classes that God is not so much impressed by our awesome music, talented singers, and great preaching, as He is by how much love we show to our brothers and sisters in Christ. Jesus put it best when He said,

> *A new commandment I give unto you, That ye love one another; as I have loved you, that ye also love one another. By this shall all men know that ye are my disciples, if ye have love one to another. (John 13:34-35)*

MIDDLE KINGDOM DYNAMICS

So far as we can tell, Abraham and Jacob's covenants with God were verbal agreements. Perhaps what is so profound about the Ten Commandments, and why they are so immediately identifiable in our collective minds, is that they represent the first written covenant.

In the remote regions of Sinai is an ancient temple called Serabit el-Khadim, which means "Heights of the Slave." A few minutes' hike above it will bring you to a small cave where, etched in terra cotta stone, are some of the oldest known letters ever written, discovered in 1906. They are not Egyptian but very early Semitic, dating to roughly the time of the Exodus (mid-second century BC). These proto-Sinaitic symbols, which include an ox, fish, snake, and hand, represent the dawn of the Hebrew alphabet (and all alphabets that would follow).[152]

While the Egyptian hieroglyphic influence is still there (the use of animals to depict words), what is revolutionary about the proto-Sinaitic alphabet is its use of one sound being represented by one letter. The complexity of hieroglyphics and cuneiform both make them incredibly difficult to decipher; combinations of over five hundred distinct hieroglyphs can form a myriad of sounds.[153] Egyptian writing was generally reserved for the wealthy or the priestly order. But while Moses was raised in Pharaoh's courts and well-versed in language, the newly formed Hebrew alphabet was a written word for the common man. The events on Mount Sinai did not just change the course of the nation of Israel. They did not just represent the birth of one of the world's oldest religions: Judaism. They changed the world, shaping civilization as we recognize it today.

THE TIES THAT BIND

Jewish tradition holds that God gave Moses the law fifty days after the Passover, leading to an important holiday in Jewish tradition: *Shavu'ot*. It is also known as the celebration of Pentecost, Greek for "Feast of 50."[154] It's no coincidence that before Jesus ascended into heaven, He ordered His followers to go to the upper room and wait.

> *And, being assembled together with them, commanded them that they should not depart from Jerusalem, but wait for the promise of the Father, which, saith he, ye have heard of me. (Acts 1:4)*

Just like Passover, Pentecost was a huge celebration with crowds of worshipers gathered from all over the Roman Empire, overflowing the streets of Jerusalem. Perched high above with an open window, patiently waiting for the promise of God, one hundred twenty disciples were in a perfect position to shake the world.

> *And when the day of Pentecost was fully come, they were all with one accord in one place. (Acts 2:1)*

The Holy Ghost fell on them in the form of tongues of fire, and they spoke in other languages as He gave them utterance. The sound filled the crowded streets, and many heard things in their own tongue. Some were confused, some laughed and mocked. But the glory of God could not be contained; unlike in the temple, where it was restrained in the Holiest of Holies, it spilled out of the upper room onto the streets, and thousands were saved in one day.

> *And the Lord added to the church daily such as should be saved. (Acts 2:47)*

The Day of Pentecost is to Christianity what Moses' receiving of the law on Mount Sinai is to Judaism. This is why they both fell on the same date. And the same Holy Spirit orchestrated the two. The fire that carved the Ten Commandments on the stone tablets descended in tongues and carved the New Testament Commandments on the minds of the apostles. The Holy Spirit directs us, similar to how the commandments guided the Israelites.

> *Howbeit when he, the Spirit of truth, is come, he will guide you into all truth. (John 16:13)*

That same fire is available for you too.

EXODUS 21-23

The Mosaic Law

At this point, the story took a strange turn. The breathless narration of one dramatic event after another was suddenly interrupted by three chapters of law-giving. These laws go into extraordinary detail, laying out the foundation of Israelite society. To read the next three chapters at once is overwhelming, but breaking them down section-by-section can help make them more digestible.

Exodus 21
1-11: The law concerning servants
12-27: The law concerning violence
28-36: Animal control laws

Exodus 22
1-15: The law concerning property
16-31: Moral and ceremonial principles

Exodus 23
1-9: Justice
10-13: The law concerning the Sabbath
14-19: The annual feasts
20-33: The angel of protection

For time's sake, I don't want to go into every scripture of every law in its exactness. However I do find that we can get valuable information from studying the law, as well as put certain controversial aspects of it to rest. For example, in the laws concerning servants, we find a type and shadow of our relationship to Christ as our master. While Exodus 21 starts off by telling us that a Hebrew servant is automatically freed every seven years, verse 5 presents us with a peculiar scenario of a servant that loves his master and doesn't want to leave.

Then his master shall bring him unto the judges; he shall also bring him to the door, or unto the door post; and his master shall bore his ear through with an aul; and he shall serve him for ever. (Exodus 21:6)

This sounds incomprehensible to the nonbeliever, but as Christians, we can clearly identify with the servant who longs to be brought before the Judge (the Father) and be marked forever as a servant of the good Master (Christ).

But things take a dark turn with the second set of laws. In listing the different potential crimes, God pronounces the punishment as *death*. Verse 12 sets the precedent:

He that smiteth a man, so that he die, shall be surely put to death. (Exodus 21:12)

Since capital punishment for murder is still legal today, this doesn't sound too extreme. But the further we go, the punishment remains the same while the crimes get lighter.

And he that curseth his father, or his mother, shall surely be put to death. (Exodus 21:17)

The Old Testament concept of law is defined and summed up a few verses down:

Eye for eye, tooth for tooth, hand for hand, foot for foot, Burning for burning, wound for wound, stripe for stripe. (Exodus 21:24-25)

In any debate I've had with an atheist, the harshness of the Old Testament law is a favorite go-to accusation against the Bible. To put it simply, if one claims to believe the Bible is the inspired Word of God, one is left with many Old Testament scriptures that deal out harsh punishment for seemingly trivial offenses. I'm often presented with a list of "the scariest scriptures in the Bible" (almost always laws from Leviticus or Deuteronomy), and they inevitably include Exodus 22:18:

> *Thou shalt not suffer a witch to live.*

This verse was infamously used in the Salem Witch Trials to justify putting suspected sorceresses to death.

Of course, this is a straw man argument built on a false notion and a fundamental misunderstanding of Christian theology. It assumes that believing the Bible is the Word of God means accepting that any scripture is automatically gospel, no context needed. I never find this argument convincing because it isn't an honest assessment and repudiation of my beliefs but a caricature stating what my beliefs *are*, followed by a knocking down of that caricature. It's obnoxious to be accused of wanting to sacrifice animals and burn witches, but I will take this opportunity to put the Old Testament law in its proper context.

I've said many times that no scripture in the Bible should be cut out by itself to prove anything. Any verse can be separated from its chapter and historical context to be twisted into appearing to say something it doesn't (Christians stuck in false doctrine do this too). After being confronted with "scary scriptures," my response is usually, "What chapter of what book is it in? What do the verses around it say? In what time period was it written?"

The Old Testament itself clearly states the Mosaic laws were only temporary. Atheists who accuse Christians of believing in it either intentionally ignore or are unfamiliar with Jeremiah 31:31-32:

> *Behold, the days come, saith the* LORD, *that I will make a new covenant with the house of Israel, and with the house of Judah: Not according to the covenant that I made with their fathers in the day that I took them by the hand to bring them out of the land of Egypt; which my covenant they brake, although I was an husband unto them, saith the* LORD.

In other words, if you believe that the Old Testament is part of the inspired Word of God, you *have* to believe that the Mosaic laws no longer apply! Christian and Jewish doctrines are very clear about this, and the New Testament itself contains thirty-seven scriptures stating that Christ's death (and resurrection) had undone the law.

> *For sin shall not have dominion over you: for ye are not under the law, but under grace. (Romans 6:14)*

In fact, this is why Romans was written in the first place; early Jewish converts refused to accept Gentiles as Christians in the Church of Rome because they didn't live by the Mosaic laws (including their non-kosher dietary practices).[155] Paul's letter was to inform them that God no longer cared about whether we lived by the law—rather, He cared about the condition of our hearts.

Of course, when pinned down with this realization, atheists usually fall back on the "same God" argument. If the God of the New Testament is the same as the God of the Old, He still wrote the law and its harsh penalties and is guilty of demanding total obedience. Once again, leaving out that He would later send His Son to die for our sins on the cross, let's place this in its proper historical context, where we can find a very critical ingredient missing from the equation.

The Law in Context of Child Sacrifice

In ancient times, life was brutal. Populations were subject to terrible weather, famines, droughts, plagues, and natural disasters. Because people tended to be superstitious, they turned to making sacrifices to try to appease their gods' wrath. When animals wouldn't work, they would turn to human sacrifice. When that wasn't enough, they would assume their deities were asking for supreme devotion, and then the firstborn child (favored heir of any family) was offered up in last-ditch efforts to save themselves.

This terrible, misguided practice would eventually become sacred custom. Droughts, plagues, or famines would end, yet people would still sacrifice their children on the altars to Molech, Ba'al, or Marduk. Blood-curdling cheers of people gathered to watch would fill the nights, as screaming children were thrown onto altars of fire and burned alive by their own parents under the watchful gaze of idols. The ritual would end in gruesome feasts as the families would eat the roasted remains. Some people would have children for the express purpose of sacrificing and eating them before the gods.

Archaeologists have found physical evidence for this barbaric practice. Mass graves of child skeletons, still bearing cut marks of ritual knives, have been found buried at Phoenician Carthage.[156] Excavations of the ruins of Jericho itself have revealed jars of baby remains stored in the city walls.[157]

Abraham was certainly aware of the practice when the Lord commanded him,

> *Take now thy son, thine only son Isaac, whom thou lovest, and get thee into the land of Moriah; and offer him there for a burnt offering upon one of the mountains which I will tell thee of. (Genesis 22:2)*

But when he took Isaac to the mountain, set him on the altar, and lifted his knife, God intervened and revealed that it was only a test.

> *And he said, Lay not thine hand upon the lad, neither do thou any thing unto him: for now I know that thou fearest God, seeing thou hast not withheld thy son, thine only son from me. (Genesis 22:12)*

The precedent for Abraham's descendants from then on was that God would not accept child sacrifice, setting His people apart from the rest. And this is why there are so many scriptures condemning it.

> *And thou shalt not let any of thy seed pass through the fire to Molech, neither shalt thou profane the name of thy God: I am the Lord. (Leviticus 18:21)*

> *Again, thou shalt say to the children of Israel, Whosoever he be of the children of Israel, or of the strangers that sojourn in Israel, that giveth any of his seed unto Molech; he shall surely be put to death: the people of the land shall stone him with stones. (Leviticus 20:2)*

> *Thou shalt not do so unto the Lord thy God: for every abomination to the Lord, which he hateth, have they done unto their gods; for even their sons and their daughters they have burnt in the fire to their gods. (Deuteronomy 12:31)*

> *There shall not be found among you any one that maketh his son or his daughter to pass through the fire, or that useth divination, or an observer of times, or an enchanter, or a witch. (Deuteronomy 18:10)*

> *Yea, they sacrificed their sons and their daughters unto devils, And shed innocent blood, even the blood of their sons and of their daughters, whom they sacrificed unto the idols of Canaan: and the land was polluted with blood. (Psalm 106:37-38)*

God abhorred this practice. And by Moses' time, it was an epidemic. All the nations Israel would be coming into contact with in their journey from Egypt to Canaan were killing and eating their own children in honor of false gods. Jericho, the first target on Joshua's conquest list, was one of the worst examples; one could call it the child sacrifice capital of the ancient world.

The punishment for sin was death by execution, because the situation was desperate. The Lord knew that even the tiniest influence of idolaters on His people would transform them into child-sacrificing cannibals. And if that sounds like an extreme conclusion to jump to, remember that this is *exactly* what happened every time they yielded to sin. King Manasseh had erected so many altars to false gods and increased sacrifice of children (including his own), the Bible says he covered the land with blood.

> *Moreover Manasseh shed innocent blood very much, till he had filled Jerusalem from one end to another; beside his sin wherewith he made Judah to sin, in doing that which was evil in the sight of the LORD. (2 Kings 21:16)*

When Jesus spoke about "hell" in the New Testament, the Greek word *gehenna* actually refers to the Valley of Hinnom,[158] which was known as a great killing ground with a similar reputation as Auschwitz has to us today. A shrine to Baal had once been erected here for child sacrifice. The prophet Jeremiah references it in 19:5-6:

> *They have built also the high places of Baal, to burn their sons with fire for burnt offerings unto Baal, which I commanded not, nor spake it, neither came it into my mind: Therefore, behold, the days come, saith the Lord, that this place shall no more be called Tophet, nor The valley of the son of Hinnom, but The valley of slaughter.*

Jerusalem was still haunted by the memories of screaming children thrown alive into burning flames, and there was no better illustration of hell, where the unsaved will be cast into never-ending fire. In the historical context, the disciples would have understood exactly what Jesus meant.

If God's judgment in the Old Testament seems cruel and maniacal, viewing it through the lens of child sacrifice brings it into a new light. Even Noah's Flood. I've written on my blog that the probable natural cause of the Genesis deluge was a massive volcanic eruption from the Aleutian Islands towards the end of the Ubaid period (about 3100 BC), which triggered a small ice age. Years of famine led to child cannibalism, recorded by the Sumerians in the *Atrahasis Epic:* "When the second year arrived, they [the people] had depleted the store-house. When the third year arrived, the people's looks were changed by starvation. . . . When the sixth year arrived, they served up a daughter for a meal, then served up a son for food."[159] This coincides with the Bible's description of the time period in Genesis 6:5:

> *And God saw that the wickedness of man was great in the earth, and that every imagination of the thoughts of his heart was only evil continually.*

But in this case, as well as with Jericho, why did *all* of them have to die? Were such extreme measures as killing the women and children really justified? To answer this, I have to draw an important comparison. Early in the Second World War, it was quickly evident what brutal rulers the Nazis were. One of the German army's most notorious war crimes occurred in 1941, shortly after taking the small nation of Latvia. The Jewish population of the city of Riga was rounded up into a synagogue that was then set ablaze, killing all the men, women, and children inside.[160]

Imperial Japan was no better. The 1937 invasion of China is considered one of the most barbaric attacks in human history. The Nanking massacre lasted about six weeks and ended with between 200–300,000 civilian deaths. The war crimes of the Japanese are too numerous to list here, but many young Chinese girls testified to being raped by Imperial soldiers as much as thirty times per day, driving some to insanity.[161] Putting a stop to the Axis powers' atrocities required drastic action. When America entered the war, bombing raids on Germany racked up massive civilian casualties to demoralize its military. Between 1939 and 1945, Allied planes dropped an estimated 3.4 million tons of bombs on Axis powers, killing at least 305,000 non-military citizens.[162]

Harsh, yes, but we justify it today by pointing out that winning the war quicker saved lives in the long run. After Germany surrendered, the war was brought to a swift end when the atomic bombs were dropped on Hiroshima and Nagasaki, killing an estimated two hundred thousand. We argue that the Allies weren't responsible for all those civilian deaths, but Hitler, Tojo, and Mussolini were responsible for causing the war in the first place. But this should also apply to God's declaration of war on the Canaanites to bring an end to the bloody practice of child sacrifice. It was so entrenched in their culture that the only way to end it was through scorched-earth tactics.

By comparison, Canaanite children who weren't sacrificed were raised in a culture of death. They had gleefully watched their brothers and sisters die on the altars of Molech and had gorged themselves on their flesh. Even at a very young age, these little monsters were probably armed and ready for Joshua's invading army. If left alive and incorporated into Israelite culture, the Lord knew that they would have a corrupting influence. This is proven by the fact that the Israelites ultimately failed in their mission to destroy the Canaanite cities, and within a few generations, they too were erecting shrines and sacrificing their own children to Molech and Baal.

To conclude, the harshness of the Mosaic laws, and the entire nature of God in the Old Testament times, must be viewed in the new light of His hatred of child sacrifice. When placed next to the New Testament scriptures pronouncing the law now obsolete, we realize that it was a temporary bulwark designed to keep God's people from becoming child-murdering cannibals.

EXODUS 24:1-18

Moses Brings the First Law

> *And he said unto Moses, Come up unto the* LORD, *thou, and Aaron, Nadab, and Abihu, and seventy of the elders of Israel; and worship ye afar off. And Moses alone shall come near the* LORD: *but they shall not come nigh; neither shall the people go up with him. (Exodus 24:1-2)*

Moses had received two parts of the law (the books of Leviticus and Deuteronomy would expand greatly on this, establishing the priesthood and setting up the Israelite legal system). Now he was commanded to bring up the seventy elders and Aaron and his sons to ascend the mountain. But only Moses was allowed to go up entirely into the presence of God.

> *And Moses came and told the people all the words of the LORD, and all the judgments: and all the people answered with one voice, and said, All the words which the LORD hath said will we do. (Exodus 24:3)*

The people echoed their earlier sentiment before God appeared on Mount Sinai. "All the words which the Lord hath said we will do." Perhaps in retrospect, they still desired to be in His presence. But this was as empty a promise now as it was then. There was only one chance, and they missed it. They said they never wanted to hear from God again, and God would oblige. Only Moses and the elders would ever be allowed in His presence.

We only have one shot to make the Rapture, and that time is now—before it takes place. Afterwards, it will be too late. So many people who claimed they were ready will be left behind. And once that day has come, I'm convinced that churches and altars all over the world will be filled with people crying out, "Come back, Jesus! Come back! *Now* I'm ready to receive you!" But they will have missed their last chance.

> *Then went up Moses, and Aaron, Nadab, and Abihu, and seventy of the elders of Israel: And they saw the God of Israel: and there was under his feet as it were a paved work of a sapphire stone, and as it were the body of heaven in his clearness. (Exodus 24:9-10)*

THE TIES THAT BIND

Moses and the seventy elders were given one of the greatest privileges in the entire Bible at this point, to see the throne of God Himself. The throne first appeared in Job, the oldest book (the devil appeared before the Lord to accuse Job), but it isn't recorded who saw it. It is not mentioned in Genesis whether Abraham, Jacob, or Joseph ever looked upon it. Moses was the first to see it in all its glory. The tiny glimpse of sapphire under the Lord's feet was in line with the later visions.

The prophet Micaiah witnessed the throne before pronouncing judgment on the wicked king Ahab in 1 Kings 22:19-23. Isaiah had one of the most famous visions of it in Isaiah 6, which occurred during a troubled time in Judah's history (immediately after the death of King Uzziah). The prophet Ezekiel was privileged with two visions of the throne: the first in chapter 1 by the Chebar River, where he saw four celestial wheels rocketing across the sky; the second in chapters 9 and 10. The final is John's vision while on the Isle of Patmos in Revelation 4. Interestingly enough, this first mention of the throne in Exodus only contains a brief description, and much more detail can be learned by examining each subsequent vision. I don't want to get off-topic by going into a detailed study of every vision, but you can read a 6-part series I wrote on this very thing on my blog: depthsofpentecost.com.

I do, however, want to at least mention the sapphire color described at the feet of God, because it is also described by Ezekiel in his second vision.

Sapphire is usually known as a brilliant blue-colored gemstone, and the color blue is mentioned over fifty times in the Bible (every instance in the Old Testament). Blue is one of the least-occurring colors in nature; while some birds can have blue feathers, no mammal has blue hair. It's even been proposed that all blue-eyed people have the same genetic ancestor, whose eye color was a mutation.[163] I've heard some speculate that it could represent the Holy Spirit, or God's healing power. I defer to its other appearance in Exodus, as one of the colors of the veil that would separate the Holiest of Holies. The sapphire stone would reappear on the priestly breastplate. But we'll get to that a little later.

> *And the LORD said unto Moses, Come up to me into the mount, and be there: and I will give thee tables of stone, and a law, and commandments which I have written; that thou mayest teach them. . . . And Moses went up into the mount, and a cloud covered the mount. . . . And the sight of the glory of the LORD was like devouring fire on the top of the mount in the eyes of the children of Israel. And Moses went into the midst of the cloud, and gat him up into the mount: and Moses was in the mount forty days and forty nights. (Exodus 24:12, 15, 17-18)*

The Lord beckoned Moses to press further in the cloud. Now that he had received the law, it was time for the instructions on how God wanted the tabernacle constructed to house His presence. He would be there for forty days and nights while Joshua waited just outside and the seventy elders just a little farther. From the view of the Israelites below, it looks as though Moses had disappeared in a fiery cloud, enveloping the summit of Sinai. Separation from their leader for too long would bring trouble.

EXODUS 25:10-22

The Ark of the Covenant

> *And they shall make an ark of shittim wood: two cubits and a half shall be the length thereof, and a cubit and a half the breadth thereof, and a cubit and a half the height thereof. (Exodus 25:10)*

In the first nine verses of Exodus 25, God instructed Moses that all the children of Israel should contribute the materials needed to construct the tabernacle: wool, animal skins, dye, etc. In verse 10 is born one of the most enduring mysteries of the Bible. The Ark of the Covenant is the most powerful symbol to emerge from the tale of the Exodus. Made even more famous today by the movie *Raiders of the Lost Ark*, it serves as one of archaeology's most tantalizing legends.

I can see from my own research why the mystery behind it is so frustrating. After years of reading about biblical archaeology in preparation for this and future books and classes, I'm confident about many things. I believe we can safely date the Flood and identify the probable location of Noah's Ark. I'm certain I've presented the most logical explanation for the events of the Exodus and have seen external historical evidence for the reigns of King David and the life of Christ. But there is very little on the Ark. Even the Bible gives us almost no clue; for such a critical sacred object in Jewish history, the Old Testament is surprisingly silent on its whereabouts after the Babylonian invasion. Where did it go? Every trail archaeologists have followed ends up cold.

THE TIES THAT BIND

In absence of ever finding the Ark, however, we can at least study it to gain insight into its meaning. It seemed to have supernatural powers; the Israelites saw victory whenever they carried it into battle. However I don't think there was anything special about the Ark itself but rather the power that rested *with* it so long as the children of God stayed totally obedient to Him. It symbolized the presence of God itself, and as such, I believe it is a fitting representative of the Holy Ghost. When looking at the Ark in this new light, it takes on a whole new meaning and is an even more powerful symbol of God.

In 1 Samuel 4:10-11, news reaches Eli that the Israelites had been defeated in battle, despite carrying the Ark with them.

> *And the Philistines fought, and Israel was smitten, and they fled every man into his tent: and there was a very great slaughter; for there fell of Israel thirty thousand footmen. And the ark of God was taken; and the two sons of Eli, Hophni and Phinehas, were slain.*

Pay attention to how he reacts:

> *And when Eli heard the noise of the crying, he said, What meaneth the noise of this tumult? And the man came in hastily, and told Eli. . . . And the messenger answered and said, Israel is fled before the Philistines, and there hath been also a great slaughter among the people, and thy two sons also, Hophni and Phinehas, are dead, and the ark of God is taken. (1 Samuel 4:14, 17)*

The Bible doesn't record whether or not Eli reacted to the news that his sons had been killed. But the news that the Ark had been taken truly devastated him.

> *And it came to pass, when he made mention of the ark of God, that he fell from off the seat backward by the side of the gate, and his neck brake, and he died: for he was an old man, and heavy. And he had judged Israel forty years. (1 Samuel 4:18)*

If we're not careful, the Holy Ghost can be taken from us. We have to love and treasure the Spirit; just like Jesus, we should want to cling to Him and never let go.

> *And thou shalt overlay it with pure gold, within and without shalt thou overlay it, and shalt make upon it a crown of gold round about. . . . And thou shalt make staves of shittim wood, and overlay them with gold. And thou shalt put the staves into the rings by the sides of the ark, that the ark may be borne with them. (Exodus 25:11, 13-14)*

The Ark was to be two and a half cubits long (a cubit is roughly the length of a man's middle fingertip to his elbow) and a cubit and a half deep and wide. While the frame was made of wood, the plating was overlaid with gold, and rings were fitted on either side. Long staves would be used to carry the Ark, a responsibility allowed to only the Levites.

> *At that time the LORD separated the tribe of Levi, to bear the ark of the covenant of the LORD. (Deuteronomy 10:8)*

In another controversial move by God, many years later, Uzzah was infamously killed for touching the Ark to steady it. After the Philistines were ready to surrender it back to Israel, David sent a company of men to retrieve it. Only they didn't carefully study God's law for how it should be transported.

> *And they set the ark of God upon a new cart, and brought it out of the house of Abinadab that was in Gibeah: and Uzzah and Ahio, the sons of Abinadab, drave the new cart. (2 Samuel 6:3)*

But setting the Ark on a cart to be pulled by an ox was not what God commanded. This act of carelessness led to tragedy.

> *And the anger of the LORD was kindled against Uzzah; and God smote him there for his error; and there he died by the ark of God. (2 Samuel 6:7)*

We need to be very careful trying to take shortcuts around God's commandments.

> *And thou shalt make a mercy seat of pure gold: two cubits and a half shall be the length thereof, and a cubit and a half the breadth thereof. (Exodus 25:17)*

God's presence was stronger in this room than anywhere else in the world, where the priest would enter every year to offer atonement for the sins of the people. The lid of the Ark was thought to be where God would sit, hence the name "mercy seat."

> *And thou shalt make two cherubims of gold, of beaten work shalt thou make them, in the two ends of the mercy seat. And make one cherub on the one end, and the other cherub on the other end: even of the mercy seat shall ye make the cherubims on the two ends thereof. And the cherubims shall stretch forth their wings on high, covering the mercy seat with their wings, and their faces shall look one to another; toward the mercy seat shall the faces of the cherubims be. (Exodus 25:18-20)*

The covering of the Ark, symbolizing God's throne, was adorned with two gold cherubs facing towards one another, their wings stretched out over the entire length of the Ark itself. Some artistic interpretations show them hiding *their* faces; while the Bible doesn't specifically say this, it would make sense compared to the vision of God's throne in Isaiah 6:2-3:

> *Above it stood the seraphims: each one had six wings; with twain he covered his face, and with twain he covered his feet, and with twain he did fly. And one cried unto another, and said, Holy, holy, holy, is the LORD of hosts: the whole earth is full of his glory.*

EXODUS 25:23-30

The Showbread

> *Thou shalt also make a table of shittim wood: two cubits shall be the length thereof, and a cubit the breadth thereof, and a cubit and a half the height thereof. And thou shalt overlay it with pure gold, and make thereto a crown of gold round about. . . . And thou shalt make for it four rings of gold, and put the rings in the four corners that are on the four feet thereof. Over against the border shall the rings be for places of the staves to bear the table. (Exodus 25:23-24, 26-27)*

This is the beginning of a very curious temple ritual. God instructed Moses to build a table almost the exact same dimensions as the Ark just outside of the entrance to the Holiest of Holies, by the seven candlesticks. It too was to be overlaid with gold and have four rings for staves to carry. (Remember that the tabernacle was supposed to be a portable temple, so everything had to be easily disassembled and transported.)

> *And thou shalt set upon the table shewbread before me always. (Exodus 25:30)*

Leviticus 24:5 reveals that twelve loaves total were placed upon the table, each representing one of the twelve tribes of Israel. The priests were instructed to partake of it as part of the atonement ritual; however, bread had to be on the table at all times. So Sabbath, freshly baked bread replaced the old. Though scholars are not sure of the significance of this ritual, most agree that it was an opportunity for the priests to give thanks to God for His provisions.

THE TIES THAT BIND

Years later, David violated this sacred law. On the run for his life, he entered the tabernacle as a hiding place, tired and famished, and shocked the priests by demanding they give him this holy bread to eat.

> *And David said unto Ahimelech the priest. . . . Now therefore what is under thine hand? give me five loaves of bread in mine hand, or what there is present. And the priest answered David, and said, There is no common bread under mine hand, but there is hallowed bread. . . . And David answered the priest, and said unto him . . . and the vessels of the young men are holy, and the bread is in a manner common, yea, though it were sanctified this day in the vessel. So the priest gave him hallowed bread: for there was no bread there but the shewbread, that was taken from before the LORD, to put hot bread in the day when it was taken away. (1 Samuel 21:2-6)*

Jesus would later reference this event when the Pharisees rebuked His disciples for plucking ears of corn on the Sabbath (which they considered work):

> *But he said unto them, Have ye not read what David did, when he was an hungred, and they that were with him; How he entered into the house of God, and did eat the shewbread, which was not lawful for him to eat, neither for them which were with him, but only for the priests? (Matthew 12:3-4)*

The bread, like God's presence, was off-limits during Old Testament days to all but a select few—the priests. However David had the godly authority to come in and partake of it. And it was through his seed that Christ would come into the world to make the Bread of Life available to us all.

EXODUS 25:31-40

The Menorah

> *And thou shalt make a candlestick of pure gold: of beaten work shall the candlestick be made: his shaft, and his branches, his bowls, his knops, and his flowers, shall be of the same. And six branches shall come out of the sides of it; three branches of the candlestick out of the one side, and three branches of the candlestick out of the other side: . . . Their knops and their branches shall be of the same: all it shall be one beaten work of pure gold. (Exodus 25:31-32, 36)*

The menorah (a word that never appears in the Bible) is the definitive symbol of Judaism, rivaled only perhaps by the Star of David. This ornate candelabrum contains a central candlestick, with six more on each side jutting out from beneath—seven total (God's perfect number). The Levitical priests were charged with keeping it lit at all times. The Bible indicates that the menorah was to symbolize the Word of God as the light to the world.

> *I have looked, and behold a candlestick all of gold, with a bowl upon the top of it, and his seven lamps thereon, and seven pipes to the seven lamps, which are upon the top thereof: . . . Then the angel that talked with me answered and said unto me, Knowest thou not what these be? And I said, No, my lord. Then he answered and spake unto me, saying, This is the word of the L*ORD *unto Zerubbabel, saying, Not by might, nor by power, but by my spirit, saith the L*ORD *of hosts. (Zechariah 4:2, 5-6)*

Although it remained in use through the years of the tabernacle and the first and second temples, the original seven-stick menorah no longer appears in Judaism, due to a tradition that nothing should be copied from the second temple after its destruction.[164]

In the early second century AD, the wicked Seleucid king Antiochus Epiphanes ruthlessly attacked Jerusalem, which had no army at the time. His forces were extreme in their cruelty as they sieged the city and slaughtered thousands of defenseless Jews. Women and children's bodies filled the streets. He desecrated the temple, erecting a statue of himself and demanding worship as god. He also commanded every copy of the Torah burned.

Antiochus also killed the high priest, which proved the final straw for one of his sons, Judah Maccabeus. Against all odds, Judah led an uprising against the king in what would be a bitter struggle for Judea's independence. Hopelessly outnumbered, his ragtag band of fighters slowly prevailed, and with God on their side, eventually beat back one of the world's most powerful armies.

In the climactic final battle, seven thousand Jewish fighters crushed sixty-thousand Seleucid warriors, and in 139 BC, Antiochus's forces finally retreated.[165] The Jews erupted in cheers at their newly won freedom and began rebuilding their ruined city. The most important part of this rebirth of Judaism was the removal of statues of the Greek gods and rededication of the temple to Yahweh. This would include relighting the sacred menorah, but according to tradition, they only had enough oil to last one day and one night (Jewish law required a continual burning for the temple to be cleansed of idolatry).[166] Through prayer, one cruise of oil managed to keep the candles burning continuously for *eight days.* Every year, these eight days commemorating the miracle of the oil is still celebrated as Hanukkah, one of Judaism's most important holidays. Lighting the nine-stick menorah (one candle representing the original menorah, the other eight reflecting the nights of the festival) has become a celebration not just of Jewish independence but an act of defiance against every attempt to destroy them over the years.

The light of the menorah has come to represent Jewish sovereignty, a fulfillment of Isaiah 49:6:

> *And he said, It is a light thing that thou shouldest be my servant to raise up the tribes of Jacob, and to restore the preserved of Israel: I will also give thee for a light to the Gentiles, that thou mayest be my salvation unto the end of the earth.*

At times that light has been nearly snuffed out as the darkness around it grows greater; but so long as there are Jews to keep the menorah going, the seed of Abraham survives. It is a reflection not just on Antiochus' cruel attacks but the Roman armies that destroyed the temple, the Holocaust, and the promise of Iran's mullahs to wipe Israel off the map. They endure.

These events are chronicled in both the Jewish Talmud and the book of Maccabees, which is part of the Apocrypha, a collection of books written during the centuries between the Old and New Testaments. The Apocrypha is part of the Catholic Bible but was never accepted by Protestants because the Jews never canonized it as official scripture.

Hanukkah, on the other hand, it sometimes scoffed at by Christians as the Jewish alternative to Christmas, since both are in December. However there is nothing anti-Christian about Hanukkah's message. (In fact, John 10:22 indicates that Jesus Himself celebrated it.) I think that the oil burning so bright in the menorah represents the Holy Spirit that will supply our need many times over, no matter how great it is. And if the glow of the menorah symbolizes the nation of Israel being a light to the nations, the burning flame of the Holy Ghost within us all should be the light to this sinful world.

> *Ye are the light of the world. A city that is set on an hill cannot be hid. (Matthew 5:14)*

EXODUS 26:1-30

The Tabernacle

> *Moreover thou shalt make the tabernacle with ten curtains of fine twined linen, and blue, and purple, and scarlet: with cherubims of cunning work shalt thou make them. (Exodus 26:1)*

The menorah, the showbread, and the Ark are all just pieces of a larger puzzle. The tabernacle would be the actual place that housed the presence of God. No place had existed like this before. Every act of worship in the Bible had been out in the open, before altars, constructed under desert skies. Moses' experience on Mount Sinai was the dawn of many things now recognizable with monotheism. We have the first written law of God, the beginning of many powerful symbols of worship, and now the first place that could fairly be called "God's house." In essence, the tabernacle was the first church.

If you're curious about the difference between the tabernacle and the temple, the tabernacle was a large, elaborate tent. Its canvasses, made out of dyed animal skins, formed the walls, and the exact dimensions and colors of each were given explicitly by God. The Israelites were to offer atonement every time they set camp. Since Jesus hadn't yet come, animals had to be sacrificed and their blood sprinkled on the altar as a temporary cover for the sins of the people.

> *Neither by the blood of goats and calves, but by his [Christ's] own blood he entered in once into the holy place, having obtained eternal redemption for us. (Hebrews 9:12)*

Like the later temple, the tabernacle consisted of an outer court where the priests would go through sacrificial ceremonies before the altar, washing and keeping the menorah lit. Each curtain forming the walls would hang from tent framing by fifty rings (coinciding with the fifty days from the Passover to God giving the law).

> *And thou shalt make loops of blue upon the edge of the one curtain from the selvedge in the coupling; and likewise shalt thou make in the uttermost edge of another curtain, in the coupling of the second. (Exodus 26:4)*

The tabernacle was only supposed to be a temporary mobile shelter for God's presence while the wanderers had no home. But in a sad show of lack of dedication, they failed to build a permanent temple after conquering the Promised Land. The tabernacle was stationed in Shiloh (Joshua 18:1) and served as a makeshift temple for many generations. Israelites would gather here every Day of Atonement for years until it would eventually get old, faded, and torn by the harsh climate. It (and the city of Shiloh itself) was destroyed by the Philistines in the same battle where they took the Ark, leading to the deaths of Eli and his two sons. This was referenced by the prophet Jeremiah hundreds of years later, while warning that if God's people didn't repent of their idolatry, their beloved temple would suffer the same fate.

> *Then will I make this house like Shiloh, and will make this city a curse to all the nations of the earth. (Jeremiah 26:6)*

God's presence would not have a long-term dwelling place until a temple was finally built by King Solomon (about 986 BC).

EXODUS 26:31-37

The Veil

> *And thou shalt make a vail of blue, and purple, and scarlet, and fine twined linen of cunning work: with cherubims shall it be made. (Exodus 26:31)*

The veil separated the outer court from the inner room, the Holiest of Holies. The Ark itself contained the original tablets of the Ten Commandments, a pot of manna, and Aaron's rod.

> *Which had the golden censer, and the ark of the covenant overlaid round about with gold, wherein was the golden pot that had manna, and Aaron's rod that budded, and the tables of the covenant. (Hebrews 9:4)*

The three colors of the veil are significant. The top section was blue (the same color as Aaron's ephod), representing the sky, or heavens (and according to the earlier theory, the Holy Spirit). The bottom section was scarlet red, like the blood that had been shed for atonement. The middle was purple, which is formed by mixing blue and red together, indicating a union between the two (heaven and earth coming together). While it served as a barrier between God and man, it also had the double meaning as an entryway to where the two would be joined together.

THE TIES THAT BIND

When Jesus was crucified, the veil in the temple was torn down.

> *Jesus, when he had cried again with a loud voice, yielded up the ghost. And, behold, the veil of the temple was rent in twain from the top to the bottom; and the earth did quake, and the rocks rent. (Matthew 27:50-51)*

According to Josephus, the veil was four inches thick and so strong that no human or animal could tear it apart. As high as it was, only something supernatural could have ripped it from the top down. Christ's death signified that the partition between God and man was gone; and now His presence is fully available for all.

So any veils separating us from the Lord are put up by us, not Him.

> *Behold, the Lord's hand is not shortened, that it cannot save; neither his ear heavy, that it cannot hear: But your iniquities have separated between you and your God, and your sins have hid his face from you, that he will not hear. (Isaiah 59:1-2)*

Christians often wonder why God won't answer their prayers, while refusing to examine what veils they themselves have erected that stop Him from hearing them.

Anything can be a veil; it can be as terrible as sin or as seemingly harmless as fellowshipping with unsaved loved ones. It all has to come down; but as we learned, only God could tear down the veil. We cannot tear down the veils in our own lives but must yield to the Holy Spirit so He can do it for us.

> *Nevertheless when it shall turn to the Lord, the vail shall be taken away. (2 Corinthians 3:16)*

One day there will be no more veils. Either we can tear them down today, or they will be torn down for us on the Day of Judgment. Even in the Old Testament, Isaiah knew that day would come that all would be revealed.

And he will destroy in this mountain the face of the covering cast over all people, and the vail that is spread over all nations. (Isaiah 25:7)

As Christians, let us all come together and let the veils down, so that nothing will stand between us and God's presence!

EXODUS 27:1-21
The Altar and the Outer Court

And thou shalt make an altar of shittim wood, five cubits long, and five cubits broad; the altar shall be foursquare: and the height thereof shall be three cubits. (Exodus 27:1)

God now gives the details of the outer court, where the altar and menorah were located. The altar was to be foursquare, five cubits long and wide and three cubits high.

These details are consistent with how altars were constructed by children of Abraham. The cube is a powerful symbol in Judaism, representing God's power and perfection. First of all, it is an unnatural creation. Straight lines do not appear anywhere in nature. Only a thinking being can create a perfect line, and therefore, a square.

THE TIES THAT BIND

During his journeys, Abraham built at least five altars, each one marking a significant event in his life (Genesis 12, 13, and 22). This is why the Holiest of Holies was a perfect cube—the same width and height.

And he made the most holy house, the length whereof was according to the breadth of the house, twenty cubits, and the breadth thereof twenty cubits. (2 Chronicles 3:8)

When John received the revelation of the end times, he saw the New Jerusalem coming down to Earth.

And I John saw the holy city, new Jerusalem, coming down from God out of heaven, prepared as a bride adorned for her husband. (Revelation 21:2)

This is the city where we will permanently reside with God, and it too is perfectly cube shaped.

And the city lieth foursquare, and the length is as large as the breadth: and he measured the city with the reed, twelve thousand furlongs. The length and the breadth and the height of it are equal. (Revelation 21:16)

That translates to fifteen hundred miles wide, long, and high.

A clear connection can be made between the Holiest of Holies and the New Jerusalem. The innermost chamber was the place where the presence of God dwelt the strongest, and the heavenly city will be the place in the universe where God will sit and be made one with His people.

> *For we are members of his body, of his flesh, and of his bones. (Ephesians 5:30)*

What do all of these symbolic squares in the Bible have in common?

> *The stone which the builders refused is become the head stone of the corner. (Psalm 118:22)*

Jesus was the stone that the builders rejected, the perfect cornerstone upon which the church is built. He is the firm foundation where our feet are planted. Nothing built on Him can fall.

> *And thou shalt make the court of the tabernacle: for the south side southward there shall be hangings for the court of fine twined linen of an hundred cubits long for one side: . . . The length of the court shall be an hundred cubits, and the breadth fifty every where, and the height five cubits of fine twined linen, and their sockets of brass. (Exodus 27:9, 18)*

God commanded the outer court to have a western, eastern, southern, and northern section, and gave the exact dimensions for each, followed by the total size. There are still two very important furnishings to the tabernacle yet to be mentioned, though.

EXODUS 28:1-43

The Priestly Garments

> *And thou shalt make holy garments for Aaron thy brother for glory and for beauty. And thou shalt speak unto all that are wise hearted, whom I have filled with the spirit of wisdom, that they may make Aaron's garments to consecrate him, that he may minister unto me in the priest's office. (Exodus 28:2-3)*

Aaron was the assigned high priest, one of the most sacred titles in the Old Testament. The rest of the priesthood consisted of his four sons: Nadab, Abihu, Eleazar, and Ithamar. This was the team who would go through the rituals of sacrifice. They had particular clothing that God wanted them to wear for the task—and important symbolism can also be found from studying the details of the priestly garments.

> *And these are the garments which they shall make; a breastplate, and an ephod, and a robe, and a broidered coat, a mitre, and a girdle: and they*

shall make holy garments for Aaron thy brother, and his sons, that he may minister unto me in the priest's office. (Exodus 28:4)

God gave the exact colors of each aspect of the priestly garments (the ephod, robe, broidered coat, girdle, and shoulder pieces) and what material they should be made of (fine linen). For this study, I want to focus specifically on the breastplate, though.

And thou shalt make the breastplate of judgment with cunning work; after the work of the ephod thou shalt make it; of gold, of blue, and of purple, and of scarlet, and of fine twined linen, shalt thou make it. (Exodus 28:15)

And thou shalt set in it settings of stones, even four rows of stones: the first row shall be a sardius, a topaz, and a carbuncle: this shall be the first row. And the second row shall be an emerald, a sapphire, and a diamond. And the third row a ligure, an agate, and an amethyst. And the fourth row a beryl, and an onyx, and a jasper: they shall be set in gold in their inclosings. (Exodus 28:17-20)

Aaron's breastplate was to have four rows of stones, each consisting of three—twelve stones total. The top row had a line of sardine, topaz, and carbuncle. The second row consisted of emerald, sapphire, and diamond. The third row was ligure, agate, and amethyst, while the fourth row was beryl, onyx, and jasper. Each represented one of the twelve tribes of Israel.

And Aaron shall bear the names of the children of Israel in the breastplate of judgment upon his heart, when he goeth in unto the holy place, for a memorial before the LORD continually. (Exodus 28:29)

THE TIES THAT BIND

Three of these stones stand out because they make a very particular appearance in the New Testament. In Revelation 4, John was swept up into a spectacular vision and immediately recognized Christ sitting on the throne of God.

And immediately I was in the spirit: and, behold, a throne was set in heaven, and one sat on the throne. (Revelation 4:2)

Yet when John described the sight, he invoked a curiously detailed image in verse 3:

And he that sat was to look upon like a jasper and a sardine stone: and there was a rainbow round about the throne, in sight like unto an emerald. (Revelation 4:3)

We can point to Aaron's breastplate, and the order of the stones, to figure out which tribes of Israel these descriptions were referencing. The jasper, the final stone, represents Benjamin, the last tribe of Israel. Jasper is clear and represents knowledge and understanding. In this final hour, God gives supernatural revelations of Himself and His nature from the Word. This is an exciting time to be a Christian, as He makes His divinity clearer for us!

The emerald rainbow hearkens back to the emerald stone, which symbolizes the tribe of Judah. It is brilliant and green, symbolizing life itself. One can't stare into it without the mind wandering into the beautiful greenery of Eden. Judah was the tribe through which Jesus would come into the world.

The sardine stone, a breathtaking deep red, coincides with the tribe of Reuben. Reuben was the eldest son of Jacob, and the stone symbolizes the blood of Jesus.

The connection is clear. Jesus was being foreshadowed in Aaron's breastplate, and this prophecy was fulfilled when He appeared before John in Revelation. The three stones represent the blood, life, and revelation. Jesus came to bring us all three. It's even evident in the names of the tribes that the stones were pointing the way to Christ. Reuben means "Behold the Son," while Benjamin means "Son of my right hand." Jesus sits at the right hand of the Father. It's noteworthy that the three stones symbolizing Him in order were the first, middle, and last.

> *And thou shalt put in the breastplate of judgment the Urim and the Thummim; and they shall be upon Aaron's heart, when he goeth in before the* LORD*: and Aaron shall bear the judgment of the children of Israel upon his heart before the* LORD *continually. (Exodus 28:30)*

The urim and thummim are two tantalizing mysteries from the Word of God, perhaps for no more reason than that they are barely mentioned. This naturally piques curiosity and has sparked all sorts of legends about these seemingly mystical objects. Exodus does not define what exactly they are; all we know is that they were stored in Aaron's breastplate and were to be cast like lots in seeking answers when God hadn't spoken clearly. (Personally, I see this as Moses, years in advance, preparing for his own inevitable death. Since no one else in the camp was as close to God as he was, he recognized the possibility that his successors wouldn't be as able to receive divine revelation.) Were they stones? Sticks? Did they have words on them? How was casting these two objects supposed to reveal an answer from God? Was it how they landed? Some mystics have suggested that perhaps they glowed or had magical powers.

We're not even sure of the exact meaning of their names; some translate *urim* and *thummim* as "light" and "dark," others as "cursing" and "blessing."[167] The Bible gives very little record of them ever being used. It's briefly mentioned that Saul got no answer from them in seeking guidance on what he should do about the approaching Philistine armies.

> *And when Saul enquired of the* LORD, *the* LORD *answered him not, neither by dreams, nor by Urim, nor by prophets. (1 Samuel 28:6)*

This would lead him to seek out the Witch of Endor, where his doom was sealed.

Seventy years after Jerusalem was conquered by Nebuchadnezzar of Babylon, the Jews were allowed to return to their homeland. The long trek across the wilderness is sometimes called the "second Exodus" and is the backdrop of the books of Ezra and Nehemiah. After making it back to the Promised Land, they then had to rebuild a ruined city that had been decaying in the desert for decades. Upon completing the new temple, they set about trying to reestablish the priesthood. However the lineage of Aaron and his descendants had been long lost, so Ezra consulted the urim and thummim.

> *These sought their register among those that were reckoned by genealogy, but they were not found: therefore were they, as polluted, put from the priesthood. And the Tirshatha said unto them, that they should not eat of the most holy things, till there stood up a priest with Urim and with Thummim. (Ezra 2:62-63)*

After this, the urim and thummim are never mentioned in the Bible again. Like the Ark of the Covenant, they disappeared into the unforgiving winds of biblical archaeology, relegated to long-lost mysterious objects that may never be found or understood fully. The ancient scripture is our only true record of their existence, for us to ponder and wonder about but never to truly know in their fullness.

EXODUS 29:1-46

The Sacrifices of Consecration

> *And this is the thing that thou shalt do unto them to hallow them, to minister unto me in the priest's office: Take one young bullock, and two rams without blemish, And unleavened bread, and cakes unleavened tempered with oil, and wafers unleavened anointed with oil: of wheaten flour shalt thou make them. (Exodus 29:1-2)*

Animal sacrifice is never pleasant to read about. Personally, I'm an animal lover. While I'll admit to occasionally enjoying steak or bacon, I've never been hunting, and I can't stand to see God's creatures suffer. I find Exodus 29 difficult to study for this very reason. The priest's job was tough, to say the least. I couldn't imagine holding a precious little lamb before the altar, while it perhaps tried to nuzzle in my arms, knowing that I'm about to slice the poor thing's throat. That said, I can't blame God for this unpleasant ritual; it's the price that had to be paid for man's sin.

But God also never delighted in animal sacrifice; while it paid the necessary atonement, the Bible is clear that it stank in His nostrils and He had every intention of ending it once the price had been paid by Christ.

> *To what purpose is the multitude of your sacrifices unto me? saith the LORD: I am full of the burnt offerings of rams, and the fat of fed beasts; and I delight not in the blood of bullocks, or of lambs, or of he goats. (Isaiah 1:11)*

The particular sacrifice described in this chapter involves consecrating the priest. Being a representative of God's people was a sacred role to take on and the priests had to be pure, holy, and consecrated. This required three distinct sacrifices laid out in verses 1-2: one young bull and two spotless lambs.

> *And thou shalt kill the bullock before the LORD, by the door of the tabernacle of the congregation. And thou shalt take of the blood of the bullock, and put it upon the horns of the altar with thy finger, and pour all the blood beside the bottom of the altar. (Exodus 29:11-12)*

The sacrifice had to be made at the altar outside of the tabernacle, which housed the Lord's presence; likewise, Jesus was forsaken by the Father as He was sacrificed on the cross.

> *And about the ninth hour Jesus cried with a loud voice, saying, Eli, Eli, lama sabachthani? that is to say, My God, my God, why hast thou forsaken me? (Matthew 27:46)*

The earth had just gone dark because God turned His back on the sight of His Son dying; it was the only way the plan of salvation could be complete without wiping out the human race for what it was doing.

First the bull had to be killed before the door of the tabernacle. Then the blood was taken inside and poured at the bottom of the altar. The innards were burned as a sin offering. The stench must have been horrendous, but this served as a reminder of how sin smells to God. A second offering, the flesh and dung, was burned outside the camp. The same process was repeated with the first ram.

> *Then shalt thou kill the ram, and take of his blood, and put it upon the tip of the right ear of Aaron, and upon the tip of the right ear of his sons, and upon the thumb of their right hand, and upon the great toe of their right foot, and sprinkle the blood upon the altar round about. (Exodus 29:20)*

THE PRACTICAL APPLICATION

This particular ritual was unique to the priests. Once killed, the ram's blood was put on the tip of Aaron's ear and the ears of his sons. The blood of

Jesus is more than just our deliverance from sin. It is also our direct access to the throne of God and our greatest weapon against the devil.

> *And they overcame him [Satan] by the blood of the Lamb, and by the word of their testimony; and they loved not their lives unto the death. (Revelation 12:11)*

The blood on the tip of the ear represents listening to God whenever He's ready to speak. The blood on the thumb of the right hand (remember, Jesus sits at the right hand of the Father) indicates being willing to act and do whatever God wants you to do. The blood on the toe of the right food represents being willing to go wherever He sends you.

In the Old Testament, this privilege was only available for the priests. But in the New Testament age, it no longer requires the blood of bulls or rams. In the ritual of consecration God puts us through, the blood of Jesus is applied to our ears, our hands, and our feet. We are able to hear the Father's voice directly and are immediately ready to go forth and do His work. Every one of us is a priest with His Word, being sent forth to preach the gospel unto every creature. This is the supreme calling of every Christian, and we should treat it with the same sacredness as the high priests.

> *And Aaron and his sons shall eat the flesh of the ram, and the bread that is in the basket by the door of the tabernacle of the congregation. And they shall eat those things wherewith the atonement was made, to consecrate and to sanctify them: but a stranger shall not eat thereof, because they are holy. (Exodus 29:32-33)*

Nothing was to go to waste, so the priests would then eat the remaining meat with the anointed showbread. But verse 33 is significant because it verifies that as an Old Testament ritual, only anointed people could partake of it. This is further demonstrated by verse 37:

> *Seven days thou shalt make an atonement for the altar, and sanctify it; and it shall be an altar most holy: whatsoever toucheth the altar shall be holy. (Exodus 29:37)*

The ritual of consecration for the priests was to be made every day for seven days. That meant one bull being sacrificed each day as well as a lamb in the mornings, afternoon, and evenings, according to verses 39-42. The altar was holy and could only be touched by the priests. But the cry for the New Testament age is for all to come and fall onto God's holy altar to receive forgiveness for our sins.

> *The Lord is not slack concerning his promise, as some men count slackness; but is longsuffering to us-ward, not willing that any should perish, but that all should come to repentance. (2 Peter 3:9)*

The Lord promises that if the children of Israel will continue with this ritual of atonement, His presence will be there to meet them every time to answer any needs they have.

> *And there I will meet with the children of Israel, and the tabernacle shall be sanctified by my glory. . . . And I will dwell among the children of Israel, and will be their God. (Exodus 29:43, 45)*

In the end, as gruesome as the rituals of atonement were, I'm simply grateful that we live in an age where Jesus paid the price. Just like the terrible punishments for violating the law, we have to place this in proper historical context. Critics like to say that God must be a savage creature to demand animals be sacrificed to appease His wrath; but at the time, this was far more enlightened than other cultures. Animal sacrifice was terrible but not as terrible as human sacrifice. It's what set the God of the Israelites apart from the false gods of the Canaanites.

The other thing that amazes me, though, is how complicated every rite and ritual in Old Testament times was. The amount of effort, from the dress to the slaughter to the pouring of oil, for seven days in a row, is mind-boggling. But not only is this privilege available to all, thanks to Christ, it is also much simpler. Somehow, the complex ceremonies all pointed the way to today's salvation plan; and yet, salvation is a free and simple gift. All it takes is believing on Jesus, and God takes care of the rest. You don't have to put the blood on your ears or thumbs; He does that for you. You don't have to pour the oil; He gives the Holy Ghost for you. How the priests surely would have loved the opportunity to receive all that God has with so little effort! And yet so many won't take advantage of it.

EXODUS 30:1-10

The Incense

> *And thou shalt make an altar to burn incense upon: of shittim wood shalt thou make it. (Exodus 30:1)*

Because different dimensions are listed in verses 2-5, this was clearly a separate altar from the one used for the blood sacrifices. It was to be placed by the veil.

> *And thou shalt put it before the vail that is by the ark of the testimony, before the mercy seat that is over the testimony, where I will meet with thee. (Exodus 30:6)*

The fire was never to go out, according to Leviticus 6:13:

> *The fire shall ever be burning upon the altar; it shall never go out.*

Since the incense is also a type and shadow of the Holy Ghost, we should take this scripture to heart. I'm afraid the fire has been going out of the Pentecostal churches for some years now. Is it going out on the altar of your soul? When was the last time you were filled with the Holy Ghost? If we reject the doctrine of "once-saved, always saved," we shouldn't believe in "once-filled, always-filled," either. Tongues should flow from our lips like living waters.

And Aaron shall burn thereon sweet incense every morning: when he dresseth the lamps, he shall burn incense upon it. (Exodus 30:7)

The incense would produce a sweet smell before the Lord, and He made it clear that this was not temporary—but a fire that should be kept burning throughout the generations.

And when Aaron lighteth the lamps at even, he shall burn incense upon it, a perpetual incense before the LORD throughout your generations. (Exodus 30:8)

How sad that so many Christians think the Holy Ghost was just for the early church and has no place today! That is completely contradicted by scripture.

Then Peter said unto them, Repent, and be baptized every one of you in the name of Jesus Christ for the remission of sins, and ye shall receive the gift of the Holy Ghost. For the promise is unto you, and to your children, and to all that are afar off, even as many as the LORD our God shall call. (Acts 2:38-39)

Ye shall offer no strange incense thereon, nor burnt sacrifice, nor meat offering; neither shall ye pour drink offering thereon. (Exodus 30:9)

The incense was so crucial to the ceremony that the Lord even specified the ingredients of the oil that would fuel it. The recipe was not to be tampered with. Anything else would produce a strange odor in the nostrils of God.

THE TIES THAT BIND

Unfortunately, as soon as the tabernacle rituals started, two of Aaron's sons did just that.

And Nadab and Abihu, the sons of Aaron, took either of them his censer, and put fire therein, and put incense thereon, and offered strange fire before the Lord, which he commanded them not. (Leviticus 10:1)

The fire in their censers burned from oil not made from the sacred ingredients listed in Exodus 30. This could have been either ignorance or laziness, but they clearly just threw it together, thinking, *We don't need to add this, it's just oil. God won't know the difference.* Isn't this typical of the attitude so many bring to church today? They come to His house with indifference. God has strict instructions for what should burn on the altars of our souls, but many throw in sin or worldliness that creates a foul odor to Him.

Every morning, the Lord looked forward to the sweet smell burning from the holy oil. It filled the tabernacle with the fragrance of His glory. But this time, something was different. The smell of blasphemy lingered in the air.

> *And there went out fire from the Lord, and devoured them, and they died before the Lord. (Leviticus 10:2)*

This was the fire of judgment, the same sulfurous brimstone that incinerated Sodom and Gomorrah. It was the fire of hell, and once it destroyed them, it filled the tabernacle with the putrid stench of death.

The sin of Nadab and Abihu was so great that the priests recovering them were not even allowed to touch their charred, smoking skeletons:

> *And Moses called Mishael and Elzaphan, and said unto them, Come near, carry your brethren from before the sanctuary out of the camp. So they went near, and carried them in their coats out of the camp; as Moses had said. (Leviticus 10:4-5)*

Moses realized that the camp was in a state of emergency. In verse 3, he immediately warned Aaron to say nothing in protest, even though his sons had just been killed, because God's wrath would fall on him next. Then, after the bodies were removed, he instructed Aaron, Eleazar, and Ithamar to go back in with their heads covered and reanoint and rededicate everything.

> *And ye shall not go out from the door of the tabernacle of the congregation, lest ye die: for the anointing oil of the Lord is upon you. And they did according to the word of Moses. (Leviticus 10:7)*

Later, in Numbers 16, Korah led a rebellion against Moses' leadership. Moses responded by offering Korah a challenge:

> *This do; Take you censers, Korah, and all his company; And put fire therein, and put incense in them before the Lord to morrow: and it shall be that the man whom the Lord doth choose, he shall be holy. (Numbers 16:6-7)*

Moses and Korah would each offer their own incense, and the Lord Himself would choose the leader.

The next morning, the two groups set up their offerings; but a strange fire burnt from Korah's censer, and God did not hesitate. The ground opened up, and all those who offered it fell into the earth where they were engulfed in hell for all eternity. The Israelites who had gathered to watch ran and screamed in terror.

> *And the earth opened her mouth, and swallowed them up, and their houses, and all the men that appertained unto Korah, and all their goods. They, and all that appertained to them, went down alive into the pit, and the earth closed upon them: and they perished from among the congregation. (Numbers 16:32-33)*

THE PRACTICAL APPLICATION

The strange fires offered by the sons of Aaron and Korah represent speaking in tongues at will. The real Baptism of the Holy Ghost is pure and holy, the genuine flame that fell on the Day of Pentecost. When you are completely surrendered, He will have His way as long as He wants.

> *Quench not the Spirit. (1 Thessalonians 5:19)*

But the devil has a counterfeit of every gift of God. I've seen it on TV. People speak gibberish into the air, "warming-up" their services with fake tongues. They tell members seeking the Baptism to "repeat after me" as if the real Holy Ghost can be taught. It's not a switch we can turn on and off. They are offering strange fire before the Lord. It may sound like the Spirit, but the incense offered by Nadab and Abihu looked real too. It may fool others, but you can't fool God.

When the Spirit is removed, flesh always takes over. The Pentecostal churches are replacing the true fire with strobe lights, the cloud of His glory with fog machines, and genuine dancing in the Spirit with choreographed moves. The holiness of old-time Pentecostalism has been reduced to a feel-good secular rock concert; we are offering strange fires before Him. The fates of Nadab, Abihu, and Korah serve as ominous warnings for those who play around with the Holy Ghost.

EXODUS 30:10-16

Yom Kippur and the Ransom Money

> *And Aaron shall make an atonement upon the horns of it once in a year with the blood of the sin offering of atonements: once in the year shall he make atonement upon it throughout your generations: it is most holy unto the LORD. (Exodus 30:10)*

According to tradition, the first Day of Atonement took place after Moses brought the law from Sinai and found Aaron and the Israelites worshiping the golden calf. The order for this holiday had already been given, but the grievous sin of the people mandated that the first atonement be immediately afterwards. The modern holiday of Yom Kippur typically falls on "the 10th Day of Tishrei," according to the lunar calendar, right after the Jewish New Year, Rosh Hashanah.[168]

We've covered the traditions of the Day of Atonement pretty thoroughly. However the casual reader is left with a puzzling question I've been asked while teaching some of my classes: Since the law requires animal sacrifice, why do the Jews no longer observe it?

There really is no easy answer, as this serves as a moral dilemma for modern (rabbinical) Judaism. According to the law, sacrifice could only be made in the tabernacle, followed by Solomon's temple. This is why Israelites would make the pilgrimage to Jerusalem every year. But Solomon's temple was destroyed by Nebuchadnezzar's army in 586 BC. The Ark of the Covenant played an important role in the rituals of atonement, and as a symbol of the physical presence of God, its disappearance was devastating. After the Jews returned to their homeland from the Babylonian exile, they rebuilt the temple under Ezra and Nehemiah's leadership, launching the Second Temple period.

However the Ark was and is still missing. Some returning Jews were angry at the audacity of restarting the Day of Atonement without the Ark and refused to participate. We have record of a secretive cult of radical Jews called the Essenes who formed a community at the city of Qumran next to the Dead Sea. The Essenic Jews fought hard to preserve what they considered a purer form of Judaism, keeping to themselves and thoroughly copying the Old Testament books for future preservation. For centuries, they hid these scrolls in the caves around the Dead Sea to be discovered many thousands of years later as the Dead Sea Scrolls.

Whether or not is was blasphemous, the Jews still made sacrifices at Yom Kippur every year throughout the entire Second Temple period, including the life of Christ. In AD 70, however, the second temple was destroyed by the Roman emperor Titus, and the Jews were scattered all throughout the empire, never to see their homeland again. It wouldn't be until 1949, in the aftermath of the Holocaust, that they regathered and the nation of Israel was reborn (but they are still missing the Ark, and the Muslim Dome of the Rock mosque is where the temple once stood).

The dispersed Jews had to revise their approach to the Day of Atonement. With the temple gone, they could no longer come to offer animal sacrifices. (Christians argue that Christ's death was sufficient for God to put a stop to the practice.) Their adopted mindset was to consider the Day of Atonement less about a temple ritual and more about a personal atonement. Jews typically spend the week before Yom Kippur forsaking all earthly pleasures and focusing intensely on prayer and fasting for forgiveness of their sins. Until the temple can be restored, this will have to do.

MOUNT SINAI

> *And the LORD spake unto Moses, saying, When thou takest the sum of the children of Israel after their number, then shall they give every man a ransom for his soul unto the LORD, when thou numberest them; that there be no plague among them, when thou numberest them. (Exodus 30:11-12)*

If the tabernacle was the first church, this was the first offering. Taking part in the rituals would require a price, and that money was considered a gift to God. In the future, King Josiah would cleverly use the same principle to pay for the temple renovations (2 Chronicles 34-36). God referred to this as a "ransom" paid for each and every soul. He ordered a census to make sure all had contributed the appropriate amount (this will be covered in the following book of Numbers, hence the name).

If it sounds terrible that God would count our souls worth a value of money, consider the upside: each and every gift you give to the church, He can take and use to win souls to His kingdom. Imagine meeting people in heaven approaching you to say, "Thank you." They're there because of each little gift you gave, even the ones you had forgotten about. We were all bought with a price at Calvary, which is why Isaiah calls us the "ransomed of the Lord."

> *And the ransomed of the LORD shall return, and come to Zion with songs and everlasting joy upon their heads: they shall obtain joy and gladness, and sorrow and sighing shall flee away. (Isaiah 35:10)*

> *Every one that passeth among them that are numbered, from twenty years old and above, shall give an offering unto the LORD. (Exodus 30:14)*

While many churches require tithing, giving in the offering plate is usually optional. When people complain about being expected to give, we should point out to them that under the Mosaic law, it was mandatory.

The concept of biblical tithing is first found in Genesis 14. Abraham was either accepted or rejected by local cities during his travels. Melchizedek, king of Salem, was not only a ruler but a priest to the same God.

> *And Melchizedek king of Salem brought forth bread and wine: and he was the priest of the most high God. And he blessed him, and said, Blessed be Abram of the most high God, possessor of heaven and earth. (Genesis 14:18-19)*

"Bringing forth bread and wine" indicates his hospitality towards Abraham. The city of Salem would eventually become Jerusalem, the capital city of Israel. (If you study ancient maps, you'll notice many cities bear a name derivative of "Ur," such as "Uruk" or "Uru." *Ur* is an old Sumerian word for "city." Therefore *Uru-Shalem* means "The City of Shalem").[169] As a priest and king of the most high God, it's no wonder that the city over which Melchizedek ruled would become the center of God's chosen nation.

Abraham gave the king a tenth of everything he owned to show his gratitude.

> *And blessed be the most high God, which hath delivered thine enemies into thy hand. And he gave him tithes of all. (Genesis 14:20)*

Melchizedek preceded the law and even Abraham himself, meaning that he was outside the legal commandment that all priests be Levites. Since Jesus was of the tribe of Judah, He was outside of the Levitical priesthood; yet He is our High Priest before the Father, which is why the Bible refers to Him as the "Priest out of the order of Melchizedek" (Hebrews 7:17).

> *And thou shalt take the atonement money of the children of Israel, and shalt appoint it for the service of the tabernacle of the congregation; that it may be a memorial unto the children of Israel before the LORD, to make an atonement for your souls. (Exodus 30:16)*

THE TIES THAT BIND

If we closely examine the summary of the Old Testament, we notice a disturbing pattern. The Israelites were warned in Exodus that if they worshiped idol gods, the Lord would punish them. Over time it would inevitably happen. The books of the prophets are full of warnings to repent. Finally, He would release His protection, and disaster would befall them.

After returning to Jerusalem to rebuild the temple under Ezra and Nehemiah, they were blessed again for a short while. In fact, idolatry was forsaken for good at this point. Never would they struggle with worshiping idols or erecting pagan altars to sacrifice and eat their own children. But Malachi, the last book of the Old Testament, indicates that their spiritual problems were still not over.

> *Will a man rob God? Yet ye have robbed me. But ye say, Wherein have we robbed thee? In tithes and offerings. (Malachi 3:8)*

Idolatry had been replaced by a new one: greed.

They weren't paying their tithes to the storehouse, and God was angrier about this than He had ever been over idolatry. If they gave in to false gods, judgment could bring them back. But what could God do with greed? I can't help but wonder if the ugly, unfair stereotype of Jews as "greedy" or money-grubbing bankers secretly controlling the world isn't a result of this terrible time.

Once they became greedy and held back their tithes, He simply left them. Malachi is the last book of the Old Testament, and God never spoke to them again. There were no more prophets. No more warnings. Four hundred years would pass between the Old Testament and the arrival of Christ. Perhaps this is an even worse punishment than horrifying judgment: being abandoned by God (seemingly) forever.

THE TIES THAT BIND

This is how serious God is about tithing. If you are being greedy with God's money, you are in extreme danger. He provided you with your income. Tithing isn't giving to God, because it's already His. As long as you keep it, you have a curse over your finances. Treat it like it's radioactive. Some Christians say they don't tithe because they can't afford to. I know it's cliché, but the old saying is still true: they can't afford not to.

Some smart-aleck Christians have pointed out to me that tithing is an Old Testament requirement and not mandated in the New. I counter them by pointing out that they probably don't want to live under the New Testament standards like they think. In Malachi's time, the people *only* gave ten percent. In the New Testament, they gave it all.

> *And all that believed were together, and had all things common; And sold their possessions and goods, and parted them to all men, as every man had need. . . . And laid them down at the apostles' feet: and distribution was made unto every man according as he had need. (Acts 2:44-45; 4:35)*

As they rejoiced, selling all their possessions and laying them down at the apostles' feet, the church lacked for nothing.

Under this great outpouring of glory and finances, Ananias and Sapphira were killed for selling only part of their possessions—keeping the rest and claiming they had given all.

> *But Peter said, Ananias, why hath Satan filled thine heart to lie to the Holy Ghost, and to keep back part of the price of the land? . . . And Ananias hearing these words fell down, and gave up the ghost: and great fear came on all them that heard these things. (Acts 5:3, 5)*

When Christians today question whether or not we're required to tithe, I detect that blasphemous spirit of Ananias and Sapphira lurking under the surface. They better be very careful with their atoning money. Churches need it to continue the Lord's work. This is a dangerous game to play.

EXODUS 30:17-21

The Laver

> *And the LORD spake unto Moses, saying, Thou shalt also make a laver of brass, and his foot also of brass, to wash withal: and thou shalt put it*

> *between the tabernacle of the congregation and the altar, and thou shalt put water therein. (Exodus 30:17-18)*

The laver was a brass tub placed just outside the tabernacle between the altar and the entrance. Like a perfect procession, a ram was sacrificed at the outer altar while the people watched. Then the priests entered the outer court to the brazen altar where the burnt offerings were made. But before they could go through the entrance, they had to wash the blood off, dipping their hands in the water before going inside to perform the rest of the sacred ritual. Death could strike any priest who entered the tabernacle without being completely spotless.

> *For Aaron and his sons shall wash their hands and their feet thereat: When they go into the tabernacle of the congregation, they shall wash with water, that they die not; or when they come near to the altar to minister, to burn offering made by fire unto the LORD: So they shall wash their hands and their feet, that they die not: and it shall be a statute for ever to them, even to him and to his seed throughout their generations. (Exodus 30:19-20)*

THE PRACTICAL APPLICATION

Pentecostals are unique in describing the "three acts of grace": being saved, sanctified, and filled with the Holy Ghost. We consider Calvary the first step in the Christian walk. We place great importance on the Baptism of the Holy Ghost with the initial evidence of speaking in tongues. But we need to be very careful to not let ourselves get the two mixed up, because there is a particular order to God's plan of salvation. Far too many Christians achieve Calvary but never press on to Pentecost, which is spiritual laziness. But trying to bypass Calvary and go straight to Pentecost is fanaticism and not of God.

Fire has a purifying effect. When we put precious metals into fire, it burns out the impurities. The Baptism of the Holy Ghost sets our souls on fire. This is why the burnt offering separated the unclean and the clean parts of the animal. The intestines and dung were taken outside the camp while the cleaner meat was taken into the tabernacle and burned before God. The Holy Spirit's job is to burn out any aspect of our personalities that are not like Christ. But going into the fire is frightening and uncomfortable, which is why so many Christians are afraid of Pentecost and don't want to venture beyond Calvary. They become content to be saved and coast their way into heaven, and this is a dangerous mentality to have.

However, we tend to overlook the process of sanctification, the step between Calvary and Pentecost. Some speak in tongues for the first time shortly after giving their hearts to Jesus, and that's wonderful. But being sanctified has to happen at some point. It's more than just the experience of water baptism, which was clearly foreshadowed by the hand washing in the laver. God will not allow any uncleanness in His presence, and that hasn't changed.

Sanctification is washing away all filth before going into the presence of God. It represents getting rid of everything from which the Lord delivered us. If you're bound by pornography, but get saved at church, you go home and destroy everything that would lead you back into it. If you're delivered from alcoholism, pour out every bottle when you get home, destroying any chance of being tempted to go back into it. A girl who testified at our church once told of being freed from years of drug addiction. After she got saved at a revival, she came home and flushed every drug down the toilet. Her friends would come back to her house, but she would turn out the lights and lock the doors and pray in another room for God to give her strength. All ties had to be cut off. Eventually her so-called friends gave up and left her alone for good. She never did another drug again because of this sanctification process.

We all have to do this once we've come to Jesus, no matter how painful it is. It may require removing things that will hurt so bad, they'll seem like chopping one's own limbs off. Sanctification may even require cutting off friends or family. It's what Jesus meant when He said,

> *And if thy right eye offend thee, pluck it out, and cast it from thee: for it is profitable for thee that one of thy members should perish, and not that thy whole body should be cast into hell. And if thy right hand offend thee, cut it off, and cast it from thee: for it is profitable for thee that one of thy members should perish, and not that thy whole body should be cast into hell. (Matthew 5:29-30)*

This doesn't mean God expects us to literally cut off our own hands or gouge out our own eyes; rather, we must take whatever extreme measures necessary to remove sin from our lives. Hell just simply isn't worth it.

THE TIES THAT BIND

When the tabernacle was replaced by the temple, King Solomon created what was called a molten sea to take the place of the laver.

> *And he made a molten sea, ten cubits from the one brim to the other: it was round all about, and his height was five cubits: and a line of thirty cubits did compass it round about. (1 Kings 7:23)*

This structure was much larger and more magnificent, a humongous tub filled with water, with twelve brass oxen holding it up, three facing each direction. The base was magnificently ornate, decorated with palm trees, angels, and animals.

> *For on the plates of the ledges thereof, and on the borders thereof, he graved cherubims, lions, and palm trees, according to the proportion of every one, and additions round about. (1 Kings 7:36)*

In 2 Corinthians 12, Paul described a vision of what he called the third heaven. While he seems to be explaining that he "knew" someone this had happened to, verse 1 indicates Paul was actually referring to himself.

> *I knew a man in Christ above fourteen years ago, (whether in the body, I cannot tell; or whether out of the body, I cannot tell. . .) . How that he was caught up into paradise, and heard unspeakable words, which it is not lawful for a man to utter. (2 Corinthians 12:2-4)*

He saw heaven and heard "unspeakable words," which could not be repeated to anyone. John would have the same experience years later:

> *And when the seven thunders had uttered their voices, I was about to write: and I heard a voice from heaven saying unto me, Seal up those things which the seven thunders uttered, and write them not. (Revelation 10:4)*

The first heaven is the limits of the earth's atmosphere, just past the sky and clouds. The Word tells us that God uses this to control the weather.

> *The Lord shall open unto thee his good treasure, the heaven to give the rain unto thy land in his season, and to bless all the work of thine hand: and thou shalt lend unto many nations, and thou shalt not borrow. (Deuteronomy 28:12)*

The second heaven is outer space, where He has control over the sun, moon, and stars.

> *The heavens declare the glory of God; and the firmament sheweth his handywork. (Psalm 19:1)*

The third heaven, which Paul and John were both privileged to see, is the holy place where God actually dwells. Here is where the souls of the righteous go after death. Sin cannot enter here. Imagine a gigantic glass barrier standing between the physical universe and the entrance to heaven.

> *And I saw as it were a sea of glass mingled with fire: and them that had gotten the victory over the beast, and over his image, and over his mark, and over the number of his name, stand on the sea of glass, having the harps of God. (Revelation 15:2)*

This "sea of glass" separates the second and third heavens. All impurities must be removed before one can enter the holiness of God.

When the devil appeared before God to accuse Job, I doubt very much that he was allowed beyond the sea of glass.

The tabernacle, then, is a reflection of the throne of God itself. The outer court represented the first heaven, the sky. The inner court symbolized the second heaven, outer space. The third heaven is represented by the Holiest of Holies. A glass barrier stands between the second and third heavens, covering the entrance to heaven itself, and we can see it in the Old Testament in the laver in the tabernacle and the molten sea in the temple, where the priests had to wash off all impurities before crossing over into the holy place.

EXODUS 30:22-38

The Anointing Oil

> *Moreover the Lord spake unto Moses, saying, Take thou also unto thee principal spices, of pure myrrh five hundred shekels, and of sweet cinnamon half so much, even two hundred and fifty shekels, and of sweet calamus two hundred and fifty shekels. (Exodus 30:22-23)*

Today, Christians refer to "the anointing" as the special, heavenly feeling that comes from being touched by God.

> *But the anointing which ye have received of him abideth in you. (1 John 2:27)*

While I love to feel it, I believe we've missed the point when we try focus on it as "feeling" God, forgetting that the Old Testament concept of "anointed" meant "called." Priests or kings had to have the oil poured on their heads, usually by a prophet, signifying they were ready for their calling.

> *And thou shalt make it an oil of holy ointment, an ointment compound after the art of the apothecary: it shall be an holy anointing oil. (Exodus 30:25)*

The anointing oil was usually stored and carried in a ram's horn.

> *And the Lord said unto Samuel, How long wilt thou mourn for Saul, seeing I have rejected him from reigning over Israel? fill thine horn with oil, and go, I will send thee to Jesse the Bethlehemite: for I have provided me a king among his sons. (1 Samuel 16:1)*

Samuel had his oil ready when he met David, and the Lord told him this young man was to be anointed king.

> *Then Samuel took the horn of oil, and anointed him in the midst of his brethren: and the Spirit of the Lord came upon David from that day forward. So Samuel rose up, and went to Ramah. (1 Samuel 16:13)*

The oil was used to anoint the entire tabernacle.

As a summary of everything discussed so far, God listed all the structure and its furnishings in verses 26-28, from the candlesticks to the tent walls to the veil and even the Ark itself.

> *And thou shalt speak unto the children of Israel, saying, This shall be an holy anointing oil unto me throughout your generations. (Exodus 30:31)*

It's clear that the Lord doesn't just want the anointing oil to be used for the time of Moses and Aaron but for all future generations. He would also someday declare that the anointing of the Holy Spirit is a promise to all future generations, not just those that experienced Pentecost.

THE PRACTICAL APPLICATION

As evidence of how the restrictive bonds were broken in the New Testament, anointing oil was used to pray for the sick and perform miracles and healings in the New Testament.

> *Is any sick among you? let him call for the elders of the church; and let them pray over him, anointing him with oil in the name of the Lord. (James 5:14)*

It was no longer reserved for just the priests but for every believer!

There's no reason for this healing power to not be available today. A young couple at my church once had a baby who was unfortunately born with an inoperable tumor on its kidney. After a series of tests, the doctors gave them the devastating news that the baby wouldn't survive more than a few days, and there was nothing they could do. Our congregation gathered together and anointed a blanket with oil, praying over it and believing that God's miracle power would provide a point of contact. The blanket was taken to the hospital and wrapped over the baby while it slept overnight. The next morning, the baby made a miraculous recovery. The doctors redid all the tests to find that the tumor had vanished! They were all stunned and at a loss to explain. The child was taken home and is a happy, healthy, living child today. God is still in the healing business!

EXODUS 32:1-11

Appointing the Craftsmen

> *And the Lord spake unto Moses, saying, See, I have called by name Bezaleel the son of Uri, the son of Hur, of the tribe of Judah: And I have filled him with the spirit of God, in wisdom, and in understanding, and in knowledge, and in all manner of workmanship, To devise cunning*

works, to work in gold, and in silver, and in brass, And in cutting of stones, to set them, and in carving of timber, to work in all manner of workmanship. (Exodus 32:1-5)

Constructing the tabernacle and its furnishings would be a major undertaking, but He had anointed someone for the job. Bezaleel, whose name means "in the shadow of God," was a Judahite.[170] According to 1 Chronicles 2:19-20, he was the grandson of Caleb:

And when Azubah was dead, Caleb took unto him Ephrath, which bare him Hur. And Hur begat Uri, and Uri begat Bezaleel.

We can assume, then, that he was very young at this point in the story but still gifted by God in craftsmanship—in carpentry, masonry, and metalworking. But he didn't just have the perfect skillset; the scripture is clear that He had been filled with the Spirit of God (Exodus 31:2).

And I, behold, I have given with him Aholiab, the son of Ahisamach, of the tribe of Dan: and in the hearts of all that are wise hearted I have put wisdom, that they may make all that I have commanded thee. (Exodus 31:6)

Aholiab, a Danite, would be Bezaleel's assistant. His name bears a similar meaning: "The Father is my tent."[171] This doesn't just refer to his tent-making skills: it indicates that He dwelled in the "tent" of God's presence. Just as Bezaleel was "overshadowed" by the Lord's presence, Aholiab was protected by a shelter of His glory.

THE TIES THAT BIND

A consistent narrative throughout the Word of God is that men who are called to do great things have to be not just appointed but *filled* with the Holy Spirit. We can see it replayed in Acts 6: as Greeks were converting to Christianity, they became upset that their widows were going hungry while Jewish widows were being given favorable treatment.

And in those days, when the number of the disciples was multiplied, there arose a murmuring of the Grecians against the Hebrews, because their widows were neglected in the daily ministration. (Acts 6:1)

While the apostles recognized the need, they realized that it was too much for them to bear while preaching the gospel was being neglected.

It is not reason that we should leave the word of God, and serve tables. (Acts 6:2)

In an interesting parallel with Moses' appointment of seventy elders, the apostles chose particular men to take care of these smaller tasks. But notice a very small detail in verse 3:

> *Wherefore, brethren, look ye out among you seven men of honest report, full of the Holy Ghost and wisdom, whom we may appoint over this business. (Acts 6:3)*

This sheds a profound light on something seemingly inconsequential. Serving Gentile widows was perhaps the lowliest job in the early church; but even these workers needed to be filled with the Holy Ghost. This ties to the main point of Exodus 31: the Holy Spirit is what binds us all together—from head to tail. He plays a crucial role in the lives of both pastor and laborer. No, speaking in tongues didn't exist in Old Testament days, but the very meaning of his name suggests that Bezaleel was completely overshadowed by the Holy Spirit.

EXODUS 31:12-18

Remember the Sabbath

> *Speak thou also unto the children of Israel, saying, Verily my sabbaths ye shall keep: for it is a sign between me and you throughout your generations; that ye may know that I am the LORD that doth sanctify you. (Exodus 31:13)*

Traditionally, the Jewish Sabbath occurs on Saturday. In the New Testament, we can actually pinpoint the moment when the Christian day of worship switched to Sunday:

> *And upon the first day of the week, when the disciples came together to break bread, Paul preached unto them, ready to depart on the morrow; and continued his speech until midnight. (Acts 20:7)*

Since Saturday constituted the seventh day, on Sunday the Christians met to "break bread" (perhaps having communion) and hear Paul preach—the first day of the week. Tradition has long held that the transition became permanent because Jesus had been resurrected on a Sunday, making that the most important day of the week in Christianity.

Remembering the Sabbath is the fourth commandment, and here God reaffirms its importance. I can't help but think that this order is immediately after the appointment of Bezaleel and Aholiab as a reminder that even in constructing the tabernacle, they were not exempt. In fact, Exodus 31:14-18 gives the usual dire pronouncement to anyone violating this rule: death. As God rested on the seventh day of Creation, one of the signs of His people is that they will rest every seventh day.

It is a sign between me and the children of Israel for ever: for in six days the LORD made heaven and earth, and on the seventh day he rested, and was refreshed. (Exodus 31:17)

THE TIES THAT BIND

But this leads to a question: how exactly does one define "work"?

An inevitable problem would eventually arise. In dilemmas like this, the best thing to do is pray for wisdom. A clear sign of a legalistic mindset is when we start attaching our own rules to God's law. Instead of seeking the Spirit, the Israelites, over time, began to define "work" their own way. Over the centuries, the rules of what was and wasn't permitted on the Sabbath became ridiculous. One ancient Jewish teaching even limited the number of steps one could take (the exact number varies; by some accounts, it was three hundred; in others, it was up to one thousand).[172] This is why the religious leaders in Jesus' time were quick to criticize Him for healing on the Sabbath, defining it as "work."

As Jesus pointed out, the religious rules they had created had caused them to miss the entire point of the law. But if we're not careful, we can get into this same mindset when we start adding or subtracting from God's Word.

EXODUS 32:1-35

The Golden Calf

And when the people saw that Moses delayed to come down out of the mount, the people gathered themselves together unto Aaron, and said unto him, Up, make us gods, which shall go before us; for as for this Moses, the man that brought us up out of the land of Egypt, we wot not what is become of him. (Exodus 32:1)

An old saying is that you could take the Israelites out of Egypt, but you couldn't take Egypt out of the Israelites. They had already demonstrated this by yearning to go back where they "had it easy." In their minds, Moses' death brought an easy way out. His leadership was synonymous with following God. Now they were ready to commit to the gods of Egypt.

The reason idolatry is enticing can be seen in this first verse: "Make us gods, which shall go before us." The God they were following could not be seen. Belief requires faith.

But without faith it is impossible to please him. (Hebrews 11:6)

Idolatry requires no faith. People want to see the god they are worshiping. It's spiritually lazy. Isaiah mocked the logical errors of idolatry.

> *The smith with the tongs both worketh in the coals, and fashioneth it with hammers, and worketh it with the strength of his arms: yea, he is hungry, and his strength faileth: he drinketh no water, and is faint. (Isaiah 44:12).*

A smith, who is human and prone to getting tired, builds an idol with his bare hands, then has the audacity to claim that idol is the creator of all things.

> *And the residue thereof he maketh a god, even his graven image: he falleth down unto it, and worshippeth it, and prayeth unto it, and saith, Deliver me; for thou art my god. (Isaiah 44:17)*

It's insanity! Yet it's a trap the Israelites would fall into over and over again.

> *And Aaron said unto them, Break off the golden earrings, which are in the ears of your wives, of your sons, and of your daughters, and bring them unto me. And all the people brake off the golden earrings which were in their ears, and brought them unto Aaron. And he received them at their hand, and fashioned it with a graving tool, after he had made it a molten calf: and they said, These be thy gods, O Israel, which brought thee up out of the land of Egypt. (Exodus 32:2-4)*

There's clearly more to the story than meets the eye here. The pure Israelites who had escaped Egypt were probably not alone on their journey. Judges 1:16 gives us a clue:

> *And the children of the Kenite, Moses' father in law, went up out of the city of palm trees with the children of Judah into the wilderness of Judah, which lieth in the south of Arad; and they went and dwelt among the people.*

While Moses' father-in-law, Jethro, was Midianite, his kin, who joined and mixed with the Israelites at Mount Sinai, are called *Kenites*. This comes from the Hebrew word *Kayin*, which means "metal smith."[173] Jethro's tribe were clearly expert metal-workers. The ghostly ruins of ancient turquoise and copper mines on the edge of the Sinai Peninsula's border with Egypt suggests that other Semitic tribes joined the Israelites once they crossed the Red Sea.[174] They probably influenced the Israelites into worshiping the golden calf. It's interesting how this is juxtaposed in the aftermath of God anointing two specific men for crafting the Ark, the tabernacle, and all its furnishings.

> *And when Aaron saw it, he built an altar before it; and Aaron made proclamation, and said, To morrow is a feast to the LORD. And they rose up early on the morrow, and offered burnt offerings, and brought peace offerings; and the people sat down to eat and to drink, and rose up to play. (Exodus 32:5-6)*

MIDDLE KINGDOM DYNAMICS

Why a golden calf? Most biblical scholars have assumed that the creation was some sort of young bull, as the Hebrew *agalim* refers to male calves.[175] However Josephus and the Septuagint both translated the word *heifer* to the Greek *damaleis*, indicating a female deity.[176] The phrase reappears later in the Bible. After the death of Solomon, his son Jeroboam claimed rightful heir to kingship of Israel. Before the king's death, he had been exiled to Egypt and had even married into the family of Pharaoh.

> *Whereupon the king took counsel, and made two calves of gold, and said unto them, It is too much for you to go up to Jerusalem: behold thy gods, O Israel, which brought thee up out of the land of Egypt. (1 Kings 12:28)*

Just like Aaron and the Kenites, Jeroboam credited a golden calf for being the deliverer from Egypt! The fact that he paraded two around the kingdom shows how the devil can resurrect double the amount of sin we've been delivered from years ago.

This indicates that the golden calf was the Egyptian goddess Hathor, ruler of love and fertility.[177] In the chapter on the ten plagues, I mentioned that the devastation of the livestock disputed Hathor. She had the head of a cow; the Egyptians interpreted abundance of crops and livestock as a sign that she was pleased. The Kenites, living close to the border and perhaps even slaving away in mines for the Egyptians, came to worship her (this is supported by images of Hathor found in the ruins of the previously mentioned mines).[178] Since the Israelites had complained about the lack of food and water and were clearly concerned about the well-being of their livestock, one can see the temptation to submit to this goddess.

> *And the LORD said unto Moses, I have seen this people, and, behold, it is a stiffnecked people: Now therefore let me alone, that my wrath may wax hot against them, and that I may consume them: and I will make of thee a great nation. And Moses besought the LORD his God, and said, LORD, why doth thy wrath wax hot against thy people, which thou hast brought forth out of the land of Egypt with great power, and with a mighty hand? (Exodus 32:9-11)*

The Lord was ready to take drastic action; He would wipe out the Israelites altogether. However, remembering His covenant with Abraham, He was willing to spare Moses so that his descendants would still be numerous as the stars. In his plea for their lives, Moses reminds the Lord of His love for Isaac, Jacob, and Joseph. How could He do such a thing to their children? Furthermore, news of how He had supernaturally delivered the Israelite slaves from Egypt was spreading throughout the ancient world.

And ultimately, if He killed them all, they would be proven right in their complaints that He and Moses had led them into the wilderness just to die.

THE PRACTICAL APPLICATION

In the twenty-second chapter of Ezekiel, God sentenced judgment on Jerusalem for its many sins.

> *Yea, I will gather you, and blow upon you in the fire of my wrath, and ye shall be melted in the midst therof. (Ezekiel 22:21)*

But most surprising is the real reason the city was doomed:

> *And I sought for a man among them, that should make up the hedge, and stand in the gap before me for the land, that I should not destroy it: but I found none. (Ezekiel 22:30)*

We tend to think of intercession as gathering to pray for special needs—maybe a church member standing in for someone else while we lay hands on them at the altar. But have we truly gone deep in the Word to understand the true nature of this biblical principle?

To "stand in the gap" means to place oneself between the punishment and the perpetrator, stopping judgment dead in its tracks. Sound extreme? It's the attitude that hung Jesus to the cross. Being a Christian means being willing to take on the personality of Jesus, and His most definable trait was His willingness to die for our sins.

> *Greater love hath no man than this, that a man lay down his life for his friends. (John 15:13)*

No one was there for Jerusalem, and Ezekiel's prophecy fell on deaf ears. But what will be the case for the Christian Church in America today?

> *Wherefore he is able also to save them to the uttermost that come unto God by him, seeing he ever liveth to make intercession for them. (Hebrews 7:25)*

> *And it came to pass, as soon as he came nigh unto the camp, that he saw the calf, and the dancing: and Moses' anger waxed hot, and he cast the tables out of his hands, and brake them beneath the mount. (Exodus 32:19)*

In the movie *The Ten Commandments*, Moses actually throws the tablets at the calf and it bursts into flames. While it is satisfying to imagine the Word of God destroying sin this way, the biblical account is grimmer. He could have been worn out from leading the ungrateful Israelites, but Moses was beginning to show tendencies of a bad temper. This was in contrast to how he just served as an intercessor, saving the people's lives from God's wrath. He seemed calm when explaining to Joshua what was going on, but as soon as he stepped down from the mountain and saw the idolatry for himself, his emotions overcame him.

THE PRACTICAL APPLICATION

Preachers and teachers need to be careful with the Word of God. Every time I teach, I spend the prior week intensely studying and preparing. When I deliver the message to the people, I think of myself as Moses carrying the tablets down from the mountain. I don't want to be careless with the Word. If I haven't prayed enough and am not full of the Holy Spirit, I could be prone to stuttering or failing to properly teach in some way. I would be like Moses dropping the tablets. We have to hold His Word to our bosoms with tender love and care.

> *And he took the calf which they had made, and burnt it in the fire, and ground it to powder, and strawed it upon the water, and made the children of Israel drink of it. (Exodus 32:20)*

The narration here is a bit strange. Moses took the calf and burned it, grinded it to powder, and put it in water that he forced all those who worshiped to drink. The amount of time this would take makes the logistics hard to place into the story. I haven't seen a movie version include this moment. Whether or not the powder proved poisonous is never mentioned—probably not, since in the coming verses those who chose Hathor would be killed in an act of God's vengeance. The moment seemed to only serve to show how sin may have a certain pleasure at first, but that pleasure very soon turns into bitter waters to drink. Jeroboam's altar to Baal would suffer a similar fate in 2 Kings 23:4.

> *And Moses said unto Aaron, What did this people unto thee, that thou hast brought so great a sin upon them? And Aaron said, Let not the anger of my lord wax hot: thou knowest the people, that they are set on mischief. For they said unto me, Make us gods, which shall go before us: for as for this Moses, the man that brought us up out of the land of Egypt, we wot not what is become of him. And I said unto them, Whosoever hath any gold, let them break it off. So they gave it me: then I cast it into the fire, and there came out this calf. (Exodus 32:21-24)*

Aaron's response to Moses was beyond stupid. First, he refused to own up to his mistake, blaming the people for pressuring him into fashioning the golden calf. Then, he made the absurd claim that he threw gold into the fire, and somehow, a golden calf popped out. Of course, Moses knows full well that a melting blob of gold doesn't shape itself into a calf.

THE TIES THAT BIND

Aaron's sin, blaming others for his own mistake, goes back to the dawn of time itself. The same spirit was in Adam and Eve's words when God asked who was responsible for eating the forbidden fruit:

> *And the man said, The woman whom thou gavest to be with me, she gave me of the tree, and I did eat. And the LORD God said unto the woman, What is this that thou hast done? And the woman said, The serpent beguiled me, and I did eat. (Genesis 3:12-13)*

Adam blamed Eve (with a subtle jab at God), and Eve blamed the serpent. Man has a tendency to make excuses and point fingers for his own sin. So many blame the devil for their wrongdoings—which, if you study Revelation carefully, explains why the devil won't be present on the Day of Judgment. He will already be cast into the Lake of Fire when the wicked stand before God on that terrible day.

> *Then Moses stood in the gate of the camp, and said, Who is on the LORD's side? let him come unto me. And all the sons of Levi gathered themselves together unto him. And he said unto them, Thus saith the LORD God of Israel, Put every man his sword by his side, and go in and out from gate to gate throughout the camp, and slay every man his brother, and every man his companion, and every man his neighbour. And the children of Levi did according to the word of Moses: and there fell of the people that day about three thousand men. (Exodus 32:26-28)*

This was the first of many mass deaths that would occur as a result of sin. Consider Moses' first words in Exodus 32:26: "Who is on the Lord's side? Let him come unto me." Earlier we saw how the scriptures depict Moses as a Christ figure, standing as an intercessor on behalf of the people before God's wrath. Now he fulfilled that completely by offering a choice: "Come unto me!" No Israelite had to die at this point. Those who committed idolatry had every opportunity to stand by Moses. The Bible only tells us how many made the wrong choice here, not how many originally worshiped Hathor. Maybe some repented. All we know is that three thousand were willing to die for the wrong choice.

Just like Moses went from intercessor to a judge, Christ is merciful now. He died on the cross so that each and every one of us could receive salvation. Jesus has cried, "Who is on the Lord's side? Let him come unto me!" ever since Calvary. But soon, that cry will be heard no more, and judgment will come. The Levites, anointed as priests of mercy for the sins of the people, will become avenging angels. They will draw their swords, and hell will come to those who favor sin.

> *For Moses had said, Consecrate yourselves today to the* LORD*, even every man upon his son, and upon his brother; that he may bestow upon you a blessing this day. And it came to pass on the morrow, that Moses said unto the people, Ye have sinned a great sin: and now I will go up unto the* LORD*; peradventure I shall make an atonement for your sin. And Moses returned unto the* LORD*, and said, Oh, this people have sinned a great sin, and have made them gods of gold. (Exodus 32:29-31)*

In the aftermath of sin, the first Day of Atonement began. Moses had to go into the presence of the Lord. This was supposed to be Aaron's job, but he had demonstrated to be not up to the task yet (and would probably need to go under intense consecration for leading the people in idolatry). According to tradition, Yom Kippur is to take place in the month of Tishrei, which falls somewhere between September and October on today's Gregorian calendar,[179] ten days after Rosh Hashanah, the Jewish New Year. The Jews are encouraged to pray for forgiveness of their sins during this period (similar to the Catholic period of Lent), culminating in a twenty-five-hour fast. It all started in this verse at the foot of Mount Sinai due to the mistake of bowing to a golden calf. It's amazing to ponder on the perseverance of a people who still honor traditions dating back more than thirty-four hundred years.

> *Yet now, if thou wilt forgive their sin--; and if not, blot me, I pray thee, out of thy book which thou hast written. And the* LORD *said unto Moses, Whosoever hath sinned against me, him will I blot out of my book. (Exodus 32:32-33)*

Once again playing the role of intercessor, Moses demonstrated his love for the Israelites by being willing to suffer not just judgment but *eternal* judgment, if God would not forgive them. He requested to be stricken from the Book of Life, but the Lord quickly corrected him that only the three thousand who chose to serve Hathor would be wiped out (suffering eternity in hell).

THE TIES THAT BIND

The New Testament is filled with breathless descriptions of the afterlife and the Day of Judgment. The Old Testament, however, is much vaguer. Critics suggest that biblical ideas of heaven and hell were invented by Christians and were perhaps a result of extra-Judaic influence from the Greeks or Romans. So few and far between are the references to the afterlife in the Old Testament that at least one sect of the Jewish religious order, the Sadducees, didn't even believe in it.

However look a little closer and you'll see this isn't the case. Many centuries before Christ, the promise that eternal fire awaited those who rejected God after death began seeping into the Old Testament writings.

> *The wicked shall be turned into hell, and all the nations that forget God. (Psalm 9:17)*

As far back as Exodus, the second book in the Bible, we find the first mention of a book that bears the names of all the righteous. The fate of whoever's name is blotted out of this book is eerily not revealed yet. Slowly but surely, the Bible is sprinkled with puzzle pieces that we can put together for the bigger picture. The first time it is referred to as a "book of life" is in Psalm 69:28:

> *Let them be blotted out of the book of the living, and not be written with the righteous.*

The book is mentioned at least fourteen times in the Bible (that I could find), and like so many other topics, more is revealed as we get closer to the end. There certainly will also be a Day of Judgment, when everyone who's ever lived will stand before God and account for their lives. Daniel (whose name means "God is my Judge"[180]) made it very clear that there will only be two possible outcomes.

> *And many of them that sleep in the dust of the earth shall awake, some to everlasting life, and some to shame and everlasting contempt. (Daniel 12:2)*

In Revelation (the New Testament companion to Daniel), we learn that the Book of Life will be present on Judgment Day, and whoever's name isn't found there will receive eternal damnation.

> *And I saw the dead, small and great, stand before God; and the books were opened: and another book was opened, which is the book of life: and the dead were judged out of those things which were written in the books, according to their works. . . . And whosoever was not found written in the book of life was cast into the lake of fire. (Revelation 20:12, 15)*

CONCLUSION

Sinai began in hope and ended in tragedy. This would be the sad story plaguing the Israelites until they reached the Promised Land. But here, in these chapters, what matters most is the seismic moment in history this represents. The nature of theism itself changed forever at Mount Sinai. The birthplace of monotheism in the modern world is more than just about worshiping one God. From here on, it would be about how people should live their lives. In the ancient world, conquest had decided whose gods were the most powerful. But this new faith was about morality.

The Ten Commandments form the foundation of the religious world ever since. The law is no longer a verbal discussion but a written contract between God and man. As Gunther Plaut said, "The story in all its brevity achieves one major goal: to convey to some degree the awesomeness of that moment when the Lord of the universe showed His Glory to Israel and when He made His covenant with them, changing their history and the history of all men as well."[181]

Chapter 9

LEAVING SINAI

INTRODUCTION

The latter half of Exodus, from the flight from Egypt onward, is punctuated by two major events: the Red Sea and Mount Sinai. Both are radically different in nature, but both show the overall arc of the story. While Moses was certainly the central character, the Israelites themselves were now going through the most dramatic transformation. At the Red Sea, they were baptized, going into the water oppressed slaves and emerging a victorious nation. At Mount Sinai, they received a law that emphasized the central tenet of a new faith: righteousness and morality as their foundation as a people.

But that's where the similarities end. The Red Sea was a terrifying event where divine intervention saved at the last minute. Mount Sinai was a place to gather and worship God. The aftermath of each was radically different. The other side of the Red Sea was filled with celebration. Surely nothing but goodness lay ahead in the wilderness! But it was to be short-lived.

God Himself appeared on this mountain, yet they were terrified and never wanted to see Him again (a bad sign for the future). Then, the law was given; but the people couldn't wait for Moses to reappear and worshiped a golden calf. Now the atmosphere was one of mourning. Three thousand had died. Rather than instruments ringing into the night, a broken people had to bury their dead and clean up the mess caused by sin. No optimism would accompany them as they ventured into the desert this time.

> *And when the people heard these evil tidings, they mourned: and no man did put on him his ornaments. (Exodus 33:4)*

Yet in the smoldering ruins of defeat, there was still reason to be hopeful. God was not abandoning them. He would help them rebuild. Moses would receive new tablets. The tabernacle would be built, and the rituals of atonement would begin. The priests would be consecrated. The Ark would lead them on.

In this final chapter, we'll look into the somber aftermath of Mount Sinai and how the Lord prepared His people for the long journey ahead.

EXODUS 33:1-23

Consecrating the People

> *And the LORD said unto Moses, Depart, and go up hence, thou and the people which thou hast brought up out of the land of Egypt, unto the land which I sware unto Abraham, to Isaac, and to Jacob, saying, Unto thy seed will I give it: And I will send an angel before thee; and I will drive out the Canaanite, the Amorite, and the Hittite, and the Perizzite, the Hivite, and the Jebusite: Unto a land flowing with milk and honey: for I will not go up in the midst of thee; for thou art a stiffnecked people: lest I consume thee in the way. (Exodus 33:1-3)*

The tragedy of this verse is the revelation of the original plan. If the Israelites had completely obeyed, the angel of the Lord would have gone before them to drive out the Canaanites. Now they would have to fight the battle themselves. This started the downward spiral of what God had ordained. The next step down would be the realization that the army wasn't ready to face them. This, along with more grumbling and complaining, would destroy all hope of claiming the Promised Land any time soon.

> *For the LORD had said unto Moses, Say unto the children of Israel, Ye are a stiffnecked people: I will come up into the midst of thee in a moment, and consume thee: therefore now put off thy ornaments from thee, that I may know what to do unto thee. And the children of Israel stripped themselves of their ornaments by the mount Horeb. (Exodus 33:5-6)*

This mirrors the terrible mistake earlier. They had used the spoils of Egypt—earrings, bracelets, etcetera—to fashion the golden calf. But not everything. Now they paid a bigger price by getting to keep less of their possessions. The remaining spoils, their "ornaments," were stripped from all over the camp to be used in the construction of the Ark, tabernacle, and its furnishings. They were willing to make a small sacrifice for an idol.

If they had never worshiped the calf, they may not have been stripped of *all*. But now God required a greater sacrifice to build His house.

> *And it came to pass, as Moses entered into the tabernacle, the cloudy pillar descended, and stood at the door of the tabernacle, and the Lord talked with Moses. And all the people saw the cloudy pillar stand at the tabernacle door: and all the people rose up and worshiped, every man in his tent door. (Exodus 33:9-10)*

Again, the narration here gets a little confusing. The scriptures had not said at any point that the tabernacle had been built. In Exodus 33:7, it seems to just appear. After the ornaments were stripped from the people, the construction must have been completed between verses 6 and 7. However it seems more important to skip to the moment Moses (still not Aaron, who clearly cannot be allowed to be priest yet due to his sins) entered. The cloud of God's glory descended in a pillar and met him there. In a sign of spiritual change since the golden calf, the Israelites gathered at the sight and worshiped the cloud.

THE TIES THAT BIND

This scene would be played out again when Solomon dedicated the temple as the permanent dwelling place of God many centuries later.

The glory was so powerful that only Moses could enter. Likewise, when the temple was complete, the same cloud filled the building and even the priests had to stay outside.

> *And it came to pass, when the priests were come out of the holy place, that the cloud filled the house of the LORD, So that the priests could not stand to minister because of the cloud: for the glory of the LORD had filled the house of the LORD. (1 Kings 8:10-11)*

Recall back that immediately after the flight from Egypt, a cloud led the Israelites by day and a pillar of fire by night. The cloud and fire appeared in successive order. Once the cloud appeared, fire descended in the temple.

> *Now when Solomon had made an end of praying, the fire came down from heaven, and consumed the burnt offering and the sacrifices; and the glory of the LORD filled the house. (2 Chronicles 7:1)*

The priests could not come close enough to light the brazen altar due to the glory of God, so the Lord sent His holy fire down Himself. And the fire led the people to worship the one true God.

> *And when all the children of Israel saw how the fire came down, and the glory of the LORD upon the house, they bowed themselves with their faces*

> *to the ground upon the pavement, and worshiped, and praised the* LORD, *saying, For he is good; for his mercy endureth for ever. (2 Chronicles 7:3)*

We have well established by now that fire in the Bible is a symbol of the Holy Ghost. In this case, the fire of God led the people to worship Him. Likewise, today, the Spirit convicts sinners to Calvary.

We've already studied how the construction of the tabernacle and the temple mirror the throne of God Himself. We also see the cloud appearing in the holiest place of heaven, surrounding His throne.

> *And the temple was filled with smoke from the glory of God, and from his power; and no man was able to enter into the temple, till the seven plagues of the seven angels were fulfilled. (Revelation 15:8)*

Just like on earth, the cloud is a power so strong that no man or angel can be inside it.

> *And the* LORD *spake unto Moses face to face, as a man speaketh unto his friend. And he turned again into the camp: but his servant Joshua, the son of Nun, a young man, departed not out of the tabernacle. (Exodus 33:11)*

Some critics have claimed that the idea of being "intimate" with God is a relatively new and unbiblical idea in church history. I completely disagree. God came down and walked with Adam and Eve every day in the cool of the evening. Ever since the Fall, He has longed to restore that relationship with us. That's why it's so important that He came down and spoke to Moses "as a man speaketh unto his friend."

THE TIES THAT BIND

> *And it shall be at that day, saith the* LORD, *that thou shalt call me Ishi; and shalt call me no more Baali. (Hosea 2:16)*

Baali means "my Lord," and *ishi* means "husband,"[182] indicating that God wants His people to view Him less as a ruler and more like how a wife would regard her husband. He wants their service not out of blind obedience but love. This is against the backdrop of the book of Hosea, where the Lord ordered a prophet to marry a prostitute who kept going back into her adulterous ways, illustrating the tormented relationship He had with Israel. Jesus echoed Isaiah 29:13 when He said,

> *Ye hypocrites, well did Esaias prophesy of you, saying, This people draweth nigh unto me with their mouth, and honoureth me with their lips; but their heart is far from me. (Matthew 15:7-8)*

God is not as interested in our adherence to religious rituals as He is to whether we love Him with all our hearts.

> *And he said, My presence shall go with thee, and I will give thee rest. And he said unto him, If thy presence go not with me, carry us not up hence. (Exodus 33:14-15)*

One of the most difficult things to do is just let God move. As humans, we tend to want to control our environment and situations. Facing the unknown can be frightening. But God promised Moses that His presence would go with them. When it was time to rest, they would rest. When it was time to go, the cloud would lead the way. God warned them never to travel without the cloud. Going ahead of God's glory is taking the path to destruction. We must be careful not to get ahead of Him.

> *And he said, I will make all my goodness pass before thee, and I will proclaim the name of the* LORD *before thee; and will be gracious to whom I will be gracious, and will shew mercy on whom I will shew mercy. And he said, Thou canst not see my face: for there shall no man see me, and live. . . . And it shall come to pass, while my glory passeth by, that I will put thee in a clift of the rock, and will cover thee with my hand while I pass by: And I will take away mine hand, and thou shalt see my back parts: but my face shall not be seen. (Exodus 33:19-20, 22-23)*

Despite Moses being privileged to be closer to God than anyone since Eden, no man can actually see His face and live.

THE PRACTICAL APPLICATION

On October 13, 2017, I took a short break from my weekly blog and asked my friend Jason Shuler to share his testimony as a fill-in. In 1987, when he was ten, his family was in a devastating car accident. He was thrown from the vehicle and landed face-first on the asphalt, ripping his face almost completely off and nearly killing him. In the hospital, the doctors told his parents that if he survived, he would need dramatic reconstructive surgery. His father, a pastor, had people all over the state praying. Within one week, Jason was completely recovered.

He did later need a minor operation on his nose, and he shared the story as follows:

> This broken nose led to something that's even more amazing than God healing and restoring my face. As I was only 10 years old all I really knew of the Bible was what I learned in Sunday school and children's church. As I had to have a minor surgery to set my nose, I was scared of them knocking me out with the gas I had to breathe. As the doctor told me to relax and breathe,

I was soon watching myself being operated on. I could see the doctors all around my face working on my nose, but didn't quite understand what I was seeing. There was no fear, no worry; it was the greatest peace I have ever felt in my entire life still to this day. I then noticed someone standing to the left of me. As I turned to look this is what I saw:

> Daniel 10:5-6: *I lifted up my eyes and looked, and behold, a man clothed in linen, with a belt of fine gold from Uphaz around his waist. His body was like beryl, his face like the appearance of lightning . . . his arms and legs like the gleam of burnished bronze . . .*

As I left the hospital that day I remember sitting in the back of the vehicle my dad was driving, and quietly telling my parents I believe I saw my guardian angel. My mother turned around and asked me to describe what I saw. Then she asked if I had seen a face. I remember replying, "No, it was just a bright light." I will never forget her next words: "Jason, that was God."

I went into a complete awe thinking of how God had shown Himself to a 10 year-old. The song "Jesus Loves the Little Children" took on a whole new meaning for me.

This is a testimony I will never forget. I pray that it may somehow bless your life such as God has blessed mine.[183]

EXODUS 34:1-35

The New Commandments

> *And the* LORD *said unto Moses, Hew thee two tables of stone like unto the first: and I will write upon these tables the words that were in the first tables, which thou brakest. And be ready in the morning, and come up in the morning unto mount Sinai, and present thyself there to me in the top of the mount. And no man shall come up with thee, neither let any man be seen throughout all the mount; neither let the flocks nor herds feed before that mount. (Exodus 34:1-3)*

Moses broke the first commandments, but God had given him the opportunity to climb back up and receive the law again. This time, the finger of God would not create the tablets; Moses must carve them out himself. Having tablets hewn by the hands of a man is still a little less special. Just like the first time, he alone was welcome into the cloud of glory covering the summit. No one, not even their livestock, was to touch even the foot of the mountain, or they would die.

> *And the LORD descended in the cloud, and stood with him there, and proclaimed the name of the LORD. And the LORD passed by before him, and proclaimed, The LORD, The LORD God, merciful and gracious, longsuffering, and abundant in goodness and truth, Keeping mercy for thousands, forgiving iniquity and transgression and sin, and that will by no means clear the guilty; visiting the iniquity of the fathers upon the children, and upon the children's children, unto the third and to the fourth generation. (Exodus 34:5-7)*

Once Moses was enveloped in glory, it tells us that the Lord passed before him and then gave observations of praise. The words remind us of God's abundant mercy. This gives the perspective that the Lord *only* killed three thousand; He had every right to kill more. He had even wanted to destroy them all and start over with Moses. Yet He helped them rebuild and consecrate so they could move on. Throughout even the Old Testament, we can stand in awe of just how patient and merciful He really was.

A careless reader will look over this and assume that God was praising Himself. Personally, I think this is one of the few instances where the Trinity is hinted at in the Torah. During Creation, God referred to Himself in plural form:

> *And God said, Let us make man in our image, after our likeness. (Genesis 1:26)*

Here, the Lord passed before Moses and then praises *the Lord*. This being a cloud of glory Moses was in, I can't help but imagine the Holy Spirit appearing to remind him that the Father and Son are to be praised for the restraint they've shown in judging the Israelites for their sin.

THE PRACTICAL APPLICATION

It also establishes an important standard in communication with God that Jesus spelled out in Matthew 6:9:

> *After this manner therefore pray ye: Our Father which art in heaven, Hallowed be thy name.*

The Lord's Prayer is not something to just recite; it is a blueprint for how our daily prayers should be structured. The first step is praise. You should begin and end your prayers in it. Before you bring any needs before the Lord, glorify His name. Recognize that you are before His very throne, in the highest courts of heaven, where even angels fear to tread. Praise Him for your house, your church, your family: but most of all, for salvation, for which you could never thank Him enough.

> *By him therefore let us offer the sacrifice of praise to God continually, that is, the fruit of our lips giving thanks to his name. (Hebrews 13:15)*

> *And Moses made haste, and bowed his head toward the earth, and worshiped. And he said, If now I have found grace in thy sight, O LORD, let my LORD, I pray thee, go among us; for it is a stiffnecked people; and pardon our iniquity and our sin, and take us for thine inheritance. (Exodus 34:8-9)*

Moses' first request was, *if* he had found grace in the Lord's sight, to let the Spirit go "among us." By *us*, he included himself with the Israelites. He acknowledged that they were a stiff-necked people but attached himself to them. God was willing to destroy Israel—but not Moses. Moses saw that the special bond he had with God could be to the people's advantage. It showed that no matter what they did, Moses still loved his people. The man who was cast out of the court of Pharaoh had found a new family in the Israelites. They were one. This had to be brought to God's attention before he could ask for pardon from "our" sin and "our" iniquity (something Moses had no need to ask for, since he didn't worship the golden calf). Once again, we see Moses, the one who did no wrong, joining himself with the people and including himself with the punishment for their iniquity, just as Christ would one day do for all humanity.

> *And he said, Behold, I make a covenant: before all thy people I will do marvels, such as have not been done in all the earth, nor in any nation: and all the people among which thou art shall see the work of the LORD: for it is a terrible thing that I will do with thee. Observe thou that which I command thee this day: behold, I drive out before thee the Amorite, and the Canaanite, and the Hittite, and the Perizzite, and the Hivite, and the Jebusite. (Exodus 34:10-11)*

In this one-on-one conversation, the Lord responded with a covenant; He would do marvels through Israel unlike any the earth had seen (other translations interpret the phrase *terrible things* as "awesome"). *Terrible* may not be inaccurate, however, when we consider the destruction coming to Canaan. We again catch a glimpse of the original plan that God was to drive the enemy out of the Promised Land for them. If they had been obedient, Joshua would have never had to lead them into bloody battle. As it stands, sin and disobedience would lead to forty years in the desert followed by the curse of war.

> *But ye shall destroy their altars, break their images, and cut down their groves: For thou shalt worship no other god: for the LORD, whose name is Jealous, is a jealous God. (Exodus 34:13-14)*

God reaffirmed His jealousy—but not just for the worship of His children. In the end, all people, even the Gentiles, are His. And He despised idolatry from them just as much from the Israelites and was intent on destroying it. He promised to fight the battle; but in return, all He asked is they destroy all idols and cut down their "groves." In Old Testament times, shrines to false gods were often placed on hilltops, which is why they are sometimes also referred to as "high places." Destroying these is not just important for purifying the land; it is about preventing future idolatry.

Exodus 34:15 tell us why this is so important:

Lest thou make a covenant with the inhabitants of the land, and they go a whoring after their gods, and do sacrifice unto their gods, and one call thee, and thou eat of his sacrifice.

This was so serious that they were not allowed to mix-breed with any other idolatrous people.

And thou take of their daughters unto thy sons, and their daughters go a whoring after their gods, and make thy sons go a whoring after their gods. (Exodus 34:16)

Just like the process of sanctification, this was about destroying the paths of future sin. Sin polluted the land and brought a curse. It's why God hated Jericho so much that He commanded all its citizens killed and the city burned so its ruins could never be occupied again.

With these introductory formalities out of the way, God was now ready to give the second law.

The feast of unleavened bread shalt thou keep. Seven days thou shalt eat unleavened bread, as I commanded thee, in the time of the month Abib: for in the month Abib thou camest out from Egypt. (Exodus 34:18)

First, the people were to observe the feast of unleavened bread (which coincides with the Passover celebration) every year. This, immediately after the commandment to not worship any other gods, is the second commandment. I don't know that this is necessarily second in importance but more of a chronological reminder of how they should act.

All that openeth the matrix is mine; and every firstling among thy cattle, whether ox or sheep, that is male. (Exodus 34:19)

Matrix refers to "womb," which means that everything alive born among the Israelites belonged to God. If they truly honored the covenant with Him, they wouldn't consider any of their possessions to actually be theirs. This was even true with the livestock. In our own lives, we should have this attitude about what we have. Our house, cars, jobs, and even marriages were all provided by God. Therefore, with an attitude of thanks, we should consider it His anyway. And we can't truly be servants of the Lord until we have.

> *Six days thou shalt work, but on the seventh day thou shalt rest: in earing time and in harvest thou shalt rest. (Exodus 34:21)*

That the Sabbath was to be observed during "earing" and "harvest" time showed how important it was. Collecting as much as possible during the harvest season was important to prepare for future seasons of famine. But even then, the Sabbath must be respected. To make an exception showed lack of faith. Picking ears of corn, no matter how important that may seem, indicated unwillingness to trust in God to provide miraculously under any circumstance.

> *And he was there with the LORD forty days and forty nights; he did neither eat bread, nor drink water. And he wrote upon the tables the words of the covenant, the ten commandments. (Exodus 34:28)*

Moses was on the summit of Mount Sinai in God's presence for forty days and nights. The Lord sustained his life; he didn't need food or water. This fast foreshadowed the forty days Jesus would endure without food in the wilderness before starting His ministry. But while Moses was completely protected by the glory of God, Christ suffered temptation by the enemy. Forty days is the maximum length of fasting in the Bible. Anyone who fasts any longer is not fasting biblically (and putting their lives in danger, I might add). In this instance, Moses also drank no water. I have never met a Christian who successfully went without drinking water for more than a few days, and it isn't mentioned that Jesus abstained from it. I would therefore not advise any Christian to avoid water during a fast.

> *And it came to pass, when Moses came down from mount Sinai with the two tables of testimony in Moses' hand, when he came down from the mount, that Moses wist not that the skin of his face shone while he talked with him. And when Aaron and all the children of Israel saw Moses, behold, the skin of his face shone; and they were afraid to come nigh him. (Exodus 34:29-30)*

How awesome that God's presence was so strong that the glory shone from Moses' face when he stepped down the mountain! But the people were so afraid when they saw it that Moses put on a veil to hide it.

> *And till Moses had done speaking with them, he put a vail on his face. But when Moses went in before the Lord to speak with him, he took the vail off, until he came out. And he came out, and spake unto the children of Israel that which he was commanded. And the children of Israel saw the face of Moses, that the skin of Moses' face shone: and Moses put the vail upon his face again, until he went in to speak with him. (Exodus 34:33-35)*

This served the same purpose as the veil in the tabernacle, a physical barrier between God's presence and man. In this case, the presence shining from Moses' face was being blocked off from the people. This was the last thing he should have done, because the glory of God was exactly what they needed to look to as they followed him.

> *Seeing then that we have such hope, we use great plainness of speech: And not as Moses, which put a veil over his face, that the children of Israel could not stedfastly look to the end of that which is abolished: But their minds were blinded: for until this day remaineth the same vail untaken away in the reading of the old testament; which vail is done away in Christ. (2 Corinthians 3:12-14)*

When we Christians are in God's presence, the glory of God will shine from our faces like Moses when he came down from Mount Sinai. But we must not hide that glory; the world needs to see it so they will recognize there's something different about us. And they will know that they need what we have.

EXODUS 40:1-38

Reviewing the Ceremony

You might notice a gigantic leap in the commentary from chapter 34 to 40. Chapters 35 through 39 of Exodus are basically a word-for-word repeat of the law that God gave the first time. I therefore decided that it wasn't necessary to rehash all we've covered. However the order of the temple ceremony was based on God's instructions to build the furnishings for the tabernacle, and the resulting picture is a bit scrambled. It seems logical to give a simple review of the tabernacle ceremony based on the order in which it was performed, using the concluding chapter of Exodus to provide a summary.

I will be going back to chapters 34-39 for reference as necessary, as there are some gaps in the ceremony review from chapter 40.

> *And it came to pass in the first month in the second year, on the first day of the month, that the tabernacle was reared up. And Moses reared up the tabernacle, and fastened his sockets, and set up the boards thereof, and put in the bars thereof, and reared up his pillars. And he spread abroad the tent over the tabernacle, and put the covering of the tent above upon it; as the L*ORD *commanded Moses. (Exodus 40:17-19)*

Presumably, this means the tabernacle was erected the first day of the first month the year after they had escaped Egypt.

> *According to all that the L*ORD *commanded Moses, so the children of Israel made all the work. (Exodus 39:42)*

For all the complicated methods going into its construction, it seems strange that they would have it set up within a day. However Ellicott's commentary points out that the craft of tent-making would have a cultural history among the Semites dating back to the time of Abraham:

> The Tabernacle was so constructed as to be capable of being rapidly both put together and taken to pieces. The erection of the framework, and the stretching upon it of the fine linen and goats'-hair coverings, must have been the main difficulty. But the family of Abraham had been familiar with tent life from the time of its quitting Ur of the Chaldees to the descent into Egypt, and its location in Egypt on the borders of the desert, in close neighborhood to various nomadic races, had kept up its familiarity with tents, their structure, and the most approved methods of pitching and striking them. Thus it is not surprising that the first erection was completed in less than a day.[184]

To recap, the tabernacle contained three main sections: the outer court, where the people gathered to worship and where sacrifices were made; the inner court—the outer part inside the tent itself, where only the priests were allowed; the innermost room—the Holiest of Holies, guarded by a thick veil. Only the high priest could enter once a year to make atonement for the sins of the people.

First came the sacrifice itself. The ram was killed and its blood shed on the altar (which ultimately points to Christ's blood running down the cross).

> *Then shall he kill the goat of the sin offering, that is for the people, and bring his blood within the vail, and do with that blood as he did with the blood of the bullock, and sprinkle it upon the mercy seat, and before the mercy seat. (Leviticus 16:15)*

The blood was collected to be used at the end of the ceremony.

> *And thou shalt set the altar of the burnt offering before the door of the tabernacle of the tent of the congregation. (Exodus 40:6)*

The brazen altar, where the burnt sacrifices were made, was before the entrance to the tent (as was the laver). Its dimensions are given in Exodus 38:1:

> *And he made the altar of burnt offering of shittim wood: five cubits was the length thereof, and five cubits the breadth thereof; it was foursquare; and three cubits the height thereof.*

The clean meat was separated from the unclean (the bowels and dung), one burned on the holy altar and the other taken outside the camp, signifying the purifying fire of the Holy Ghost Baptism.

> *And thou shalt set the laver between the tent of the congregation and the altar, and shalt put water therein. (Exodus 40:7)*

The priests had to be spotless before entering the tabernacle, where God's presence was. They washed the blood off their hands in the laver, a brass tub full of water. Later, in the temple, this would be replaced by the molten sea (which was much larger and more ornate). The laver represented sanctification, removing all things from one's life after salvation that could one day lead back into sin. God is holy and will not allow sin in His presence; this is why He is coming back for a bride without spot, wrinkle, blemish, or any such thing. This is also why there is a sea of glass under His throne separating the second and third heavens.

> *And thou shalt set the altar of gold for the incense before the ark of the testimony, and put the hanging of the door to the tabernacle. (Exodus 40:5)*

The golden altar of incense was inside the inner court, near the "hanging door" to the tabernacle. The incense was a holy fire burning from oil made out of specific ingredients. This was not just for the yearly atonement, but Aaron and his sons were to enter every morning to wave it before the Lord. The ascending smoke of incense represented the prayers of the people rising to the throne of God. Two of his sons would be killed in the temple for offering strange fire, or incense made from the wrong ingredients.

> *And he put the candlestick in the tent of the congregation, over against the table, on the side of the tabernacle southward. And he lighted the lamps before the LORD; as the LORD commanded Moses. (Exodus 40:24-25)*

The menorah, with its seven candlesticks, was next to the table of showbread before the veil. While not part of the yearly ceremony of atonement, the flames of this iconic symbol of Judaism were to be kept burning continually. The incense and the candlesticks both signified the fire of the Holy Ghost burning in the Christian at all times. It was blasphemous for the priests to ever allow the light to die out, and we too should never allow the fire of the Holy Ghost to fade out on the altar of our souls.

> *And he put the table in the tent of the congregation, upon the side of the tabernacle northward, without the vail. And he set the bread in order upon it before the LORD; as the LORD had commanded Moses. (Exodus 40:22-23)*

The table of showbread was before the veil, which separated the outer court from the Holiest of Holies. The bread was to be kept on the table at all times and could only be eaten by the priests. On the Day of Atonement, the priests also ate the cooked meat of the sacrifice along with the showbread. This was a sacred part of the daily rituals that were violated by David when he entered the tabernacle famished and requested to eat the anointed bread. But the reason he wasn't slain by God for this is that it served as a prophecy that through his lineage, Jesus would make the Bread of Life available to *all*, not just the priests. The showbread ritual was also a type and shadow of the Last Supper when Jesus revealed that He was the Bread of Life.

> *And thou shalt take the anointing oil, and anoint the tabernacle, and all that is therein, and shalt hallow it, and all the vessels thereof: and it shall be holy. (Exodus 40:9)*

Before any ceremony could take place, the priests and the entire tabernacle had to be consecrated with anointing oil. The oil symbolized the anointing, the physical presence of God that we feel when we are called or operating under the gifts of the Spirit. Each priest had oil poured on him and it was applied to every wall, door, and furnishing within the tabernacle. The anointing of God has to be in every aspect of our lives before we can act on His calling in our lives.

> *And thou shalt put therein the ark of the testimony, and cover the ark with the vail. (Exodus 40:3)*

The veil separated the Holiest of Holies, the innermost room where God's glory dwelt the strongest on earth. It represented the physical partition between God and man, which is why it was torn apart when Christ was crucified.

> *And he made a vail of blue, and purple, and scarlet, and fine twined linen: with cherubims made he it of cunning work. (Exodus 36:35)*

> *And of the blue, and purple, and scarlet, they made cloths of service, to do service in the holy place, and made the holy garments for Aaron; as the LORD commanded Moses. (Exodus 39:1)*

The presence of God was so strong in the innermost chamber that the high priest had to wear a rope with bells attached so that if he died, his body could be safely dragged out without entering in to retrieve it.

> *And they made bells of pure gold, and put the bells between the pomegranates upon the hem of the robe, round about between the pomegranates. (Exodus 39:25)*

After the veil was torn, the innermost chamber was moved from the temple to the upper room. The veil could contain the glory of God, but the upper room could not, as the Holy Spirit overflowed into the streets of Jerusalem and saved thousands every day.

In the final step of the atonement ceremony, the high priest sprinkled the blood of the sacrifice on the mercy seat, the lid of the Ark of the Covenant.

> *Then shall he kill the goat of the sin offering, that is for the people, and bring his blood within the vail, and do with that blood as he did with the blood of the bullock, and sprinkle it upon the mercy seat, and before the mercy seat. (Leviticus 16:15)*

The Ark contained Aaron's rod, a pot of manna, and the tablets containing the Ten Commandments (Hebrews 9:4). Animal sacrifice provided a yearly cover for the sins of the Israelites but could not completely wash sin away (Hebrews 10:4). Only a perfect sacrifice from the Perfect One would be able to accomplish that.

> *By the which will we are sanctified through the offering of the body of Jesus Christ once for all. (Hebrews 10:10)*

And just like in the temple, the throne of God Himself contains an altar before it where the blood of Jesus has been sprinkled as a covering for sin. When we face God on Judgment Day, those who have their names written in the Lamb's Book of Life will be pointed to the altar. The blood has covered our sins, and we will hear that sweet and wonderful voice:

> *Well done, thou good and faithful servant: thou hast been faithful over a few things, I will make thee ruler over many things: enter thou into the joy of thy lord. (Matthew 25:21)*

CONCLUSION

Exodus 40:33 ends with five simple words:

> *So Moses finished the work.*

The tabernacle was complete, the priestly garments were fashioned, the priests had all been consecrated, and the furnishings had been built. The atonement sacrifice could now begin. Before they could enter the Promised Land, the priests and all the people must be anointed before the Lord. Moses' understanding of the importance of consecration explains why he led them to this holy mountain in the first place.

> *Then a cloud covered the tent of the congregation, and the glory of the LORD filled the tabernacle. And Moses was not able to enter into the tent of the congregation, because the cloud abode thereon, and the glory of the LORD filled the tabernacle. (Exodus 40:34-35)*

As a sign that God was pleased, the glory appeared again; but this time it was so powerful even Moses could not enter. He stood at a distance and watched in awe as the cloud filled the tent. A new era had begun. A few individuals had been able to make sacrifices here and there, but this was the first time a nation could come together and receive atonement for sin. The next step in God's plan to restore His relationship with man was complete. It all pointed to Calvary.

The golden calf was now a distant memory. The people had come together and completed the work according to His divine will. Only a few more times in history would this kind of unity bring the fullness of His glory. They would see it again forty years later while conquering Jericho. It would come again in the long-distant future, when the twelve hundred were gathered in the upper room, obediently seeking the Holy Spirit. But when it was poured without measure then, unlike with Moses and the Israelites, they would be inside it. To be baptized doesn't just mean to be submerged; it means to be *immersed*, inside and out. When a cup is submerged in water, it is not just surrounded but *filled*.

The Jews call it the Shekinah glory, a word that derives from the Hebrew shekinot, loosely referring to "a dwelling place."[185] The Lord's presence is not some distant unreachable concept but actually, at times, dwells with man. The way we think of the Shekinah is a little different from the original meaning. We envision some sort of ethereal halo of light emanating around God, but the Hebrew word for "glory," *kavod*, more accurately translates to "weight" or "heaviness."[186] It wasn't metaphysical but reality with weight and dimension. To be near God isn't to just feel His presence but to experience the weight of it.

We tell stories of great moves of God from years ago and resign that God "just doesn't move like that anymore." But God hasn't changed; He was pouring out His Shekinah glory thousands of years before Jesus. And He can use us to shake this earth even more today.

Every church must be the house of God, and every child of God His temple. The glory fills our churches and our innermost beings completely. We are vessels.

> *But we have this treasure in earthen vessels, that the excellency of the power may be of God, and not of us. (2 Corinthians 4:7)*

And we are not enough to hold it back as it is poured out continually into the world.

> *And when the cloud was taken up from over the tabernacle, the children of Israel went onward in all their journeys: But if the cloud were not taken up, then they journeyed not till the day that it was taken up. For the cloud of the LORD was upon the tabernacle by day, and fire was on it by*

night, in the sight of all the house of Israel, throughout all their journeys. (Exodus 40:36-38)

These final three verses conclude the book of Exodus, and rightfully so. It started forty long chapters ago by listing the names of the sons of Jacob. Now it ends with a people who had been both liberated and judged. They had been freed from the chains of Egypt and decimated at the base of Sinai. They had been baptized in both water at the Red Sea and fire in God's judgment for worshiping the golden calf. Like a precious metal being burned with a terrible fire but submerged in cooling water, they had gone from formless raw material to the chosen people of God.

They had built the first dwelling place for the Lord in this world. They had started a new system of worship that atones for the sins of man and were under a law that established morality and justice over conquest and brute strength. Now, ready or not, it was time to follow the cloud. As the cloud moved, they moved. As it was taken up, they stopped, set camp, and atoned for sin. They would observe new customs and traditions every year.

Sinai was an unforgettable place. After spending so much time camped in its shadow, it had become a place of safety. But eventually, the time of refuge had come to an end. They had to move out of their comfort zone and into a foreboding wilderness, whatever it may hold. The path would be fraught with danger. They had to trust the Spirit to lead them.

And so do we.

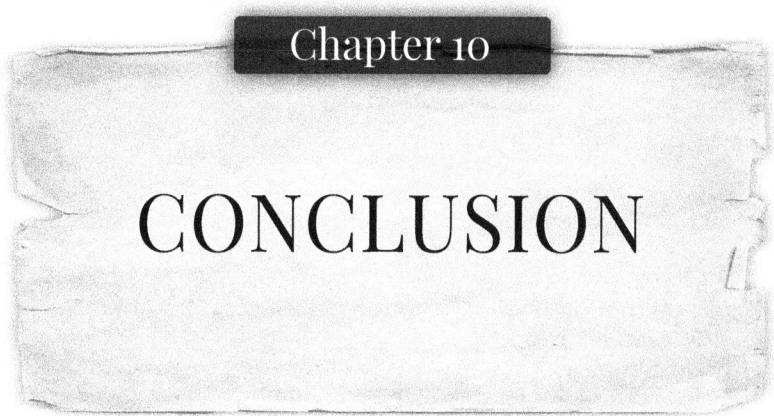

Chapter 10

CONCLUSION

The book of Exodus itself ends on a positive note; the Shekinah glory of God had anointed the tabernacle and now the children of Israel followed it into the wilderness. However I feel the story of the Exodus didn't end here but far into the book of Numbers. And this ending wasn't nearly as hopeful. Perhaps even more tragic than Sinai, where three thousand died, is a place called Kadesh Barnea.

> *And Moses sent them to spy out the land of Canaan, and said unto them, Get you up this way southward, and go up into the mountain: And see the land, what it is, and the people that dwelleth therein, whether they be strong or weak, few or many. (Numbers 13:17-18)*

After a long journey, the Israelites arrived in Kadesh and set camp just outside of the Promised Land. The spies snuck into Canaan and scouted ways to attack.

> *And they went and came to Moses, and to Aaron, and to all the congregation of the children of Israel, unto the wilderness of Paran, to Kadesh; and brought back word unto them, and unto all the congregation, and shewed them the fruit of the land. (Numbers 13:26)*

When they returned, they gave vastly different reports. Caleb, who trusted God enough to see past the obstacles at the wonderful blessings ahead, remembered that the Lord promised to fight for them.

> *And Caleb stilled the people before Moses, and said, Let us go up at once, and possess it; for we are well able to overcome it. (Numbers 13:30)*

The other spies, however, gave a dour report.

But the men that went up with him said, We be not able to go up against the people; for they are stronger than we. And they brought up an evil report of the land which they had searched unto the children of Israel, saying, The land, through which we have gone to search it, is a land that eateth up the inhabitants thereof; and all the people that we saw in it are men of a great stature. (Numbers 13:31-32)

Rather than seeing what God can do, these fear-mongers scared the people into focusing on the seemingly impossible task ahead.

The following scripture is often misquoted to ridicule the Bible:

And there we saw the giants, the sons of Anak, which come of the giants: and we were in our own sight as grasshoppers, and so we were in their sight. (Numbers 13:33)

While the Bible does speak of giants such as the Nephilim or Goliath, it doesn't usually give exact height, and some critics use this scripture to claim that it describes men so tall that others are like grasshoppers next to them. This is of course a complete mischaracterization (the fear-struck spies were clearly exaggerating, made clear by the fact that they described themselves as grasshoppers "in our own sight"). It also completely misses the point that not trusting in God can have disastrous consequences.

Overcome with fear and panic, the Israelites reverted back to complaining.

And all the children of Israel murmured against Moses and against Aaron: and the whole congregation said unto them, Would God that we had died in the land of Egypt! or would God we had died in this wilderness. (Numbers 14:2)

If this sounds familiar, it's because we heard it after the crossing of the Red Sea. Only this time, they had pushed God too far.

And they said one to another, Let us make a captain, and let us return into Egypt. (Numbers 14:4)

After seeing God smite Egypt with ten plagues, drown Pharaoh's army in the Red Sea, and lead them with a cloud of glory by night and pillar of fire by day, they still doubted. The desire to return to Egypt, like our old lives of sin, had been bubbling under the surface all along. Now it had fully boiled over. They even sought to kill Moses and Aaron, completing the mutiny.

But all the congregation bade stone them with stones. And the glory of the LORD appeared in the tabernacle of the congregation before all the children of Israel. Fortunately, the glory steps in to save them. (Numbers 14:10)

CONCLUSION

Rebellion is as the sin of witchcraft, and it shows that Israel was just not ready to take the Promised Land. They always saw insurmountable obstacles and never the bigger picture of how God wanted to pave the way for them. But now, the sin of rebellion had brought them further than they ever thought it would. Grumbling and complaining had festered into a desire to murder their leaders and return to slavery.

Judgment at Sinai would pale in comparison to the curse that had come.

> *As truly as I live, saith the LORD, as ye have spoken in mine ears, so will I do to you: Your carcases shall fall in this wilderness; and all that were numbered of you, according to your whole number, from twenty years old and upward which have murmured against me. Doubtless ye shall not come into the land, concerning which I sware to make you dwell therein, save Caleb the son of Jephunneh, and Joshua the son of Nun. (Numbers 14:28-30)*

This effectively ends the story of the Exodus. It sadly reflects the beginning and the end of Genesis, which started with an explosion of life and creation and ended with Joseph dead in his casket. Exodus started with a promise that God would deliver His people from bondage, honoring the covenant He made with their long-distant ancestor. But it ended with a curse being placed on them. They would wander aimlessly in the burning desert until their bones bleached under a pitiless sun. Only those twenty years old and under, as well as Joshua and Caleb, would ever see Canaan. While at the cusp of all they had been promised, they had to turn and walk away into oblivion.

Their only hope for survival as a people was to go live on pure faith for the next four decades. As the old generation that grew up in slavery died, a new generation that was used to God miraculously supplying every need would take its place. The subsequent book of Joshua, which details Israel's great military victories over the Canaanites, is one of the few books in the Bible where we see the results of total obedience. When we come together as one, there is no limit to what God can do through us.

Even in tragic endings, the theme of hope for the future permeates the entire Word of God. As soon as man sinned, the Lord promised the serpent that one day a Savior would bruise his head. Through years of idolatry, violence, and bloodshed during the reigns of the kings of Israel and Judah, there was always at least a remnant of people who chose to serve God.

> *Yet I have left me seven thousand in Israel, all the knees which have not bowed unto Baal, and every mouth which hath not kissed him. (1 Kings 19:18)*

Even when all the disciples had fled, John still stayed by Jesus' side to the end. Since he was the last apostle alive on the Isle of Patmos, perhaps it was all the more prophetic when Jesus said,

> *But he that shall endure unto the end, the same shall be saved. (Matthew 24:13)*

Fast forward many years. A new generation of Israelites, stronger in faith, arrived at the borders of Canaan. The Torah had been almost completed. Moses could not go into the Promised Land due to striking the rock. But as the final act of his life, the Lord had allowed him to ascend Mount Nebo to see it for himself.

> *And Moses went up from the plains of Moab unto the mountain of Nebo, to the top of Pisgah, that is over against Jericho. (Deuteronomy 34:1)*

From there, as he drew his last breath at the age of one hundred twenty, this legendary figure of the Old Testament, the central character and author of the Torah, was granted the view of everything he had wanted for his people. Two-thirds of his life was to bring the children of Abraham to their promised land. Perhaps himself being there was less important as completing the work of ushering them through a wilderness of fire while God purged out all doubt and iniquity.

> *And the LORD said unto him, This is the land which I sware unto Abraham, unto Isaac, and unto Jacob, saying, I will give it unto thy seed: I have caused thee to see it with thine eyes, but thou shalt not go over thither. (Deuteronomy 34:4)*

And there, the prophet and leader died. In his final eulogy, Deuteronomy concludes by telling us,

> *And there arose not a prophet since in Israel like unto Moses, whom the LORD knew face to face, In all the signs and the wonders, which the LORD sent him to do in the land of Egypt to Pharaoh, and to all his servants, and to all his land, And in all that mighty hand, and in all the great terror which Moses shewed in the sight of all Israel. (Deuteronomy 34:10-11)*

In *Walking the Bible: A Journey by Land through the Five Books of Moses* (you may notice this book appears many times in my sources), author Bruce Feiler climbed Mount Nebo and camped out overnight at the summit, getting a general idea of the beautiful landscape Moses saw in his final moments. He noticed, with great poignancy, that due to the curvature of the earth, not all of the cities described in Deuteronomy 34:1-3 are visible from the summit. It was through divine vision that God showed Moses what the entire Promised Land, from the far reaches of North, South, East, and West, would look like. Perhaps fittingly, Moses passed away in a vision from the Lord.

To the very end, let's always look forward, through eyes of divinity, to what God has in store—not just for us, but for our future generations.

AUTHOR'S AFTERWORD

When I was growing up, my mother read from a thick volume of illustrated Bible stories for children as my bedtime story every night. Until I was old enough to understand the Bible for myself, it was a great way to teach me the basics. In simple language, it covered story after story with vivid, colorful illustrations. I grew up not just with a thorough comprehension of almost every Bible story but with indelible mental images that are still with me: the serpent tempting Eve; Jonah treading water—a giant, ominous sea creature with open maw below him; Christ hanging on the cross.

Every Easter my family watched *The Ten Commandments*. I've also seen the excellent animated movie *The Prince of Egypt*. It was years before I learned just how different the movies are from the actual scriptures. The love triangle between Ramses, Nefretiri, and Moses was a creative liberty. At one time not too long ago, I was absolutely certain that somewhere the Bible named Ramses as the Exodus Pharaoh.

But it all changed when I saw a Netflix documentary: *Exodus: Patterns of Evidence*. This started a chain reaction that led to an obsession with archaeology (combined with a passion for studying and teaching the Word of God) that led me to ordering dozens of books and watching countless documentaries to learn all I could about biblical history. As of the time of this writing, this has been going on for about two and a half years. I also taught a twelve-part series at my church on biblical archaeology. But this book is perhaps the most profound thing to come out of it so far.

My mental images have changed. The unforgettable imprints of illustrated Bible stories and Yule Brenner watching his army drown under two collapsing walls of water are still there, don't get me wrong. But through this study, God has shown me past the larger-than-life myths we've exaggerated these stories into—to the real historical events that inspired them. The Exodus has been brought from the shroud of mythological archetypes back to the light of history.

Does it really matter? This is the question I'm sure many fellow theists have asked about the premise for this book. It's the thought process behind many believers on historical apologetics. The archaeological evidence for the Bible is fine, but does it really matter as long as we have faith in the Word of God? I mean after all, we know the Bible says what it says, so if we truly have faith, can't we go along with that?

This is actually the case with other religions and philosophies. If you ask a Buddhist whether some of the mythical fables of Buddha actually happened, he or she will probably respond with, "Who cares?" This is also true for Aesop's fables. Whether or not a tortoise actually beat a hare in a race is irrelevant to the lesson we learn from the story.

But no. This has never been the case for Christianity. Our faith is based on not just the lessons but the historicity of the Bible. And it isn't just about the Flood, the Exodus, or any other Old Testament tale. It's based on the life, death, and resurrection of Christ. He is the centerpiece of Christianity, and for us to thrive and continue, the Exodus has to be a historical event. This goes back to the very beginning. The apostle Peter himself said,

> *For we have not followed cunningly devised fables, when we made known unto you the power and coming of our Lord Jesus Christ, but were eyewitnesses of his majesty. (2 Peter 1:16)*

Even then, eyewitness accounts of the resurrection of Christ formed the bedrock of the Christian faith.

I certainly understand the "just have faith" mindset. But it bothered me over the years, especially after being confronted by non-believers. How to witness to someone who's been told by historians that the Bible is just a collection of Bronze Age fairytales? Circular reasoning like, "I believe the Bible *because* it's the Word of God," isn't going to convince anyone. On the other hand, if there *is* empirical evidence supporting the stories in the Bible, don't we have an absolute duty to proclaim it to the world?

But of course, it was never just about the archaeological evidence. I've found plenty of Bible commentaries that focus on the life lessons we can learn from Exodus. And I've seen plenty of books thoroughly and wonderfully explaining the archaeological support for the story, while completely ignoring the life applications. It occurred to me that I have not yet found a book that truly does *both*. In this discovery, I felt the Lord wanted me to craft something wholly unique: part-Bible study, part-commentary, and part-history book. This is what it really meant as the title rang from my keyboard. I wanted to bring this story to life like never before. I want to introduce you not just to the mythical ideas of Moses and the Pharaoh and the Israelites but to the real ones who lived. I want you to see the sweat on their sun-worn brows and look into the wisdom in their eyes.

And through this book, I've been with them all along. Or at least it feels that way. In the absence of time travel ever being invented, historical research is the next best thing. Any history buff will tell you that's what they experience when they immerse themselves in research. It isn't just about maps, facts, figures, and dates. It's about traveling back in time and connecting with our past. It's about closing your eyes and imagining what it was like to *be* there. What did they see? What did it sound like? How did they feel?

AUTHOR'S AFTERWORD

After writing this book, the Exodus is less mystical and more real to me than ever. I don't imagine a giant wall of water on either side of marching, singing Israelites, but a howling wind driving back a lake while a frightened, desperate tribe of desert nomads scramble across to safety. In some ways, it has shattered my preconceived notions of the Bible. Yet in doing so, the Bible is more personal, and I feel a deeper connection with God over it.

And I hope I didn't just go on that journey alone. My sincerest wish is this has educated you on ancient history. I also hope you have learned valuable life lessons in your walk with God that you can never unlearn.

And this is why I'm so excited to be authoring what I hope will be the first book in a whole new series. There are plenty more topics in the Bible to dive into. There are prophets. There are kings. There is a Creation and an ending. And there is a Savior, hanging on the cross, that it all revolves around and points to. I hope *Bringing the Exodus to Life* will be the start of something that changes the way the world perceives the Word of God, bringing hope to this lost and dying world.

INDEX

A

Aaron, 17, 38, 45, 64-65, 68, 70, 71, 74, 75-79, 81, 84, 88-89, 91-92, 94, 96, 98, 103-105, 126, 134, 136, 140, 142, 145, 160-161, 169-170, 173-176, 179-180, 186, 190, 193-195, 197-199, 203, 210, 213-214, 219-220

Abd-El, 116

Abednego, 34

Abihu, 78, 160-161, 172, 179-181

Abraham, 10, 12, 15-16, 18, 27, 44-48, 52-53, 55, 57, 60, 69, 78, 98, 110, 141, 153, 157-158, 161, 168, 171, 183, 184, 195, 202, 212, 222

Adam, 54, 73, 91, 99, 198, 204,

Aesop, 224

Africa, 7, 116, 132, 138, 142, 147

Africanus, 138

Agate, 173

Ahmose II, 26, 139

Aholiab, 191, 192

Aithiopiai, 142

Akhenaten, 114, 115, 116

Akkadian, 36-37

Akki, 36-37

Aleph, 106

Amalek, 17, 135-136, 137, 139

Amalekites, 17, 135-136, 137, 138, 139, 142

American Revolution, 127

Amethyst, 173

Ammon(ites), 58, 135

Anachronism, 21, 22, 232

Ananias and Sapphira, 185

Angel(s), 39, 52, 63, 70, 81, 83, 86, 87, 95, 98, 99, 104, 119, 145, 155, 167, 187, 198, 202, 204, 206, 207

Ankhu, 29-30

Anointing, 66, 70, 137, 141, 180, 189, 190, 194, 214

Antichrist, 51, 82, 86, 87, 96

Apocrypha, 168

April, 98, 239

Arabia, 112, 113, 144-145, 146-147, 236

Archaeology, 8, 11, 12, 14, 21, 26, 146, 162, 163, 175, 223

Ark of the Covenant, 17, 51, 94, 112, 146, 162-165, 168, 169, 170, 177, 178, 182, 190, 194, 202, 213, 214, 215, 238

Asher, 31, 33

Asiastic(s), 30, 31, 32, 33, 104, 106

Assyrian(s), 48, 90

Aten, 115, 116

Atheists, 21, 152, 155, 156, 157

Atonement, 102, 120, 164, 165, 168, 170, 176, 177, 178, 181, 182, 184, 199, 202, 212, 213, 215
  Day of, 54, 169, 181, 182, 199, 213

Atrahasis Epic, 159

Avaris, 22, 30-31, 32, 33, 34, 104, 105, 106, 111, 117, 129, 138

Axis powers, 160

Ayun Musa, 129

Azusa Street, 32

B

Ba, 80
Baal, 22, 157, 159, 160, 197, 221
Baali, 204
Babylon, 12, 13, 14, 15, 18, 36, 48, 163, 175, 182
Bahr Yussef, 29
Bedouins, 13, 132
Benjamin, 24, 31, 174
Beracah (valley of), 59
Beryl, 173, 206
Bethlehem, 41, 150, 189
Bezaleel, 190, 191, 192
Bietak, Manford, 30, 33, 106
Bir el-Mura, 128, 129
Bitter Lakes, 111, 117
Blasphemy, 64, 81-83, 93, 180, 182, 185, 213
Book of Life, 102, 199, 200, 215
Brenner, Yule, 21, 223
British, 7, 11, 117, 127, 134, 239
Bronze Age, 57, 84, 104, 110, 224
Buddha, 223

C

Cairo, 25
Caleb, 191, 219, 221
Calvary, 51, 52, 64, 71, 82, 91, 129, 183, 186, 198, 204, 216
Canaan, 9, 17, 27, 28, 30, 57, 66, 111, 125, 133, 142, 145, 158, 208, 219, 221, 222
Canaanites, 15, 55, 58, 160, 178, 202, 208, 221
Carbuncle, 173
Carter, Howard, 115
Carthage, 157
Catherine, 144
Catholic, 168, 199
Celsus, 80
Chebar River, 161
Cherubs, 165, 168, 169, 188, 214
Child sacrifice, 157-160
China, 32, 159
Christianity, 7, 8, 14, 32, 53, 65, 73, 144, 154, 191, 192, 224
Christmas, 168
Chronicles, book of, 24, 51, 58, 59, 171, 183, 191, 203, 204
Chronologies,
    Old, 22, 25, 28, 114
    New, 22, 24, 25, 26, 40, 41, 106, 116
Circumcision, 46, 68, 69, 70
Codex Sinaiticus, 144
Compositional View, 19
Constantine, 144
Constitution, 127
Creation, 10, 16, 19, 20, 72, 124, 171, 192, 195, 207, 221, 225
Crocodiles, 39, 80, 110, 111
Crucifixion, 51, 98, 99, 101, 102, 170, 214

D

Daniel, 18, 34, 39, 150, 200, 206
Dark Ages, 12
David (king), 43, 45, 82, 83, 163, 164, 166, 189, 213
Day of Pentecost, 53, 65, 121, 154, 181
Dead Sea Scrolls, 14, 182
Declaration of Independence, 127
DeMille, Cecil B., 21
Djoser, 114
Dome of the Rock, 14, 182
Dudimose II, 26, 48, 84, 107, 124, 138

E

Early Dynastic Period, 36
Easter, 98, 222
Eden, Garden of, 10, 54, 70, 73, 148, 174, 205
El Amarna, 115
Eleazar, 78, 79, 172, 180
Eli, 163, 169
Elijah, 44-45, 51, 120
Eliphaz, 135
Ellicott's commentary, 212
El-Olam, 57
El-Shaddai, 78
Emerald, 173, 174
Epic of Gilgamesh, 15, 36
Epiphanes, Antiochus, 98, 167, 168
Erythra Thalassa, 116
Essenes, 14, 182
Esther, 14
Etham, 110, 117, 128
Ethiopia, 88, 142
Europe, 11, 12, 132
Eusebius, 138
Evangelism, 15, 32
Exodus: Patterns of Evidence, 223
Ezekiel, 161, 196
Ezra, 14, 18, 175, 182, 184

F

Firstborn, 63, 68, 80, 81, 85, 88, 97, 98, 99, 104, 115, 116, 118, 124, 157,
Flood, 15, 20, 29, 36, 51, 92, 125, 159, 163, 224
Founding Fathers, 7
Frogs, 63, 80, 87-89, 92

G

Galilee, 49, 62, 102
Gandhi, 8
Gardiner, Alan, 84
Gebel el-Lawz, 112, 113, 144, 145, 147
Gebel Musa, 144
Gehenna, 159
Gem stone, 162
Genocide, 106
Gentile(s), 62, 156, 167, 192, 208,
George III, King, 7
Germany, 19, 159, 160
Gershom, 47
Gethsemane, 103, 150
Gnats, 63, 89
Gold, 14, 24, 58, 85, 96, 97, 164, 165, 166, 167, 170, 173, 181, 191, 193, 194, 195, 197, 199, 206, 213, 214
Golden Calf, 147, 181, 193-197, 199, 201, 202, 203, 208, 216, 217
Goliath, 220
Goshen, 30, 91, 93, 104, 110, 143
Grand Canyon, 112
Greek, 7, 11, 13, 25, 30, 80, 142, 144, 153, 159, 167, 191, 195, 199
Greek Orthodox, 144
Gregorian Calendar, 199
Gulf of Suez, 128, 145

H

Hagar, 44
Hanukkah, 98, 167, 168
Hapi, 80
Hathor, 80, 195, 197, 198, 199
Hatshepsut, 25
Heber, 46

Hebrew, 11, 13, 19, 21, 22, 25, 26, 34, 35, 39, 40, 41, 44, 45, 52, 54, 57, 58, 70, 71, 73, 75, 76, 78, 79, 83, 92, 98, 99, 103, 106, 110, 112, 116, 117, 129, 133, 140, 142, 153, 155, 169, 170, 184, 191, 193, 194, 195, 196, 208, 215, 216

Hekket, 80

Helena, 144

Hell, 44, 75, 77, 91, 96, 99, 123, 159, 180, 181, 187, 198, 199

Hierarchy, 103, 141

Hieroglyphics, 19, 25, 29, 153

Hinnom, Valley of, 159

Hiroshima, 160

Hitler, Adolph, 19, 48, 98, 160

Hittites, 15, 55, 58, 61

Hobab, 46

Holiest of Holies, 54, 57, 120, 149, 154, 162, 165, 169, 171, 172, 189, 212, 213, 214

Holy Ghost, 52, 53, 54, 59, 64, 65, 81, 82, 94, 120, 121, 154, 163, 164, 168, 178, 179, 181, 185, 186, 192, 204, 212, 213

Holy Grail, 112

Holy Spirit, 20, 47, 52, 54, 64, 65, 82, 98, 124, 145, 154, 162, 168, 170, 186, 190, 191, 192, 197, 207, 214, 216

Homer, 7, 11

Horeb, Mount, 50-51, 57, 78, 133, 202

Hosea, 204

Humic acid, 76

Hykau, 107

Hyksos, 26, 84, 106, 107, 138, 139

Hypocoristic, 24, 25, 29

Hyssop, 100, 101, 102

I

Iliad, 7

Imhotep, 114

Incense, 178-181, 213

Intercession, 196

Intermediate Period(s), 22, 138

Ipuwer Papyrus, 84-86, 115, 138

Isaiah, 48, 52, 53, 53, 54, 55, 161, 165, 167, 170, 171, 176, 183, 193, 194, 205

Ishmael, 46

Isis, 80, 81

Islam, 7, 98

Ismaliya, 128

Issachar, 31, 33

Ithamar, 78, 172, 180

J

Jackson, Andrew, 127

Jacob, 9, 10, 11, 16, 18, 27, 28, 30, 31, 35, 36, 47, 53, 55, 57, 60, 78, 148, 153, 161, 167, 174, 195, 202, 217, 222

Jahaziel, 59

Japan, 159

Jarvis, C.S., 134

Jasper, 173-174

Jehovah, 78, 137

Jehovah-Nissi, 137

Jericho, 11, 12, 21, 23, 139, 142, 157, 158, 159, 209, 216, 222

Jeroboam, 195, 197

Jerusalem, 12, 18, 24, 51, 59, 62, 98, 102, 113, 150, 153, 158, 159, 167, 171, 172, 175, 182, 183, 184, 195, 196, 214

Jether, 45

Jethro, 45, 46, 50, 51, 66, 74, 140, 141, 142, 194

Jezebel, 44, 45, 51

Joan of Arc, 144
Job, book of, 17, 161, 189
Jochebed, 138
John (apostle), 51, 55, 101, 102, 161, 171, 173, 174, 188, 221
John the Baptist, 42, 82
Jonah, 44, 90, 223
Joseph, 10, 11, 16, 23, 27, 28, 29, 30, 31, 32, 46, 114, 139, 161, 195, 221
Josephus, Flavius, 19, 26, 138, 170, 195
Joshua, 11, 17, 18, 70, 94, 136, 137, 139, 158, 160, 162, 169, 197, 204, 208, 221
Josiah, 22, 25, 183
Judah, 18, 24, 31, 53, 59, 60, 62, 150, 156, 158, 161, 167, 174, 184, 190, 194, 221
Judaism, 7, 13, 14, 57, 98, 121, 153, 154, 166, 167, 171, 182, 213
Judgment Day, 100, 171, 198, 199, 200, 215
Judi Dagh, 111, 112

K

Ka, 80
Kadesh Barnea, 219
Kantara, 117
Kavod, 216
Kenites, 194-195
Kenyon, Kathleen, 11, 21, 23, 26
Ketef Hinnom, 13
Keturah, 45
Khaneferre, 40
Khepri, 80
Khnum, 80
Khonsuemwaset, 124
King Agag, 139
King Manasseh, 129, 158
King, Martin Luther, 8

Kitchen, Kenneth, 21
Kohath, 38
Korah, 180-181
Kushites, 40

L

Lake Timsa, 110, 111
Lapis lazuli, 85
Last Supper, 101, 102-103, 131, 214
Latvia, 159
Laver, 185-189, 212-213, 221
Leah, 35, 36
Lent, 98, 199
Leprosy, 61-63, 142
Levites, 18, 79, 164, 184, 198
Leviticus, 17, 18, 62, 156, 160, 165, 178, 179, 180, 212, 215, 231, 234, 239
Lice, 80, 89, 92, 130, 175
Ligure, 173
Livestock, 80, 88, 92, 97, 114, 122, 139, 195, 207, 209
Locusts, 63, 81, 85, 88, 94-96, 117
Lot, 50, 60
Lot's wife, 50
Luke, 13, 49, 50, 51, 53, 62, 69, 102, 103, 150, 131
Luxor Dynasty, 30, 33

M

Maccabees, book of, 168
Maccabeus, Judah, 167
Magicians, 61, 81, 87, 89, 92
Malachi, 50, 184-185
Manetho, 107, 138-139
Manna, 7, 15, 130-134, 169, 170, 215
Marah, 128-129
Marduk, 157

Martha, 53
Masoretes, 13-14
Masoretic Text, 13-14, 231
Matrix, 209
Matzah Bread, 100, 103
Maximinus, 144
Medieval, 12
Mediterranean, 88, 117
Melchizidek, 183-184
Menahem, 33
Menorah, 166-169, 171, 213, 239
Merestekhi, 40
Merhotepre, 41
Merneptah Stela, 25
Meshach, 34
Mesopotamia, 10, 12, 15, 20, 36
Messiah, 62, 150
Middle Kingdom, 9, 22, 23, 26, 33, 40, 84, 105, 111, 114
Theory, 21, 23, 24, 26, 30, 137, 138, 139
Midian, 44, 45, 50, 66, 112, 113, 140, 142, 145
Midianite, 45, 46, 66, 130, 143, 144, 145, 147, 194, 234
Migdol, 112, 238
Mio, 40-41, 47
Miriam, 38-39, 62, 124, 126, 142
Moab, 58, 125, 135, 222
Moabites, 58
Molech, 157, 158, 160
Moller, Lennart, 146
Molten Sea, 187, 189, 213
Moshe, 40
Mount Everest, 8
Mount Olympus, 143
Mummies, 80, 81
Munius, 40

Mussolini, Benito, 160
Mysterious Numbers of the Hebrew Kings, The, 22

N

Naaman, 62
Nabatean, 147
Nadab, 78, 160, 161, 164, 172, 179, 180
Nagasaki, 160
Nanking, 159
Napoleon, 25
Nash Papyrus, 13
Nash, Walter, 13
Nazis, 159
Nebuchadnezzar, 12, 14, 175, 182
Nefertiti, 115
Nehemiah, 14, 175, 182, 184
Nephilim, 220
Netflix, 223
New Kingdom, 22, 23, 26, 33, 84, 114, 116, 138, 139
New Orleans, 127
New Testament, 18, 51, 53, 56, 79, 87, 113, 120, 121, 144, 154, 156, 157, 159, 160, 168, 173, 177, 185, 190, 192, 199, 200, 238
New York City, 43
Niebelungs, 19
Nile River, 29, 32, 35, 37, 39, 63, 80, 86, 88, 105, 138
Ninevah, 90
Nissan, 98
Noah, 15, 16, 36, 39, 73, 159
Noah's Ark, 15, 51, 111, 112, 163
Nuweiba, 111-114, 146

INDEX

O
Old Kingdom, 22, 36, 80, 114
Onyx, 173
Osiris, 80-81
Ottoman Empire, 145

P
Pa-Aneah, 29
Palmanothes, 39
Passover, 98-100, 102-103, 153, 169
Pa-Tjuf, 117
Patmos, Isle of, 161, 121
Patriarch(s), 10, 16, 19, 30, 57, 66, 100, 103
Paul, 18, 20, 44, 103, 113, 114, 157, 188, 192
Pelusiac, 32
Pentecostal(s), 32, 39, 55, 179, 181, 186
Peter, 44, 49, 51, 54, 120, 148, 150, 177, 179, 185, 224
Pharisees, 12, 13, 32, 62, 82, 166
Philistines, 139, 163, 164, 169, 174
Phoenicia, 157
Piharoth, 117
Pithom, 21, 22, 32
Plaut, Gunther, 200
Potiphar, 28
Prince of Egypt, The, 48, 223
Promised Land, 15, 42, 60, 65, 70, 110, 126, 134, 135, 142, 145, 169, 175, 200, 202, 208, 215, 219, 221, 222
Protestant(s),
Proto-Sinaitic (language), 13, 152, 168
Psalms, 43, 82, 99, 101, 103, 119, 137, 158, 172, 188, 199, 200
Puah, 34
Putiel, 45, 79

Q
Quail, 131-132
Qumran, 14, 182

R
Rachel, 35
Raiders of the Lost Ark, 162
Ramses, The Great or II, 21-26, 29, 33, 47, 84, 115, 116, 138, 223
Rapture, 50, 91, 121, 151, 161
Rephidim, 133, 135, 139, 142, 144, 237
Reuben, 31, 78, 106, 174
Reuel, 45
Revelation (book of), 9, 51, 55, 82, 83, 86, 87, 93, 95, 96, 98, 102, 161, 173, 174, 177, 188, 198, 200, 201
Riga, 159, 239
Roe v Wade, 41
Rohl, David, 22, 23
Roman Empire, 144, 147, 153, 156
Romans (book of), 7, 18, 99, 156, 199
Roosevelt, Theodore, 43
Rosh Hashanah, 182, 199

S
Sadducees, 199
Salem Witch Trials, 156
Samaria, 61, 62, 131
Samuel, 53, 82, 116, 139, 163, 164, 166, 175, 189
Sapphire stone, 161, 162, 173
Sarah, 27, 45, 52
Sarcophagus, 81
Sardine, 173, 174
Sargon of Akkad, 36-37
Saudi Arabia, 113, 144, 145, 236

Saul, 53, 82, 83, 116, 139, 174, 175, 189
Seleucid, 48, 167
Septuagint, 13, 116, 142, 195
Serabit el-Khadim, 153
Seth, 81
Shadrach, 34
Shakespeare, William, 7
Shavu'ot, 153
Sheik Abu Taleb, 136
Shekinah glory, 216, 219, 240
Shekinot, 216
Shiphrah, 33, 34
Shishack, 24-25
Shoshenk I, 24
Show bread, 165, 168, 177, 213, 214
Shur, Wilderness of, 110, 128
Silver, 46, 48, 85, 97, 191
Simeon, 31, 78
Simon, 49, 53, 150
Sinai, Mount, 50-51, 70, 79, 81, 112, 113, 129, 143-145, 147-149, 151, 153, 157, 159, 161-163, 165, 167-169, 171, 173, 175, 177, 179, 181, 183, 185, 187, 189, 191, 193-195, 197, 199, 201, 210, 211, 213, 215, 217, 219, 221
Sinai, Peninsula, 15, 113, 128, 129, 132, 134, 136, 144, 145, 194
Skeptics, 7, 11, 21, 36, 139
Sobekhotep III, 35
Sobekhotep IV, 40, 47
Sobekhotep V, 41, 48
Solomon, 14, 24, 25, 112, 119, 169, 182, 187, 195, 203
Speaking in tongues, 53, 54, 65, 121, 154, 179, 181, 186, 192
St. Catherine's monastery, 144
Succoth, 104-105, 110, 117

Suez Canal, 117
Sumerian, 36-37, 50, 159, 183
Syncellus, 138
Syrio-Canaan, 30, 57

T

Tabernacle, 141, 149, 162, 165-169, 172, 165-169, 172, 176-180, 182-184, 186-187, 189-192, 194, 202-204, 210-216, 219, 220
Tafuni, 134
Tamarisk tree, 130
Tefillin, 13
Tell el-Maskhuta, 110
Temple, 14, 16, 18, 22, 24, 25, 53-54, 62, 119, 153-154, 165, 167-170, 175, 182, 183, 189, 203-204, 213, 215, 216, 231, 232
Temple, Second, 14, 182
Ten Commandments, 13, 21, 51, 112, 120, 143, 151, 153-154, 169, 196, 200, 210, 215
Test of Time, A, 22
Tetragrammaton, the, 57
The Ten Commandments (movie), 47, 223
Thera, 88
Thiele, Edwin, 22, 24
Third heaven, 188-189
Thutmose III, 25
Timna, 135
Timothy, 20, 67
Tishrei, 182, 199
Titus (emperor), 182
Tojo, Hideki, 160
Topaz, 173
Torah, 11-13, 16-20, 22, 40, 45, 46, 62, 167, 207, 222

Transfiguration, Mount of, 51, 120
Tribulation period, 51, 86, 91, 95, 96, 121, 151
Trinity, 65, 120, 207
Tulloch, Sir Alexander, 117
Turquoise, 84, 145, 194
Tutankhamen, 114-115

U
Unleavened bread, 100, 175, 209
Uraeus, 81
Urim and thummim, 174-175
Uzzah, 164

V
Valley Forge, 7
Veil, 54, 149, 162, 169-170, 178, 190, 210-214
Volcano, 88

W
Wadi Islaf, 136
Wadi Tumilat, 128
Wadi-Feiran, 133
Wadi-Refayid, 133
War of 1812, 127
Washington, George, 7
Witch of Endor, 175
Wormwood, 86-87
Wyatt Archaeological Research, 112
Wyatt, Ron, 111-112, 114, 146-147

Y
Yam Suph, 116
YHWH (Yahweh), 57, 78, 116, 137, 147, 167
Yom Kippur, 181-182, 199

Z
Zipporah, 45, 68, 70, 140, 142

ENDNOTES

INTRODUCTION

1. Tremper Longman III and David E. Garland ed., *The Expositor's Bible Commentary: Revised Edition (Genesis-Leviticus)* (Grand Rapids: Zondervan, 2008), 335.

2. Bruce Feiler, *Walking the Bible: A Journey by Land through the Five Books of Moses* (New York, NY: HarperCollins, 2002), 96.

3. David Rohl, *Exodus: Myth or History?* (St. Louis Park: Thinking Man Media, 2015), 10.

4. Feiler, *Walking the Bible*, 97.

5. Longman, *The Expositor's Bible Commentary*, 28.

6. "Accuracy of the Torah Text," *Simpletoremember.com*, accessed March 11, 2016. www.simpletoremember.com/articles/a/torahaccuracy/.

7. Edmund Davison Soper, *The Religions of Mankind*, 3rd ed., revised (New York: Abingdon-Cokesbury Press, 1951), 198.

8. Feiler, *Walking the Bible*, 105.

9. "The Bible and Its Translations: Original Languages of the Bible," *King James Version* (Thomas Nelson Inc., 1962).

10. "Jewish Concepts: Masoretic Texts," *Jewishvirtuallibrary.com*, accessed March 21, 2016. www.jewishvirtuallibrary.org/jsource/Judaism/Masoretic.html.

11. "Nash Papyrus," *University of Cambridge Digital Library*, accessed March 21, 2016. cudl.lib.cam.ac.uk/view/MS-OR-00233/1.

12. Amiram Barkat, "Bible Texts on Silver Amulets Dated to First Temple Period," *Haaretz.com*, September 29, 2004, accessed March 24, 2016. www.haaretz.com/bible-texts-on-silver-amulets-dated-to-first-temple-period-1.136051.

13. Diane Cole, "Carbon Dating Confirms World's Oldest Torah Scroll," *Nationalgeographic.com*, May 31, 2015, accessed March 24, 2016. news.nationalgeographic.com/news/2013/05/130530-worlds-oldest-torah-scroll-bible-bologna-carbon-dating/.

14. Yosi Krausz, "What Are the Dead Sea Scrolls?" *Chabad.org*, accessed March 24, 2016. www.chabad.org/library/article_cdo/aid/1725431/jewish/What-Are-the-Dead-Sea-Scrolls.htm.

15. "The Jewish Temples: The First Temple-Solomon's Temple," *Jewishvirtuallibrary.org*, accessed March 24, 2016. www.jewishvirtuallibrary.org/jsource/Judaism/The_Temple.html.

16. "Learn About the Scrolls," *Deadseascrolls.org*, accessed March 24, 2016. www.deadseascrolls.org.il/learn-about-the-scrolls/introduction.

17. Feiler, *Walking the Bible*, 73.

18. Feiler, *Walking the Bible*, 23.

19. Longman, *The Expositor's Bible Commentary:* page 335.

20. Jack W. Hayford ed., *Spirit-Filled Life Bible For Students (New King James Version)* (Nashville: Thomas Nelson Publishers, 1995), 583.

21. Feiler, *Walking the Bible*, 212.

22. Feiler, *Walking the Bible*, 97.

23. Feiler, *Walking the Bible*, 103.

24. "Anachronism," *Merriam-Webster.com*, accessed August 22, 2016. www.merriam-webster.com/dictionary/anachronism.

25. "3c. Dynasties,"*Ushistory.org*, accessed August 23, 2016. www.ushistory.org/civ/3c.asp.

26. David Rohl, *From Eden to Exile: The 5,000-Year History of the People of the Bible* (Lebanon, TN: Greenleaf Press, 2002), 454.

27. Rohl, *From Eden to Exile*, 454.

28. Rohl, *Exodus: Myth or History?*, 57.

29. Rohl, *Exodus: Myth or History?*, 276.

30. Rohl, *Exodus: Myth or History?*, 61.

31. Rohl, *Exodus: Myth or History?*, 69.

32. Rohl, *Exodus: Myth or History?*, 24.

33. Rohl, *Exodus: Myth or History?*, 45.

34. Rohl, *Exodus: Myth or History?*, 156.

35. Rohl, *Exodus: Myth or History?*, 157.

CHAPTER 1

36. David Rohl, *Exodus: Myth or History?* (St. Louis Park: Thinking Man Media, 2015), 85.

37. Rohl, *Exodus: Myth or History?*, 90.

38. Rohl, *Exodus: Myth or History?*, 91.

39. Rohl, *Exodus: Myth or History?*, 91.

40. Rohl, *Exodus: Myth or History?*, 101.

41. Rohl, *Exodus: Myth or History?*, 104.

42. Rohl, *Exodus: Myth or History?*, 104.

43. Rohl, *Exodus: Myth or History?*, 105.

44. Rohl, *Exodus: Myth or History?*, 136.

45. David Rohl, *From Eden to Exile: The 5,000-Year History of the People of the Bible* (Lebanon, TN: Greenleaf Press, 2002), 166.

46. Rohl, *Exodus: Myth or History?*, 21.

47. Rohl, *Exodus: Myth or History?*, 122.

48. Rohl, *Exodus: Myth or History?*, 106.

49. Rohl, *Exodus: Myth or History?*, 116.

50. Rohl, *Exodus: Myth or History?*, 112.

51. Rohl, *Exodus: Myth or History?*, 121.

52. Rohl, *Exodus: Myth or History?*, 135.

53. Rohl, *Exodus: Myth or History?*, 127.

54. Rohl, *Exodus: Myth or History?*, 127.

CHAPTER 2

55. David Rohl, *From Eden to Exile: The 5,000-Year History of the People of the Bible* (Lebanon, TN: Greenleaf Press, 2002), 109.

56. Rohl, *From Eden to Exile*, 181–182.

57. David Rohl, *Exodus: Myth or History?* (St. Louis Park: Thinking Man Media, 2015), 132.

58. Eliezer Dazinger, "What Was Moses' Real Name?" *Chabad.org*, accessed Jan. 24, 2016. www.chabad.org/parshah/article_cdo/aid/627663/jewish/What-Was-Moses-Real-Name.htm.

59. Rohl, *Exodus: Myth or History?*, 138.

60. Rohl, *Exodus: Myth or History?*, 140.

61. Rohl, *Exodus: Myth or History?*, 138.

CHAPTER 3

62. "Midianite: Ancient People," *Britannica.com*, revised 4-18-2014, accessed Jan. 24, 2016. www.britannica.com/topic/Midianites.

63. "Jethro," *Jewishvirtuallibrary.org*, 2008, accessed Jan. 24, 2016. www.jewishvirtuallibrary.org/jsource/biography/Jethro.html.

64. Jack W. Hayford ed., *Spirit-Filled Life Bible for Students (New King James Version)* (Nashville: Thomas Nelson Publishers, 1995), 74.

CHAPTER 4

65. Joseph Jacobs, M. Seligsohn, & Wilhelm Bacher, "Sinai, Mount. Mount Horeb," *Jewishencyclopedia.com*, accessed February 7, 2016. www.jewishencyclopedia.com/articles/13766-sinai-mount.

66. Peter Enns, *The NIV Application Commentary: Exodus* (Grand Rapids: Zondervan, 2000), 96.

67. G. H. Parke-Taylor, *(Yehovah) Yahweh: The Divine Name in the Bible* (Waterloo, Ont.: Wilfrid Laurier University Press, 1975), 79.

68. David Rohl, *Exodus: Myth or History?* (St. Louis Park: Thinking Man Media, 2015), 218.

69. Enns, *The NIV Application Commentary: Exodus*, 109.

CHAPTER 5

70. Tremper Longman III and David E. Garland ed., *The Expositor's Bible Commentary: Revised Edition (Genesis-Leviticus)* (Grand Rapids: Zondervan, 2008), 388.

71. Jack W. Hayford ed., *Spirit-Filled Life Bible for Students (New King James Version)* (Nashville: Thomas Nelson Publishers, 1995), 78.

72. Edmund Davison Soper, *The Religions of Mankind*, 3rd ed., revised (New York: Abingdon-Cokesbury Press, 1951), 56.

73. Soper, *The Religions of Mankind*, 64.

74. Ziony Zevit, "Exodus in the Bible and the Egyptian Plagues," *Biblicalarchaeology.org*, 03-01-2015, accessed February 2, 2017. www.biblicalarchaeology.org/daily/biblical-topics/exodus/exodus-in-the-bible-and-the-egyptian-plagues/.

75. "Uraeus," *Ancient-symbols.com*, accessed February 2, 2017. www.ancient-symbols.com/symbols-directory/uraeus.html>

76. David Rohl, *Exodus: Myth or History?* (St. Louis Park: Thinking Man Media, 2015), 150.

77. Bruce Feiler, *Walking the Bible: A Journey by Land through the Five Books of Moses* (New York, NY: HarperCollins, 2002), 182.

78. Feiler, *Walking the Bible*, 182.

79. Longman, *The Expositor's Bible Commentary*, 406.

80. Longman, *The Expositor's Bible Commentary*, 410.

81. "Passover (Pesach) 2017," *Chabad.org*, accessed May 8, 2017. www.chabad.org/holidays/passover/pesach_cdo/aid/871715/jewish/What-Is-Passover.htm.

82. Merrill C. Tenny ed., *Pictorial Bible Dictionary* (Nashville: The Southwestern Company, 1968), 664.

83. William L. Coleman, *Today's Handbook of Bible Times and Customs* (Minneapolis, MN: Bethany House Publishers), 222.

84. Rohl, *Exodus: Myth or History?*, 153.

85. Rohl, *Exodus: Myth or History?*, 153.

86. Feiler, *Walking the Bible*, 206.

87. Rohl, *Exodus: Myth or History?*, 220.

88. David Rohl, *From Eden to Exile: The 5,000-Year History of the People of the Bible* (Lebanon, TN: Greenleaf Press, 2002), 251.

CHAPTER 6

89. David Rohl, *Exodus: Myth or History?* (St. Louis Park: Thinking Man Media, 2015), 168.

90. Rohl, *Exodus: Myth or History?*, 171.

91. Rohl, *Exodus: Myth or History?*, 169.

92. Rohl, *Exodus: Myth or History?*, 170.

93. "Noah's Ark-The Early Years," September 11, 2011, *Wyattmuseum.com*, accessed March 31, 2017. wyattmuseum.com/noahs-ark-the-early-years/2011-697.

94. "The Egyptian Watergate," *Wyattmuseum.com*, accessed June 2, 2017. wyattmuseum.com/the-egyptian-watergate/2011-673.

95. "Chariot Wheels in the Red Sea," *Wyattmuseum.com*, accessed June 2, 2017. wyattmuseum.com/chariot-wheels-in-the-red-sea/2011-669.

96. Donald P. Moss, "Evidence of Red Sea Crossing," *Biblebigpicture.com*, accessed June 2, 2017. www.biblebigpicture.com/biblelessons/evidenceofredseacrossing.htm.

97. "Solomon's Pillar–Israelite's Red Sea Crossing Site on Bible Study Tour," *Livingpassages.com*, accessed June 2, 2017. www.livingpassages.com/2017/03/solomons-pillar-to-show-the-crossing-site-of-the-israelites-at-the-red-sea/.

98. "Rock in Horeb found near burnt mountain in Saudi Arabia," *Wyattmuseuem.com*, accessed June 2, 2017. wyattmuseum.com/rock-in-horeb-found-near-burnt-mountain-in-saudi-arabia/2016-11856.

99. Rohl, *Exodus: Myth or History?*, 198.

100. Rohl, *Exodus: Myth or History?*, 393.

101. Rohl, *Exodus: Myth or History?*, 388.

102. "The 18th Dynasty," *Wyattmuseum.com*, accessed July 18, 2017. wyattmuseum.com/the-18th-dynasty/2011-671.

103. Lennart Moller, *The Exodus Case: New Discoveries Confirm the Historical Exodus* (Copenhagen, Denmark: Scandinavia Publishing House, 2002), 65.

104. Bruce Feiler, *Walking the Bible: A Journey By Land Through the Five Books of Moses* (New York, NY: HarperCollins, 2002), 149.

105. Feiler, *Walking the Bible*, 149.

106. Feiler, *Walking the Bible*, 149.

107. Feiler, *Walking the Bible*, 150.

108. Ker Than, "King Tut Mysteries Solved: Was Disabled, Malarial, Inbred," *Nationalgeographic.com*, February 17, 2010, accessed September 4, 2017. news.nationalgeographic.com/news/2010/02/100216-king-tut-malaria-bones-inbred-tutankhamun/.

109. Lennart Moller, *The Exodus Case* (Copenhagen, Denmark: Scandinavia Publishing House, 2002), 143.

110. David Rohl, *From Eden to Exile: The 5,000-Year History of the People of the Bible* (Lebanon, TN: Greenleaf Press, 2002), 302.

111. Rohl, *From Eden to Exile*, 302.

112. Merrill C. Tenny ed., *Pictorial Bible Dictionary* (Nashville: The Southwestern Company, 1968), 709.

113. Feiler, *Walking the Bible*, 188.

114. Rohl, *Exodus: Myth or History?*, 176.

115. Rohl, *Exodus: Myth or History?*, 189.

116. Rohl, *From Eden to Exile*, 212.

CHAPTER 7

117. David Rohl, *Exodus: Myth or History?* (St. Louis Park: Thinking Man Media, 2015), 194.

118. Rohl, *Exodus: Myth or History?*, 195.

119. Rohl, *Exodus: Myth or History?*, 195.

120. Bruce Feiler, *Walking the Bible: A Journey By Land Through the Five Books of Moses* (New York, NY: HarperCollins, 2002), 220.

121. Feiler, *Walking the Bible*, 286.

122. W. Ewing, "Rephidim," *Biblehub.com*, accessed September 18, 2017. biblehub.com/topical/r/rephidim.htm.

123. Rohl, *Exodus: Myth or History?*, 223.

124. Feiler, *Walking the Bible*, 210.

125. David Rohl, *From Eden to Exile: The 5,000-Year History of the People of the Bible* (Lebanon, TN: Greenleaf Press, 2002), 234.

126. Rohl, *Exodus: Myth or History?*, 225.

127. Jack W. Hayford ed., *Spirit-Filled Life Bible for Students (New King James Version)* (Nashville: Thomas Nelson Publishers, 1995), 96.

128. Lennart Moller, *The Exodus Case: New Discoveries Confirm the Historical Exodus* (Copenhagen, Denmark: Scandinavia Publishing House, 2002), 110.

129. Rohl, *From Eden to Exile*, 216-217.

130. Moller, *The Exodus Case*, 110.

131. Merrill C. Tenny ed., *Pictorial Bible Dictionary* (Nashville: The Southwestern Company, 1968), 262.

132. "Zipporah," *Wikipedia.com*, last edited September 11, 2017, accessed September 28, 2017. en.wikipedia.org/wiki/Zipporah#cite_note-12.

CHAPTER 8

133. Bruce Feiler, *Walking the Bible: A Journey By Land Through the Five Books of Moses* (New York, NY: HarperCollins, 2002), 260.

134. Feiler, *Walking the Bible*, 234.

135. David Rohl, *Exodus: Myth or History?* (St. Louis Park: Thinking Man Media, 2015), 236.

136. Feiler, *Walking the Bible*, 238.

137. Lennart Moller, *The Exodus Case: New Discoveries Confirm the Historical Exodus* (Copenhagen, Denmark: Scandinavia Publishing House, 2002), 267.

138. Rohl, *Exodus: Myth or History?*, 385.

139. Moller, *The Exodus Case*, 126.

140. Rohl, *Exodus: Myth or History?*, 391.

141. Carl Drews, "Crossing the Red Sea at Aqaba? No," *Migdolbrook.com*, last updated August 14, 2015, accessed October 17, 2017. migdolbook.com/crossing-red-sea-aqaba-no.html.

142. Randall Price, *Searching for the Ark of the Covenant: Latest Discoveries and Research* (Eugene, Oregon: Harvest House Publishers, 2005), 180.

143. Moller, *The Exodus Case*, 211.

144. Moller, *The Exodus Case*, page 218.

145. Moller, *The Exodus Case*, page 222.

146. Moller, *The Exodus Case*, page 225.

147. Moller, *The Exodus Case*, page 260.

148. Rohl, *Exodus: Myth or History?*, 396.

149. Moller, *The Exodus Case*, 263.

150. Rohl, *Exodus: Myth or History?*, 394.

151. Feiler, *Walking the Bible*, 257.

152. Feiler, *Walking the Bible*, 211.

153. Feiler, *Walking the Bible*, 212.

154. "Jewish Holidays: Shavu'ot," *Jewishvirtuallibrary.org*, accessed October 24, 2017. www.jewishvirtuallibrary.org/shavu-ot.

155. Frank Viola, *The Untold Story of the New Testament Church* (Shippensburg, PA: Destiny Image Publishers, Inc., 2004), 128.

156. David Rohl, *From Eden to Exile: The 5,000-Year History of the People of the Bible* (Lebanon, TN: Greenleaf Press, 2002), 125.

157. "Baby Bones Discovered in the Walls of Jericho," *Livingpassages.com*, February 22, 2016, accessed October 25, 2017. www.livingpassages.com/2016/02/baby-bones-discovered-in-the-walls-of-jericho/.

158. Francis Chan, *Erasing Hell: What God Said About Eternity, and the Things We've Made Up* (Ontario, Canada: David C Cook Distribution, 2011), 52.

ENDNOTES

159. Rohl, *From Eden to Exile*, 50.

160. "Burning of the Riga Synagogues," *Wikipedia.com*, last edited July 17, 2017, accessed October 26, 2017. en.wikipedia.org/wiki/Burning_of_the_Riga_synagogues.

161. "Nanking Massacre," *Wikipedia.com*, last edited August 17, 2017, accessed August 19, 2017. en.wikipedia.org/wiki/Nanking_Massacre.

162. "Every Bomb Dropped By the British and Americans During WW2," *Brilliantmaps.com*, April 12, 2017, accessed August 19, 2017. brilliantmaps.com/uk-us-bombs-ww2/.

163. Zach Williams, "All Blue-Eyed People Have a Single Ancestor in Common," *Businessinsider.com*, September 21, 2017, accessed October 27, 2017. www.businessinsider.com/all-people-blue-eyes-have-common-ancestor-2017-9.

164. "The Menorah," *Jewishvirtuallibrary.org*, accessed November 2, 2017. www.jewishvirtuallibrary.org/the-menorah.

165. Harry Oates, "The Maccabean Revolt,"*Ancient.edu*, October 29, 2015, accessed November 3, 2017. www.ancient.eu/article/827/the-maccabean-revolt/.

166. "The Story of Chanukah," *Chabad.org*, accessed November 3, 2017. www.chabad.org/holidays/chanukah/article_cdo/aid/102978/jewish/The-Story-of-Chanukah.htm

167. "How Did the Urim and the Thummim Function?" *Bible.org*, January 1, 2001, accessed November 10, 2017. bible.org/question/how-did-urim-and-thummim-function.

168. "What Is Yom Kippur?" *Chabad.org*, accessed November 16, 2016. www.chabad.org/holidays/JewishNewYear/template_cdo/aid/177886/jewish/What-Is-Yom-Kippur.htm.

169 Rohl, *From Eden to Exile*, 120.

170. Tremper Longman III and David E. Garland ed., *The Expositor's Bible Commentary: Revised Edition (Genesis-Leviticus)* (Grand Rapids: Zondervan, 2008), 536.

171. Longman, *The Expositor's Bible Commentary*, 536.

172. Tyler Jarvis, "Could the Jews Only Take a Limited Number of Steps on the Sabbath?" *Fakegesis*, February 27, 2015, accessed December 1, 2017. fakegesis.wordpress.com/2015/02/27/could-the-jews-only-take-a-limited-number-of-steps-on-the-sabbath/.

173. Rohl, *From Eden to Exile*, 24.

174. Rohl, *Exodus: Myth or History?*, 231.

175. Rohl, *Exodus: Myth or History?*, 232.

176. Rohl, *Exodus: Myth or History?*, 232.

177. Rohl, *Exodus: Myth or History?*, 232.

178. Rohl, *Exodus: Myth or History?*, 231.

179. "Yom Kippur," *History.com*, accessed December 12, 2017. www.history.com/topics/holidays/yom-kippur-history.

180. Jack W. Hayford ed., *Spirit-Filled Life Bible for Students (New King James Version)* (Nashville: Thomas Nelson Publishers, 1995), 1,064.

181. Feiler, *Walking the Bible*, 259.

CHAPTER 9

182. Jack W. Hayford ed., *Spirit-Filled Life Bible for Students (New King James Version)* (Nashville: Thomas Nelson Publishers, 1995), 1,089.

183. Jason Shuler, "Guest Blog: Jason Shuler's Testimony," *Depthsofpentecost.com*, October 13, 2017, accessed December 18, 2017. depthsofpentecost.com/blog/guest-blog-jason-shulers-testimony.

184. "Exodus 40:17: Ellicot's Commentary for English Readers," *Biblehub.com*, accessed December 21, 2017. biblehub.com/commentaries/exodus/40-17.htm.

185. Jack Wellman, "What Is Shekinah Glory? Is It in the Bible?" *Patheos.com*, May 17, 2014, accessed December 26, 2017. www.patheos.com/blogs/christiancrier/2014/05/17/what-is-shekinah-glory-is-this-in-the-bible/.

186. Charleeda Sprinkle, "Glory-Kavod," *Bridgesforpeace.com*, October 4, 2009, accessed December 26, 2017. www.bridgesforpeace.com/article/glory-kavod/.

www.ingramcontent.com/pod-product-compliance
Lightning Source LLC
Chambersburg PA
CBHW060124170426
43198CB00010B/1024